PARENTING A
HAPPY CHILD

*Compliments of
fa PC Ugo*

[signature]

11/23/2018

PARENTING A HAPPY CHILD

⚭

Peter Claver Ugo

Copyright © 2018 by Peter Claver Ugo.

Library of Congress Control Number: 2018912473
ISBN: Hardcover   978-1-9845-6052-0
               Softcover   978-1-9845-6051-3
               eBook   978-1-9845-6050-6

All rights reserved. No part of this book may be reproduced or transmitted in any form or by any means, electronic or mechanical, including photocopying, recording, or by any information storage and retrieval system, without permission in writing from the copyright owner.

The views expressed in this work are solely those of the author and do not necessarily reflect the views of the publisher, and the publisher hereby disclaims any responsibility for them.

Any people depicted in stock imagery provided by Getty Images are models, and such images are being used for illustrative purposes only. Certain stock imagery © Getty Images.

Print information available on the last page.

Rev. date: 10/17/2018

To order additional copies of this book, contact:
Xlibris
1-888-795-4274
www.Xlibris.com
Orders@Xlibris.com
785898

Contents

Foreword vii
Dedication xi
Acknowledgements xiii
Reviews xv
About The Author xvii

Chapter 1   Introduction 1
Chapter 2   Bio-Psychological Concerns In Parenting 18
Chapter 3   Mother-Child Attachment 36
Chapter 4   Attachment And Adolescent Emotional
            Development 51
Chapter 5   Stages Of Child Cognitive And Moral
            Development 63
Chapter 6   Types Of Parenting Styles 76
Chapter 7   Parenting And Adolescent Views On Values 116
Chapter 8   Infant And Adolescent Temperament 122
Chapter 9   Early Adolescent Anxieties 127
Chapter 10 Adolescent Storm And Stress 133
Chapter 11 Coping With Adolescent Stress And Storm 143
Chapter 12 Adolescent Social Development 151
Chapter 13 Resilience In Parenting 164
Chapter 14 Moral Internalization And Corporal
            Punishment In Parenting 171
Chapter 15 Side Effects Of Punishment 181
Chapter 16 Discipline And Adolescent Behavior
            Management 192
Chapter 17 Child Abuse And Trauma 199

Chapter 18 The Impact Of Child Abuse 211
Chapter 19 Some Perspectives In Mental Health Care
           For Abuse Victims 229
Chapter 20 The Pastoral Care Of Abuse Survivors 242

References 259

FOREWORD

EXPERIENCE THEY SAY is the best teacher, but experience is not the only way of learning or knowing. We can learn and know in so many other ways including our own mistakes and that of others. Much of the wisdom I have shared in this book is derived from my studies, readings, observations, interactions, my own family and childhood experiences with my parents and the last but not the least, my own experience as a guardian to the children who lived with me. Although this may not qualify me to be an authority in parenting, we are all teachers by the way we live and the persons we become.

My aim in writing this book is not necessarily to present a new ideas but to help the reader especially parents, would-be parents, grandparents, guardians and those in the helping profession to rediscover what might be some of the essential tools needed to raise a happy and successful child. The Church's teaching to respect human life from the moment of conception to natural death is one that has a great implication on the way and manner the child is raised after birth.

The dignity of the individual cannot be down-played at any level of human development. It takes some spiritual sense of resilience and grace to accompany the child through those developmental stages of life that will make or break the child in adulthood. While it may not be necessary that every parent must be religious, it is recommended that every would be parent have some sense of the divine or value which will be the driving force for that parent to persevere in the selfless and sacrificial act of raising a happy and successful child. It gets even better where the parent is religious which means that he or she is actively spiritual or a practicing Christian. In which case, it becomes an added tool for raising a Christian child, who will be raised in the fear and love of God and humanity.

With the family as the most basic unit of the human society and socialization we cannot but emphasize the importance of a stable family as one of those tools needed to achieve this goal. What I intend this book to do for its readers is to provoke questions as to whether parents have been intentional in the choices they make in the upbringing of their children. If lots of effort and measures are taken today to train our pet animals so that they can live with us at home, how much more should we be most intentional in preparing the ground for parenting by equipping oneself with the necessary tools required to be a good parent. By reading a book like this one in your hands and so many others, one can prepare adequately before planning to begin a family.

A Latin adage says *Dat quod non habet*, meaning "No one gives what he does not have". This wise saying makes sense in the business of parenting. We are in an age where children are begetting children due to lack of knowledge which contributes to rampant teenage pregnancy. It gets complicated when a teenager who should still needs parental care becomes a parent.

This book examines some of the fundamental precautions that should be taken from the moment of conception such as the effects of toxins or teratogens that could affect the health of the baby in the womb. Every parent who has the good of their baby in the womb should know about these toxins and avoid putting them into their body. Fundamental to parenting with resilience and grace lies in the sacred nature of the human body as presented in this book. Any form of physical and emotional abuse or addiction to alcohol and substances of abuse which can pose danger to the unborn baby or a child should be avoided. The need for the parents to form a secure attachment with the baby cannot be underestimated as insecure attachment could result to lifelong emotional and psychological imbalance in the child if not properly addressed.

This book also seeks to emphasize that no two persons are ever the same, not even identical twins. Therefore the former idea in parenting that tends to say one-size-fits-all is untenable when it comes to raising a child who can live true to his or her nature. I have in this book explored the various traits and energy movements that could inform the personality of your child and offers best practice tips to raise each child to be happy and successful. Many behavioral warning signs that could show when the child is not properly being raised or abused are discussed. Finally some measures that could be taken to arrest the effects of poor parenting and healing of a traumatized inner child are equally presented. It is my sincere hope many will find this book a good guide and reference book in raising their children.

DEDICATION

FOR MY FATHER, Livinus Ugoagwu Odom and my mother, Margaret Mary Ugo whose resilience and grace in sacrificing their own comfort to raise me and my siblings provided us a strong foundation and presented the opportunity they did not have.

ACKNOWLEDGEMENTS

I THANK GOD WHO in His wisdom and love has led me in every step of my life journey in my quest for true knowledge. It was in search of knowledge that I found my vocation to serve God. I have also come to discover that any knowledge and wisdom that does not bring one closer to him is not worth its value. He has taught me to live true to myself and keeps inspiring me to share the same with others. I can't begin to number all the people who either inspired me through their experiences, ideas, writings or the role they played in making this book a reality. I can't thank enough those men and women who completed my survey during graduate school and whose childhood experiences inspired me to work on this book. I want to thank my friend Dominick Forte, who was the first and last to edit the manuscript and whose inspiring theological books remain unique in their originality and perception.

Thanks to Karen DeCrosta who made valuable contributions in reading the manuscript. Nancy LaPonzina a Registered Nurse turned writer, provided immense help in reading through the many changes the first manuscript went through and whose expertise and suggestion led to further expansion in the ideas shared in this book. Upon completion of my writing Larry Whartenby and Donna Minafra gratefully offered their time and expertise in the final editing. To all my friends who kept asking me when the book was going to be published during the many months it was left at the burner of my agenda, thank you for never letting me quit. To my father and mother for molding me into who I am and guiding me through the grace of God and their resilience in the right direction my whole life. Finally to my numerous family and friends whose prayer, unflinching support and love have been my strength, many thanks and blessings.

REVIEWS

"PARENTING A HAPPY Child presents a thoughtful yet practical guide for parents. Drawing on his extensive research, as well as his day-to-day experience as a spiritual leader, Fr. Peter Claver Ugo enlightens parents about the value of spiritual support in raising children and points the way for them in a world often challenged by clashing values".

Karen DeCrosta

"I think the book is very well written. It is very clear and understandable. It is an excellent resource for parents and any person who works in schools, both public and private. I really liked Chapter 6, which is parenting according to an individual's nature. I wish I had this information when I was raising my children".

Donna Minafra

Father Peter Claver has provided us with a clear, concise, and incisive work on building the foundations of happy and wholesome family life. We are well served to benefit from his years of experience as a spiritual director and family counselor.

His untiring dedication to this work is a tribute to his fervent desire to making social interaction among families enhanced under the guidance and direction of God.

Dominick Forte

Raising confident productive children who possess self-awareness of their society and can contribute to a greater rapport with their world as they develop, is parent-whisperer Fr. Peter Claver Ugo's labor of love and dedication. *Parenting a Happy Child* shares guidance with parents as well as to those adults entrusted with the care of children and to successfully meet the responsibilities and challenges they will face in life.

Nancy LaPonzina RN BS

ABOUT THE AUTHOR

THE AUTHOR WAS educated at Saints Peter and Paul Major Seminary Bodija Ibadan, Nigeria where he obtained a Bachelor of Arts Degree in Philosophy from the University of Ibadan and a Bachelor of Theology Degree of Urban University Rome. On August 14, 1993 he was ordained a priest for the Catholic Diocese of Issele-Uku, Delta State of Nigeria. For twelve years he served as parochial vicar and pastor in many parishes in his home diocese Issele-Uku and Ijebu-Ode diocese where he was on mission for a number of years. In 2005 he took a study leave for graduate studies in the United States of America.

In 2008 he a obtained Master's degree in Pastoral and Mental Health Counseling at Fordham University Rose Hill Campus, Bronx and in 2012 obtained a PhD in General Psychology at Capella University Minneapolis where he carried out research on the "Impact of Childhood Attachment on the Adult Relationship Among African Americans". The results of the study hypotheses became the inspiration to write this book. While in the States, Fr Peter Claver has served in the Archdiocese of New York as hospital chaplain at St Luke's Cornwall hospital, where he also assisted various parishes and institutions in Newburgh and Cornwall New York including, the Presentation Sisters convent and the Air National Guard in Newburgh until 2014. He also taught at the Mount Saint Mary College as Adjunct Professor in Developmental Psychology.

In late 2014 he was appointed hospital chaplain at Westchester Medical Center where he has been serving as priest chaplain to date. His childhood upbringing, experiences in living with his nephews and nieces as a pastor, and learning exposed him to what it takes to parent for a happy and successful child and which contributed in writing this book. The author notes that although he may not have been fully emotionally available as biological parents would have been, in his role as guardian to those children he tried to fulfill that role and still insists that parenting should properly be the exclusive role of biological parents who are fully and emotionally available for proper upbringing of emotionally balanced and successful children. Material provision alone does not qualify anyone for parenting, but a loving emotional attachment with a child supersedes any other form of love and care a parent can provide and anyone who does not possess both may not have the qualification for parenting, the author opines. This book is a must read for parents, would be parents, grandparents, foster parents, guardians and professionals as an added tool and guide to adequately fulfill the role of parenting.

CHAPTER 1

Introduction

PARENTING HAS BECOME quite scary, owing to the digital age and latest developments in the communication industry that has evolved so much that we can access any information we need by the press of a button. Instant messaging has transformed the parts of our world that once were so separated into a global village. Despite the numerous advantages of communication technology in our time, its abuse has added to the significant burden of parenthood in the 21st century. The millennials or children who are born in this digital age and who are growing up in it are the most advantaged recipients of its benefits and at the same time, the worst victims of its shortcomings. Almost every child in the most advanced countries has all the current electronic gadgets from tablet computers to cell phones on which they chat and text all day long with their peers near and far. The problem is that many children are reading fewer books and novels that could help them develop good communication skills, and are living more sedentary lives.

The truth is that such a lifestyle is not only contributing to childhood obesity and the underdevelopment of intellectual abilities, but also exposing children to all kinds of information online, some of which parents have no idea about. This is why as a parent you may not be too sure to vouch for your child when it comes to their innocence when accused of an offense if you have not been close to that child.

As first educators and teachers to their children, parents today face the challenge of being the first to inform their children since children have ready access to all kinds of information from peers from all corners of the globe. Parents do not only need to match toe-to-toe with their children in being computer savvy but should even be a leg ahead of the child in order to minimize the adverse influence and peer pressure originating from the digital world. It calls for diligence on the part of parents to be concerned not only with their child's physical peers but also with their virtual peers, whose backgrounds and associations with their children they may be unaware of. Since you cannot live out the duty of parenting regarding strangers both real and virtual, the book you have in your hand can serve as an additional tool in your professional arsenal to help you think through and apply the best possible practices when it comes to dealing with your child or that child in your care who is transitioning from childhood to adulthood. This age can be the most interesting time and yet also be the most challenging for many parents. More so at a time when it is getting more and more unfashionable to be a stay-at-home mom or stay-at-home dad for successful upbringing of children due to the economic pressures on many families today.

This book presents the author's multidisciplinary perspective in parenting drawing from his broad philosophical, theological and psychological backgrounds. This work is partly a product of a doctoral study conducted on the "impact of attachment styles on the quality of romantic relationships as measured by support, depth and conflict," as you may have noted in chapters three and four of this book. The crucial role childhood attachment plays in the child's formation of an internal working model shapes his or her future relationships, which makes early responsive parenting critical. Like most human tasks, parenting is an arduous task that requires skill and emotional investment, yet it is rarely given sufficient attention in research and training. Parenting, from the beginning, was the exclusive reserve of adults who are presumed to be mature and knowledgeable in psychosocial developmental tasks. For the demanding nature of parenting duty, individuals who are not prepared to make the required sacrifices that it demands, often give up this responsibility to tested and trusted hands, seek the help of families and friends who act as foster parents, or lose the child to government agents like child Protective Services. This decision often derives from the fact that when the desired emotional and material maturity required for positive parenting is lacking in a couple, the resultant outcomes are often debilitating to both parents and the child. The anxiety created by the psychological and other environmental stressors arising from being ill-prepared or from some handicap could lead to wrong choices such as abortion, infanticide, child abuse, separation, divorce, and human-trafficking. For reasons such as these, there has been a subtle call from some schools of thought advocating a licensing process for would-be parents. These schools of thought argue that certification of intending parents would provide them the required skills and tools for adequate parenting as required in other professional fields. The thought of licensing parents can only point to the seriousness of the issue of parenting in the 21st century. Parenting is presented here as one all-important duty in human socialization which men and women often take for granted, seeking little or no formal coaching before embarking on it. It is for this reason that this book is written as an added tool to provide a handy reference for parents, would-be parents, and coaches. Most research findings in this field do not often get to those at the grassroots level and so they lack knowledge of new trends in parenting skills.

The family is the most fundamental component of the society and the place where new members are socialized. The connection between the family and society is fundamental in building a better society. Like the duty of governing wisely, the duty of parenting merits adequate attention. Governments at all levels should be supportive of families in carrying out their social responsibility of raising good children who eventually will become valuable members of the society. In this book I have noted that parenting begins from the moment of conception; this implies that parents of the infant have a sacred duty to nurture and nurse the child to excellent physical and psychosocial health. To create a child before thinking of proper parenting skills does not portray a readiness on the part of the parent or parents to be emotionally and otherwise prepared to welcome a new member to the family and to society. Removing all foreseeable barriers to positive and responsive parenting is the only way to ensure an adequate child-rearing experience. Preparing for responsive positive, parenting is not limited to a baby shower as practiced in American culture; it goes beyond the idea of friends and family getting together to support the expectant parents with material goods that the new infant will need. Preparing for responsive, positive parenting also sees to the provision of the emotional support the new parents need to embrace the responsibility of parenting. In this way the old African adage that says "it takes a village to raise a child" becomes realistic when all concerned play their roles.

How early is too early to start preparing for parenting? It can never be too early for parents to start the sacred duty of being the desired responsive, motivated, positive, and caring father or mother to their infant. It is imperative to keep this in mind, due to the implication that the impact of childhood maternal or paternal attachments can have on the child's interpersonal relationships through his or her lifespan as presented in chapters 3 and 4 of this book. Parenting cannot start from adolescence. It is too late for parents to begin to relate in a parent-child relationship at the adolescent stage. Parents may not do well as parents if they substitute their role of being parents for that of being friends with their children. These are two different kinds of relationships. Many parents who find parenting difficult often try in vain to make their relationships with their children like a friendship between two equals, which is not the case in successful parent-child relationships.

Finally, this book presents parents in their proper perspective not as friends, or abusers, or dictators, but as loving, firm, responsive, and caring adults. This tone must be set from the onset to avoid giving the child mixed messages. Parenting like blacksmithing or pottery making is time-sensitive; a blacksmith must shape the iron while it is hot: this implies that a child must be fashioned to our dream personality early in life. It is only by so doing that parenting can result in rearing a socially competent child. It is the opinion of this author that given the importance of parenting for a better 21st century society, parenting cannot be left to chance because nurture rather than nature makes the most difference in human life and the development of social skills. It is hoped that this book will help parents and would-be parents with additional skills and insights in parenting.

DIVINE NATURE OF HUMAN LIFE AND PARENTING

In Christianity and other world religions, God is seldom defined by gender – female or male. However, in some ancient traditional religious beliefs God is understood more in the sense of a female or mother due to the association with for instance "Mother Nature" or "Mother Earth," which in those religions refers to the "goddess of fertility". If God shares the attribute of fertility she can be described also as a god of fertility by implication, then she is also a god of nurture and parenting. This understanding provides the basis in Christianity that all fatherhood or motherhood derives its beginning and origin from God who is the Father or parent of all. It is from this background that one can form the image of God from the perspective of a parent- father and mother. It is for this reason that in parenting, biological parents model for the child "a God image". This means that the first impression of the attributes and temperament of God is perceived or understood by the child from the earliest childhood interaction with his or her parents. The first impression could be kind, loving, compassionate, and responsive or it could be uncharitable, punishing, unforgiving or repulsive. Whatever impression the parent makes on the child leaves a very good or a very bad taste with the child. The disposition of a good or very bad parent may translate to an image of a good or bad God for the child. Consciously or unconsciously, parenting would amount to modeling an image of God to the child. However, does any parent think herself or himself a god? Absolutely not. Does any child think her dad or mom is a god? Probably yes. As a priest, I know a particular child of about two years old who kept calling me God, even though her parents consistently corrected her by telling her that I was not a god. Eventually, the parents prevailed in making her understand that I was not a god but a priest of God and human like herself. This situation may make the issue of parenting and modeling for a pure and innocent child very challenging.

At the core of this all-important undertaking and sacred duty of parenting is the sacred nature of the human person. The human person's body is made up of body, soul, and spirit. This is why the perspective of this book is not only to explore the nature of parenting from the psychological perspective, but more importantly to explore the core fundamentals for positive parenting from the theological point of view. Theology is not only a study of God. Theology also seeks to define the meaning of humankind's existence and value. Hence, John Paul II, (1984), commenting about the true meaning and value of human sexuality and love, says "it is an illusion to think we can build a true culture of human life if we do not …accept and experience sexuality and love and the whole of life according to their true meaning and their close inter-connection" (n.97).

Secondly, we should also rely on human experience as John Paul II proposed. At the basis of integral human nurturing and care giving is the conviction among Christian theologians and thinkers that humankind is "Imago Dei," that is, in the "Image of God." Herein lies the true meaning of humankind as John Paul II demonstrated in his *Theology of the Body*. No study of the nature of the human person could therefore be complete if it is isolated from its divine origin, just as there can be no study of all created things without reference to their divine origin and essence. Humankind is considered the crown of God's creation because man is the only creature that resembles God and so is deserving of all respect and dignity. In parenting, the caregiver must be mindful of this. The Bible as the word of God provides the basic framework which informs other tools and skills we learn from the social and behavioral sciences for parenting.

The theology of the body is basically founded in the biblical account of creation that humankind is created in the image and likeness of God (Genesis 1:27) and therefore should be treated with dignity and respect from the moment of conception to natural death. This creationist view of human life as divine, acts against the evolutionist view that life gradually evolved from a single cell which had originated from dead matter and is fundamental in understanding the human role as co-creator and custodian of human life. Parenting as tender loving care begins before conception. It implies that intending parents must lovingly desire to bring forth a child into the world. This deep seated love could be likened to the divine love and care of which the prophet Jeremiah spoke, "before I formed you in the womb, I knew you..." (1:5). Unconditional responsive loving care is desirable in parenting as it seeks to offer nothing but the best to the child. Again, in a like manner, the prophet makes God's best wishes for good life and happiness for all His children typified in His covenant with Israel.

In both Christian religions and other world religions, life is considered to be sacred. Most religions and cultures affirm that life is a gift from God, and thus life belongs to God. Nurturing life is equally viewed as a sacred duty and a violation of this sacredness of human life is often considered a serious and ungodly act. True parenting takes into consideration this sacred nature of the totality of the human person and the preservation of the sanctity of human life from conception to natural death. Abortion, which is early termination of human life, and all other forms of physical or moral violence, would be considered dehumanizing.

A CHRISTIAN UNDERSTANDING OF THE NATURE OF THE HUMAN BODY FOR PARENTING

The human body is often understood to symbolize human sexuality because human sexuality is a major topic in academia and entertainment in modern times. Sex is also used or abused to gain love or acceptance in a relationship, to dominate or hurt others or even to sell merchandise, contrary to the practice in the Victorian period when modern societies avoided any mention of all parts of the body covered by clothing. During this period, for example, male doctors examined female patients in totally dark rooms, and some females covered piano legs for propriety (Allan, 2000; Money, 1985a). This is no longer the case in the twentieth-first century. Our concern here is to examine the value of the divine gift of the human body and sexuality as part of parenting.

The sacred nature of human life is derived from the Christian theology of the human body. The rationale behind the theology of the human body is both to expound on the sacred nature of the human body and to use new methods and approaches to present a teaching in human sexuality aimed at countering the modern day sexual revolution which is posing enormous challenges to the sacred nature of the human body and sexuality today. For example, a recent study of nine thousand students with an average age of thirteen in London, UK, found that one in every fourteen of those surveyed had had sex by the time he or she had reached thirteen (Percy, 2006, p.9). One of the research studies reviewed in this book found that out of 5,473 US female navy recruits surveyed 1,267, or twenty-four percent of respondents, admitted having been sexually abused at one time or another (Merill et al. 2003, pp.987-996). With all this information there is no doubt that we have a problem which parents and would-be parents stand to learn from if they pay attention to the new trends in child abuse in recent times. It is the challenges of issues like these posed to society that would have informed John Paul II's writings on human sexuality and most importantly made the Pope adopt a modern method of presenting his teaching on human sexuality. In times past, the Church simply stated her sexual teaching. She has always taught that sex before marriage, masturbation, adultery and contraception, for example, are sinful and harmful acts. The Church leaders and teachers would speak the truth of sexual issues and people were asked to trust the teaching of the Church without much explanation. This was acceptable when there was a prevailing atmosphere of trust in the Church and in society in general. But since the 1960s and the age of liberation theology and the sexual revolution, this approach has proved quite unsuccessful. Percy (2006) posits that people view most institutions with a good deal of suspicion, especially the Church. Hence, a new approach is called for in the Church's moral teaching (p.10). In the past, too, the Church's teachings on human sexuality were not always presented positively. On many occasions they were presented as a series of do nots or "thou shall nots." For example, the reasons as to why intending couples should not sleep together before marriage or the evils of sex abuse were not always forthcoming. The fear of sexual sin rather than reasonable explanations was the main weapon the Church had at her disposal to discourage such practices among its members. This approach was effective to an extent at that material time, but today, this method of teaching no longer carries much weight, just as it would not forcefully impress a teenager if the parent just tells him or her not to sleep with a man for it is sinful.

Parents and would-be parents will have a better case to make in teaching their teens about their sexuality if they take a cue from John Paul II's method. As Percy (2006) observed, John Paul II addressed the shortcomings and critical concerns about the way we traditionally understand and communicate the truths about human sexuality with his theology of the body. He introduces us into a new understanding of the human body and sexuality in a way that is positive, responsible, and conversational (p.10). Some of the questions I would like to answer in this book are as follows: Where does sex fit in our lives? What values are associated with it? Is it intimate and sacred? Or is it simply "a casual indoor sport?" Theology of the body says that sex means something fundamentally valuable and that is what I intend to explore here against the backdrop of sexual abuse in all its ramifications. Theology of the body gives us an adequate response to the myriads of sexual abuse incidents facing humankind in the 21st century of which parents and would-be parents should be aware.

SACRED NATURE OF THE HUMAN BODY

The origin of the sacred nature of the human body is derived from the narrative of Genesis. From the text of Genesis (2:23) and from the whole context of Genesis it is clearly seen that humankind was created as a particular value before God. "God saw everything that He had made, and behold, it was very good" (1:31). In the first chapter of the *Bible*, the narrative of creation affirms that man was created in the image of God as male and female. The function of the image is to reflect the one who is the model, to reproduce its own prototype.

John Paul II (1979) says that "from the beginning, man is not only an image in which the solitude of a person who rules the world is reflected, but also, and essentially, an image of an inscrutable divine communion of persons"(p.46). He posits that the first expression of man "flesh of my flesh," contains a reference to what makes that body truly human. Therefore, at the very core of the anthropological reality is the human body, which is not only anthropological, but also essentially theological because of its divine origin, at least for Christian theologians. Right from the beginning, the theology of the body is bound up with the creation of man in the image of God. "It becomes in a way, the theology of sex, or rather the theology of masculinity and femininity, which has its starting point here in Genesis as I observed earlier (p.47).

Furthermore, there is a deep connection between the mystery of creation, as a gift springing from love, and that beautifying "beginning" of the essence of man as male and female, in the whole truth of their body and their sex, which is a pure and simple truth of communion between persons. When the first man exclaimed, at the sight of the woman: "This one is bone of my bones, and flesh of my flesh" (Gn. 2:23), he merely affirmed the human identity of both. Exclaiming in this way, he seems to say that here is a body that expresses the person. The Yahwist text presupposes that the body reveals man as a "living soul," when God-Yahweh breathed life into him. This resulted in his solitude before all other living beings, thereby making humankind distinct from other living beings (p. 61). The human body and sexuality are at the center of our relationship with God and one another because of their importance.

As human beings we are created in the image and likeness of God. As a matter of fact, the dignity and respect due to every human person is not assigned by any group of people, nor granted by a government. According to Kurtz (2006), human dignity "is not contingent on what we own, or even on what we do. We cannot buy it or sell it. This dignity and worth comes from God as a complete and inestimable gift to humankind" (p.4). In this way we share God's nature; we share in His immortality and holiness. Like God, we have a rational nature, the ability to reason, to love and to be loved.

HUMAN BODY AND HUMAN SEXUALITY

The dignity of the human person includes our sexuality, which is more than our gender and an inseparable part of our person. Sexuality is part and parcel of human life. This we know from experience. The sexual urge is a very powerful human emotion. John Paul II, though, holds that humankind is more relational than we are sexual. Woman and man from the account of creation are gifts to one another, meant for one another. This mutual interpenetration of the "self" of the human persons, of the man and woman, according to John Paul II, seems to subjectively exclude any reduction to an object. This reveals the subjective profile of that love. For Percy (2006), it can be said that this love "is objective" to the depths, since it is nourished by the mutual "objectivity" of the gift.

Following the relational nature of humankind, John Paul posits that the human body is profoundly relational. Thus, humankind is by nature, called to associate with others, accept others, affirm others, give ourselves to others and to develop intimate and enduring relations with others (Percy 2006, p.4). In short, our vocation is to love and to accept love as demonstrated in marriage and conjugal love, through which humankind shares in the love and creativity of God. This does not mean that we are necessarily called to have sex with others. In this way, John Paul makes a distinction between our bodies and our sexuality as not being the same. Sexuality for him is to serve a true and lasting communion between men and women and to lead us into a true and lasting communion with God, thereby making sexuality a noble and sacred part of our being. Hence, he describes it as nuptial. The discovery of the nuptial meaning of the body ceases to be a simple reality of revelation and grace.

THE ROLE OF LUST AND CONCUPISCENCE IN HUMAN SEXUALITY

Due to the fall of humankind's first parents, man and woman lost the grace of original innocence, which resulted in lust and concupiscence. Lust and concupiscence refer to an inordinate desire in humankind which indicates the fallen nature of humankind. On the other hand, West (2003), referring to Sirach 23, describes concupiscence as a "burning fire" that heats the soul and "will not be quenched until it is consumed" (p.171). It refers to the whole revealed truth about humankind and is important in the theology of the body. John Paul II (1997) remarked that for all that is in the world, the lust of the flesh -- the lust of the eyes and the pride of life -- is not of God but of the world (pp. 108-109). They are not part of humankind from the beginning but fruit of the tree of knowledge of good and evil in humankind's heart (Gn 2:17). These three forms of lust fructified the breaking of the first covenant with the Creator, and this covenant was broken in humankind's heart by accepting the motivation suggested by the tempter. This act changed the original innocence of humankind. Lust and concupiscence therefore show man's new situation after sin and the new state of human nature. It suggests the beginning of lust in humankind's heart (p.111).

John Paul II (1997), develops this description with a remarkably keen phenomenological analysis of lust. This "flaring up in man," invades his senses, excites his body, involves his feelings and, in a certain sense, takes possession of his heart. It also causes the "external man" to reduce the "internal man" to silence. Because passion aims at satisfaction, "it blunts reflective activity and pays no attention to the voice of conscience (p.171). Once the "external man" (like Freud's ego) has suffocated the voice of conscience (superego) and given his passion free reign, he remains restless until he satisfies the insistent need of the body and the senses for gratification. It is at this state of mind that abuses occur, even though psychological theorists, different from theologians, will attribute the cause to some psychological dispositions. What may be certain here is that any form of human abuse results from some kind of psychosocial disorder. However, West (2003) maintains that if we allow our passions to "undergo a radical transformation, they can become, once again, the desire to love as God loves. The contrary, which is lust, destroys that revealed value, dignity and goodness which humankind saw when Adam and Eve first saw one another in their original innocence" (p.173). However, the indelible meaning of this gift will remain in the heart of man as the ethos of the gift and a distant echo of original innocence. Through the veil of shame, man will continually rediscover himself as the guardian of the mystery of the subject that is the freedom of the gift and, by so doing, will defend it from any reduction to the position of a mere object (p.75).

Speaking of the birth of lust, on the basis of Genesis, we realized that the original meaning of shame first appeared with the original sin. This shame induces man and woman to hide their bodies from each other and especially their sexual differentiation. This shame confirms that the original capacity of communicating themselves to each other, which Genesis (Gn. 2:25) speaks of, has been shattered.

The radical change of the meaning of original nakedness leads us to presume negative changes in the whole interpersonal man-woman relationship. Lust of the body in particular attacks this "sincere giving." It deprives man of the dignity of giving, which is expressed by his body through femininity and masculinity. In a way it depersonalizes man, making him an object "for the other." Instead of being "together with the other" a subject in unity, in the sacramental unity of the body, man becomes an object for man, the female for the male and vice versa.

Violating the dimension of the mutual giving of the man and the woman, concupiscence also calls into question the fact that each of them was willed by the Creator "for his own sake." In a certain sense, the subjectivity of the person gives way to the objectivity of the body. Owing to this the female body becomes an object for man and the male body an object for the female. Concupiscence means that the personal relations of man and of woman are unilaterally and reductively linked with the body and sex, in the sense that these relations become almost incapable of accepting the mutual gift of the person. There is a loss of the interior freedom of the gift. Concupiscence limits interiorly and reduces self-control. Together with that, the beauty that the human body possesses in its male and female aspects as an expression of the spirit is obscured. The body therefore remains an object of lust and, therefore, as a "field of appropriation" of the other human being (p.127), leading to abuse and all manner of sexual irresponsibility as we are witnessing today.

We have learned that our humanity has a theological basis. It is founded on the truth about God and, more specifically, the truth that God made man. An adequate anthropology then must ultimately be a theological anthropology, just as an adequate anthropology must be a "theology of the body." As John Paul says, man's vocation "springs from the eternal mystery of the person, which is the image of God incarnate in the visible and corporeal fact of the masculinity or femininity of the human person." This is the body's great dignity; it incarnates God's mystery, which is love. Thus man's vocation is to love as God loves, and it is revealed through the nuptial meaning of his body (West, 2003. p.225). The theology of the human body also teaches that the Creator has assigned the body and the gift of sexuality to man as a task. It is the task of discovering the truth of our humanity and the dignity of the person. It is the task of embracing our redemption and growing in purity so that we can fulfill ourselves and bring joy to others through the sincere gift of ourselves- the sincere gift of our bodies which affords a true interpersonal communion. This is lived out particularly in marriage, but marriage is not the only way to live the sincere gift of self.

However, we cannot understand and live the truth about life if lust fills our hearts and our behavior contradicts the dignity of the person. The pedagogy of the body, as taught by John Paul II, also provides an anthropology that adequately explains the moral order regarding human sexuality. The Christian theology of the human body, therefore, considers any act that violates the divinity and spirituality of the human body as offensive to God and humankind. It is worthy to note here Sigmund Freud's statement that the "abandonment of the reproductive function is the common feature of all sexual perversions" (Introduction Lecture in Psychoanalysis, p.266). Though Freud was not strictly speaking theologically, he did however, made a point that strongly affirms the primary function of human sexuality as procreation. However, sexual relationship need not be inherently related to procreation as long as such a relationship does not in any way degrade procreation.

From the foregoing one can deduce why any form of human abuse is inherently degrading and an absolute violation of human dignity. Sexual abuse is a product of lust and concupiscence which treat the opposite sex as a means toward selfish gratification. According to John Paul (1993), in humankind's fallen state, mere excitement and emotion (here is where abusers fit in) often stems from a utilitarian outlook contrary to the very nature of love as self-donation (p.139). Enslavement to concupiscence is the basic and fundamental force disrupting the relationship of the sexes and, in turn, the dignity and balance of human life (p.468). It will be noted here that theology of the human body does not specifically address the issues concerning all kinds of sexual abuse, but, in general, considers any form of human abuse, whether physical or sexual, as degrading and violating divine human dignity. Any form of human abuse could be associated with the fallen human nature of humankind and is worsened by psychological problems. As important and fundamental as our human sexuality is in human relationships, it is crucial that parents be aware of the various horrific abuses that could manifest in the forms of physical abuse, sexual abuse, rape, exploitation of young boys and girls, crimes of passion, pornography, and modern day human trafficking of women and children. All these illustrate this fallen aspect of our human nature. It is my belief that good parenting could reverse this ugly trend and the developmental consequences it could have on the mental health of children and survivors. The following chapter discusses the basic biological preparations for good parenting and stages of psychosocial development which provide parents with needed insight into parenting expectations and proper responses in child rearing.

CHAPTER 2

Bio-Psychological Concerns In Parenting

PARENTING STARTS BEFORE the moment of conception. This means that would-be parents and parents would need to predispose themselves or comply with some of the vital information that would promote a child's healthy conception and delivery. This necessitates the need for the prenatal education of would-be mothers and expectant mothers who may be new to the challenges of pregnancy and the necessary precautions expectant mothers should take to ensure the health of the baby in the womb as well as what is needed to successfully carry the infant to term. Another phase of the responsibility of weaning the child to a healthy physical and emotional development begins after birth through the critical stages of development from infancy to young adulthood. Each phase of psychosocial development of the child presents its own challenge. If properly resolved through responsive parenting, the child will become his or her best despite the natural endowment. Proficient parenting and nurturing could positively alter the nature of the infant's temperament. However, abstaining from consumption of toxic beverages that could endanger the life and healthy development of the child in the womb and avoidance of an emotionally toxic and uncaring parenting attitude are to be preferred to professional intervention to resolve any problem that could arise as a result later in the child's life due to parental negligence. A proficient style is critical because attachment theory hypothesizes that the infant's early experiences with the mother or primary caregiver will predict expectations and beliefs of the child's social perceptions, attitude, and future adult relationships. Another parenting failure that could impact the psychosocial well-being of the child through adulthood is physical or sexual abuse of children. Signs and symptoms of abuse, stigmatization and intervention can provide a guide for the required professional intervention in the subsequent chapters.

PREPARATIONS FOR GOOD PARENTING

As earlier stated, good parenting begins before conception. From the beginning, would-be mothers are advised to avoid all forms of teratogens, i.e. agents and conditions that can impair prenatal development and result in birth defects or even death (Berger, 2013). Teratogens include all harmful ingestion, infections, environmental hazards or emotional stress that could be harmful to the healthy development of the fetus. The expectant parent is to avoid ingestion of drugs, alcohol, tobacco, cocaine, and marijuana, among other harmful ingestions. Further, she must avoid any food, drink or drugs, legal or illegal, which will have a harmful effect on the fetus. Ingestion of such items could harm the fetus through the placenta because it serves as the vessel that carries nutrients from the mother's blood and also removes waste through the mother's blood, thereby exposing the fetus to danger; hence, pregnant women are advised to avoid certain food and beverages especially during the fourth or fifth week of pregnancy because it is during this period that most of the major organs are developed. Ingestion of alcohol at this time, for example, could have serious effects resulting in cardiac, skeletal, and urogenital abnormalities. Others defects could be dental abnormalities, growth deficiencies, metacognitive deficits, attentional problems, social perception problems, language deficits, and learning problems (Broderick, 2010). Use of tobacco could also result in low weight due to restricted blood circulation, reduced nutrition, prematurity, respiratory problems, hyperactivity, and disruptive behaviors. In addition, the use of cocaine could lead to drug withdrawal after birth, irritability, restlessness, tremors, learning problems, and ADHD.

Marijuana, equally could result in neurological consequences. Teratogens can take the form of infections such as HIV and AIDS which can be transmitted to the fetus through the placenta and can also infect the fetus through contact with the mother's blood through the placenta. Such viruses can cause damage to the neonates' immune system, and can cause growth problems, brain disorders and developmental delays (Broderick, 2010). Environmental hazards such as lead poisoning and use of PCB's can result in premature birth, low birth weight, brain damage, mental retardation, cognitive impairments *etc.*. The extent of birth defects arising from teratogens cannot be determined by one individual factor but depends on many. While one may not be exposed to all the teratogens enumerated here, ingestion of any of the items above, infection or exposition to environmental hazards can cause irreparable damage to the fetus at the prenatal stage since there can be no safe dosage for pregnant women. No level of infection and lead poisoning is safe for the fetus. However, both the mother's and baby's genes could be a determinant factor as to the resistance or severity of abnormalities caused by teratogens. Teratogens affect both mother's and her infant's development differently. Since one cannot determine such effects, the best practice would be prevention instead of regret. Berger (2013) description of a girl whose expectant mother was drinking and smoking cigarettes while pregnant brings clarity on effects teratogens on unborn babies. When the young girl of nine heard her mother announce that she was pregnant she was elated at the eventuality of having a baby sister or brother. She had once asker her mother why she smokes and drinks. Her mother simply say to her that she does not know or have control over her life style. While in the fifth grade the girl had watched a film with her classmates about birth defects associated with smoking and drinking in expectant mothers and was afraid her mother was going to give birth to a fetal alcohol syndrome (FAS) infant. The baby was born after full term and the doctors said that her baby brother was a healthy baby. On hearing that she felt what she had watched in the film was misleading. She quickly concluded that her speculation was wrong though young. No sooner than later she observed that her newborn baby brother would not show any interest in what makes babies giggle, like toys. He would not babble or get a word out of his mouth and had no common sense. The message of the film on the dangers of drinking and smoking during pregnancy was believable and her fears were after all real.

One would wonder why this expectant mother would want to take such a chance, knowing the probable consequence of her actions on the baby. Many would wonder why anyone would engage in behaviors that can hurt those who cannot defend themselves. This question can only be answered by knowledge of the individual's genes, postnatal experiences, and her understanding of the magnitude of the risks teratogens could have on the developing fetus. One crucial factor that can increase the risk of harm is timing or the age of the developing organism when it is exposed to the teratogen. While some teratogens cause damage only during a critical period, when particular parts of the body are forming, most obstetricians would recommend that before pregnancy women should avoid drugs and especially alcohol. This is because preconception health is as important as health during pregnancy. It is recommended that women take adequate supplements and a balanced diet with extra folic acid, iron, and other crucial vitamins, and update their immunizations.

A second factor that could affect the harm from any teratogen is the dose or frequency of exposure because some teratogens have a threshold effect, that is, they are harmless until exposure reaches a certain level and becomes damaging. Some substances are, however, beneficial in small amounts but dangerously toxic in large quantities. For example, vitamin A is essential for healthy development, but 50,000 units per day (in pills) can cause many abnormalities (Naude, *et al.*, 2007). Genes of the developing organism are another factor that can determine the healthy development of the fetus. When a woman carrying dizygotic twins drinks alcohol, for instance, the twins' blood alcohol levels are equal, yet one twin may be more severely affected than the other. The reason could be as a result of the fact that only one twin has an allele that affects the enzyme that metabolizes alcohol. Genetic vulnerability is suspected for many birth defects. Although life entails risks, knowing which risks are worth taking and how to minimize the chance of harm makes this chapter very important for all expectant and would-be mothers.

Developmental psychology, as a part of prevention psychology, intends to be proactive by raising awareness so that counselors, with the cooperation of other health providers, can educate nursing mothers and would-be mothers on the dangers and long-term effects of undue exposition to teratogens. Adequate awareness of the dangers of ingesting substances of abuse and alcohol while pregnant is fundamental to adequate parenting. Educating expectant mothers on the dangers of lead poisoning through the use of objects that could expose the unborn babies to such dangers is also encouraged by counseling psychologists. The objective should be to help women realize how damaging it could be to have babies when infected with HIV and/or AIDS virus. Most people still believe that the baby's chance for contracting the disease is remote and so would want to try their luck. The emphasis here is the fact that prevention is better than cure.

Investing time and resources in spreading the information among expectant mothers on the risks of exposition to teratogens will be the beginning of the turn of the tide in good parenting. Counseling on the mother's diet during pregnancy is paramount in avoidance of teratogens since whatever the mother ingests goes into her bloodstream and affects the fetus. This means that the infant in the womb eats whatever the mother eats. Healthy eating is encouraged during pregnancy since it contributes significantly to the health of the fetus.

Although it has been established that biological and physiological factors could affect pre-natal development due to the mother's exposure to them, stress also has an important part to play in the overall health of the mother. A healthy expectant mother is a healthy baby. It is crucial that expectant mothers are aware of the adverse impact emotional stress can have on them and invariably on the well-being of the unborn child. Everyone experiences one kind of stress or another. Expectant mothers should do whatever it takes to avoid high stress levels that result from frustrations, conflicts, pressures, or negative events that people experience daily, either occasionally or chronically (Broderick, 2010). Such stress conditions very often determine whether a woman is able to carry the baby to term or not. When there is physical or psychological stress, the body responds by an outpouring of chemicals that mobilize its rapid response system and then recede once the threat has subsided. This may deplete the body's stress resistance if the stress becomes chronic. Chemicals such as epinephrine or adrenaline, and norepinephrine are released both in the brain and body, arousing the body. It is noted that stress also activates the hypothalamus-pituitary-adrenal (HPA) axis of the brain that detects and communicates with the hypothalamus when there is danger. The chemical that carries this message is the corticotrophin releasing factor (CRF). This causes the pituitary gland to release the adrenorcorticotropic hormone or ACTH.

Expectant mothers are encouraged to minimize stresses that are avoidable as some of the chemicals the body releases through early trauma resulting from such incidents as accident, death in the family, loss of job, painful divorce or serious illness could affect general mental and emotional functioning. Abnormalities in chemical messengers could, in the long run, cause depression. Chronic stress may also cause permanent damage to the individual by altering her resistance resource and making the individual sensitive to stress. Another important stress hormone is called cortisol which acts to increase blood glucose and to suppress the immune response after a short-term boost. The cortisol returns to the hypothalamus, but when stress is prolonged, it leads to the hypothalamus not being able to shut down stress response effectively, causing the individual stress system to become chronically activated. This leads to allostatic load, thereby weakening the body's ability to fight infection, suppressing growth hormone, and finally, leading to long-term cardiovascular and nervous system functioning problems.

An expectant mother who experiences chronic stress will experience increased levels of stress hormones. The secretion of these hormones will eventually cross the placenta barrier. Consequently, this may affect the developing child in so many ways (Broderick, 2010). Hormones influence the genes and development of the child and contribute in shaping the infant's neuroendocrine system which influences responsivity to stimulation, activity rhythms, and the ability to modulate and regulate behavior. Parental exposure to stress can lead to a child's hyperactivity to stress later in life. A relationship between maternal stress and neonatal hyperactivity and irritability has been well supported by many studies in humans (Levine, 1969). Again, an increased level of maternal epinephrine decreases blood flow to the uterus. And, consequently, the placenta, thereby reducing oxygen flow to the fetus. Another study in animals suggests that sexual orientation may be altered by severe maternal stress during pregnancy. It is also noted that length of stress and release of stress hormones interfere with fetal testosterone production and may affect the sexual orientation of male offspring (Ward, 1992). Finally, ongoing studies relate maternal stress during pregnancy with children's increased risk of psychopathology even when controlling for other risk factors. However, positive postnatal environmental factors such as a sound child-rearing style and experience could modify the harmful effects of pre-natal stress exposure. Such effort will help in preventing the epidemic of mental health issues, as well as developmental, cognitive and other health complications in the later part of the child's life.

GENES AND GENDER

All living things are made up of tiny cells and the work of these cells is done by proteins. Each cell manufactures proteins according to instructions stored by molecules of deoxyribonucleic acid (DNA). At the center of each cell is a chromosome which contains cells and genes that together form the human body. Humans have twenty-three pairs of chromosomes or forty-six chromosomes. The chromosomes contain the instructions to make all the proteins that a person needs and are organized in units called genes. Most genes have thousands of precise base pairs arranged in precise triplets making twenty types of amino acids needed for development into a human being. The codes for each gene can vary, although not often. Some genes have alternate versions of base pairs, with transpositions, deletions, or repetitions of base pairs not found in other versions of the same gene. Each of these variations is called an allele of that gene. Most alleles cause only minor differences, for example, the shape of an eyebrow, and some significant and notable differences such as an enzyme (monoamine oxidase A, abbreviated MAOA). This is the enzyme that affects neurotransmitters (chemicals in the brain). This gene comes in two versions, producing people with lower or higher levels of the enzyme. Both versions are normal and about one-third have low MAOA. Researchers have found that boys who were mistreated by their parents were about twice as likely to be overly aggressive, to develop a conduct disorder, to be violent, to be antisocial, and eventually to be convicted of a violent crime if, and only if, they had the low-MAOA gene instead of the high-MAOA one (Caspi et al., 2002). However, boys who were not maltreated and had the low-MAOA gene were more likely than those with the high-MAOA gene to become law-abiding and peaceable adults.

All mammals have most of the same genes and every person equally has almost all the same genes as any other. However, everyone also has some significant alleles which make everyone genetically unique.

MALE OR FEMALE

Development begins at conception when a male reproductive cell or sperm penetrates the membrane of a female reproductive cell, the ovum, to create a new cell called a zygote. Each of the human reproductive cells, or gametes, contains twenty-three chromosomes which is half of the forty-six of the zygote. This one-celled zygote copies itself again and again to create an embryo, a fetus, a baby, and eventually an adult with trillions of cells that contain the same forty-six chromosomes of the original zygote. Most human cells have all forty-six chromosomes of the zygote that began that particular person although each gamete has only twenty-three chromosomes. In every sperm or ova, a cell splits in half, with each half having only one of the two chromosomes at each location. A gamete also has one chromosome number 10, although the man or woman who formed it has two chromosomes at the 10th site. Each zygote will have a pair of number 10 chromosomes, one from the mother and one from the father. Each member of the chromosome pair on a given gamete is randomly selected. Each person can produce 223 different gametes or more than eight million of his or her own forty-six chromosomes. This means that if a man and woman conceived a billion children, each child would be genetically different from the others because of the chromosomes of the particular sperm and ovum that created the child. The genes on the chromosomes constitute the organism's genetic inheritance, or genotype, which endures throughout lifespan.

The 23rd pair of chromosomes is a special case. These two are the sex chromosomes. In females, the 23rd pair is composed of two X-shaped chromosomes. In males, the 23rd pair has one X-shaped chromosome and one Y-shaped chromosome, and is called XY. For the reason that the female's 23rd pair is XX, every ovum contains either one X or the other. On the other hand, the male's 23rd pair is XY, half of the male sperm carrying an X chromosome and half carrying a Y chromosome. It should be noted that the X chromosome is bigger and has more genes whereas the Y chromosome has a crucial gene, called SRY, that directs the fetus to make male organs and hormones. It therefore means that the sex of the baby depends on which sperm penetrates the ovum. A Y-shaped sperm with the SRY gene creates a boy (XY) whereas an X-shaped sperm creates a girl (XX). This information is fundamental to disabuse the minds of the males who would accuse the females of being responsible for all girl births, especially in those cultures where the male children are valued more than females.

Prenatal sex selection is possible as a way to address the issue of too many girls as often complained about in cultures where parents prefer boys. Some ways to prevent female births are by inactivating X sperm before conception or through the use of in vitro fertilization (IVF), and by sorting sperm which is a method to change the proportion of X and Y sperm before insemination. This technique works for humans about 85 percent of the time (Karabinus, 2009). Most parents today agree that sorting and sex selection is a reproductive right that should be accessible to couples everywhere (Karabinus, 2009). Although gender selection is natural and mostly dependent on the sex chromosome of the males (XY), still in cultures where the male gender is preferred to female gender, women have often been vilified by the men folk who at times seek for separation or outright divorce from the woman whom they accuse being responsible for the reproduction of all females in the family.

Although every trait, psychological or physical, is influenced by genes, human characteristics have been found to be influenced more by environmental factors which surround the genes, thereby affecting the genetic expression. Such influence occurs in the first hours of the beginning of life when the biochemical elements present in the body alters or silence certain genes in a process called methylation. Research has found that methylation changes the expression of the genes over one's life span (Mazin, 2009). Why people get old, develop cancer or die is attributed to epigenetic. The elderly have the same genes they had as newborns but methylation changes the expression of those genes as time goes on. Again, it has been found that all diseases known to be genetic such as cancer, schizophrenia, and autism are actually epigenetic (Saey, 2008). While certain environmental factors such as injury, extreme temperatures, and drug abuse can impede genetic development, others such as nourishing food, loving care, and play can facilitate development of genes. Thus, no human trait such as blood pressure is determined by genes alone, rather, that trait is mediated through altered genes.

Knowing the important contribution of the environment raises the awareness to avoid situations whenever a genetic vulnerability is apparent, especially with teratogens. For example, if alcoholism is in the genes, parents can keep alcohol away from their home and children, which might let the potential alcoholic become cognitively and socially mature before drinking. Ignoring the power of nature – nurture interaction could be a dangerous thing to do as genetic expression can be directed or deflected, depending on the culture and society as well as on the individual and family.

CHILD PSYCHOSOCIAL DEVELOPMENT

Basic to proper parenting is the knowledge of the basic stages of human development. Sigmund Freud posited that the complex functioning of adult personality presupposes the processes within the psychosexual stages of childhood development. Parental knowledge of the various stages of child development is critical for the child's personality development at each stage. It is for this reason that childhood psychosexual development should be given close attention since each developmental stage cannot be repeated once that stage passes unresolved, even though personal identity and interpersonal behavior evolve through a lifespan. In the mid-1900s, the psychosocial developmental theories of Freud, Erickson and Piaget made important contributions to developmental psychology. Erikson's eight psychosocial stages, which emphasize the ego rather than the id as more rational and the driving force for all human behaviors, are preferred in discussing human development and provide a fuller understanding of the stages of human development. Piaget observed that human development also undergoes several stages of changes in cognitive, rational thinking and problem-solving from childhood through adolescence. Thus, parents should be concerned with the psychological, moral, and cognitive development of the child.

Erikson, a "neo-Freudian" developmental theorist, reshaped Freud's five stages of personality development into eight psychosocial stages that deemphasized id as the driving force for all human behaviors and emphasized the ego as a more rational driving force for human behavior. While the first five stages correspond to Freud's theory, the last three stages centered on adult life stages. This shows that personal identity and interpersonal behavior evolve from birth to death (Broderick & Blewitt, 2010). Both theories distinguish clear stages of personality development with different motivations and probable outcomes for personality development. The developmental stages found in both Freud's and Erikson's theories pose different kinds of crises or conflicts relating to a specific developmental task. Parents should be familiar with these tasks and crises and know what to expect at each stage and how to respond to these corresponding changes in the child's behavior or expectations.

The first stage in Freud's developmental theory starts at the first year of life when the infant possesses an incredible amount of id energy drive that is satisfied through the mouth. This is manifested in the infant's voracious eating, drinking, and even engaging in nonnutritive sucking which provides much pleasure at this stage of the infant's life. The experiences with feeding and the extent to which this parental practice promotes or prevents the oral pleasure in the baby can determine how much interest in food the baby will develop in the future. Denying the child the oral pleasure of sucking his or her thumbs by tying the baby's hand to the side of the crib at night on the grounds that it is bad for babies to suck their thumbs, for example, would predict what Freud in his theory described as oral fixation. This fixation could manifest itself during the baby's adult life. The child might grow up to desire excessive oral pleasures, more than most adults, manifested further by overeating, becoming obsessively talkative, or becoming a chain smoker. Among grown women it might be exhibited by behaviors or feelings in adulthood that are characteristic of babies, like crying easily or experiencing overwhelming feeling of helplessness. Freud maintained that fixation in a stage of development can be a result either of denial of the child's needs or overindulgence of those needs. Defense mechanisms such as "reaction formation" or "repression" can be associated with the conflict that may arise at any stage of human development (Broderick & Blewitt, 2010). Erikson maintains that infants must resolve the crisis of trust and mistrust in their first stage of life, when they take in whatever nourishment they are given by parents and receive emotional attention. If caregivers and parents do not consistently meet these needs, the infant might begin to mistrust other's response to their needs rather than trust them. This topic will be broadly discussed under the patterns of attachment later in this book.

The second psychosexual stage is called the anal stage. This stage takes place from ages two to three. This is a change resulting from biological development in the infant because at this age the anal area is the greatest locus of pleasure. When the child develops control over the anal sphincter, the child enjoys holding on and off. According to Freud, parenting practices that overemphasize over controlling or overindulgent practices relating to toilet training, for example, can have a lasting effect on the child's personality development or what Freud described as "anal personality" resulting from anal fixation. This, he predicts result in the withholding of material or emotional resources, or being compulsively cautious in keeping things clean and in order. Freud's anal fixation theory also predicts that an adult can become very messy and disorganized or one who lets go very easily. In Erikson's perspective, the toddler at this stage faces the crisis of autonomy versus shame and doubt. Infants will fail to establish basic trust as valuable at this stage if parents and caregivers do not meet their nutritional or emotional needs. Parents should at this stage be gentle in teaching the child proper toilet use while at the same time reinforcing their readiness to provide nourishment and emotional affection to the child, as mistrust of parents in these areas would lead to the development of mistrust of others and self and difficulty in achieving a sense of autonomy later in life. With the child's maturing muscular control and cognitive and language skills, unlike helpless infants, toddlers will learn to control their elimination and also to feed, dress, express themselves with some accuracy, and move around their environment without help, thereby developing a sense of control of their own destiny. Parents must be cognizant of the child's need for independence at this stage and at the same time exercise sufficient control to keep the child safe and to help the child learn self-control. Parents' failure to strike the right balance at this stage may deny the child the needed sense of autonomy, which should assure him or her of sense of "I can do it myself." Otherwise the child might end up with a sense of shame or self-doubt when making any attempts.

The third stage of development, called the phallic stage, takes place from the third year to the sixth year. At this stage, the id energy shifts again. This time it is focused on the genital region. Children from the ages of three to six are found to derive special pleasure by fondling their genitals. This early sexual urge leads children to complex emotions which motivate them to desire physical closeness to the parent of the opposite sex. Freud called these the Oedipus and Electra complexes. It is at this stage that children begin to feel the full force of parental discipline followed by the emergence of guilt feelings and the development of superego. How parents deal with the child at this difficult emotional stage will also predict how the child will deal with his or her post-pubertal sexual needs. Excessive punishment when children are caught masturbating or when they compete jealously for the affection of the opposite parent could result in strong internalized inhibitions against sexual behaviors or in the asserting of oneself in adulthood. However, seductive indulgent action by parents can cause a selfish and flirtatious adulthood and a feeling of guilt over thoughts and actions.

Erikson described this psychosocial developmental stage as initiative versus guilt. This stage is found to be the period when the child wants to exercise more grown-up responsibility. In this preschool age, toddlers develop a sense of self-awareness and independence; they continually assert their wills by saying "no, no," and "me, me." They want to feed themselves, take their own bath or even cook their own food and accomplish so many other initiatives on their own. Parents who graciously handle this early attempt at independence with patience and encouragement help their toddlers to develop a sense of power, autonomy, and self-confidence, whereas if parents were discouraging, impatient, or controlling, the child may develop a sense of uncertainty and doubt that he could do things by himself which would result in a feeling of shame and doubt.

The fourth stage of development is called the latency stage. According to Freud, the latency stage occurs from ages six through twelve when the energy of the Id is no longer directed to any particular part of the body. The new personality of the child continues to develop following the styles of development formed from the first three stages of the child's development. Sexual desires are repressed at this stage and energy is directed into work and play. Erikson described this stage of development as a stage of industry versus inferiority. At this time, children develop a sense of industry and competency as they begin to put into practice skills that they will need for a productive life. This is also the elementary school age, when children learn to read, write, count, and learn other productive skills as their culture and society requires of them. Children should be encouraged and not inhibited from trying their hands in all manner of skills, for example playing of musical instruments, participating in sports, gymnastics etc. The way parents and society respond to the child's success or failure in learning those basic skills will determine whether the child will develop feelings of competency and industriousness or feelings of insecurity and inferiority.

The fifth stage of Freud's psychosexual development is the genital stage. The genital stage occurs between puberty and adulthood or ages twelve to twenty. At this stage of development, the Id energy is invested in sexual impulses which dominate and motivate behaviors. The child engages in certain activities and seeks to fulfill this need through participation in socially acceptable activities, such as work, friendship, or marriage with a partner who will substitute for the early object of desire or the opposite-sex parent. Erikson describes this stage of psychosocial development as a period of identity versus role confusion. At this stage the individual develops a personal identity from a period of serious soul-searching and questioning. During this stage of identity crisis, adolescents attempt to discover who they are, the kind of skills they possess, and the kind of role they are most capable of performing for the rest of their lives. Since no two children could ever develop all their potentials equally, parents will be proactive if they seek help for more needy children, such as the help of a guidance counselor or career counselor who will assess the child's abilities and assist the child in making a choice for a college major or career that best suits the child. Failure to resolve this stage of identity crisis can result in the adolescent's lack of a stable identity, delinquency, or even developing a problem in maintaining an intimate relationship later in life.

At the sixth stage of Erik Erikson's stage of psychosocial development it is assumed the individual had established a firm sense of identity. This is the period of young adulthood which ranges from the age of twenty to thirty. This is when sexual instinct is no longer repressible, but the individual is ready to meet the challenges of intimacy versus isolation. If the individual succeeds in forming a close bond with a significant other, a sense of intimacy will have been achieved. Otherwise the individual may avoid committed relationships with consequent feeling of isolation. Parents should encourage their children to form healthy friendships and relationships with their peers. This is not only to avoid the pitfall or crisis of isolation but also to encourage social learning since children learn best from their peers.

The seventh stage which occurs between the ages of 30 and 65 is the period of generativity versus stagnation. This is a period in human development when the individual thinks less of self or immediate family. The feeling of love and concern for others and community expands. Individuals who have no children of their own at this stage undertake the responsibility of raising and mentoring other children in their community or volunteering their time and energy to work for the good of others. The driving factor at this age is that all adults wish to leave behind a lasting contribution for the next generation. Individuals who do not develop this selfless and expansive love for other's wellbeing may stagnate or stop being productive in the sense that they may develop a new obsession for acquisition of more material things and become preoccupied with personal wellbeing.

The eighth and last stage in Erikson's psychosocial development is the period of ego integrity versus despair. This stage occurs through the entire late adulthood and it is the period when individuals who have been able to resolve their earlier psychosocial crises look back at their lives with feelings of fulfillment and accomplishment. Asked if there is anything they would like to go back in life to change, their answer is in the negative because they feel they have no regrets about the way their lives unfolded. However, those who resolved their earlier developmental crises negatively and considered their lives as fruitless and self-centered may deeply regret lost opportunities and become despondent as it would be too late for a do- over in their old age. According to Soren Kierkegaard, "life is lived forward, but understood backward." This stage is a period of wisdom and regret. Adults come to terms with the realities of successes and failures during the twilight of life. Both Freud and Erikson's developmental theories have their limitations because neither can easily be tested scientifically. However, Erikson's developmental theory was more widely accepted because it was not focused on sexual drive as is Freud's. Rather, it proposed psychosocial developmental stages that continue even beyond adolescence. However, the concentration here will be the adolescent stage of human development which has been considered as the most difficult stage of human development. In the following chapter, I will discuss attachment theory as a critical foundation for raising a healthy and happy child.

CHAPTER 3

Mother-Child Attachment

PARENTING IS BASICALLY about a parent-child bonding relationship without which other parent-child relationships may be difficult. The introduction of attachment theory and its application to the social and emotional development of an infant was a result of the pioneering work of Bowlby (1969/1982b, 1973, 1980). Bowlby (1969/1982b) observed that infants are naturally drawn to maintain proximity with the adult primary caregivers for protection due to their vulnerability in times of distress. This explains the infant's disposition to seek closeness and protection from the attachment figure whenever the need arises. Articulating the various thoughts from his medical and psychoanalytic background, Bowlby (1969/1982b) defined *attachment* as

> a way of conceptualizing the propensity of human beings to make strong affectional bonds to particular others and of explaining the many forms

of emotional distress, personality disturbance, including anxiety, anger, depression, and emotional detachment, to which unwilling separation and loss give rise (p. 201).

Bowlby (1969/1982b) maintained that a warm, intimate, and consistent relationship with the mother or caregiver is critical for the mental health development of an infant or a young child. It also includes an atmosphere in which the mother and child derive mutual security and satisfaction. Warm and continuous relationships with a caregiver promote psychological health throughout the infant's lifetime (Bowlby, 1969/1982b). Humans and other primates were found to possess organized cognitive, emotional, and behavioral systems which intrinsically enable helpless infants and mothers or caregivers to remain close (Bowlby, 1969/1982b). The identifiable variables that can trigger or activate attachment behaviors are the needs of the child and the condition of the environment surrounding the child. For example, infants and children experience separation anxiety when they are threatened and the attachment figure is not available to provide security and support (Bowlby, 1973; Bretherton, 1992).

From the experiential knowledge of attachment separation, Bowlby and Robertson (as cited in Bretherton, 1992) described three stages of separation anxiety: protest, despair, and denial. The protest stage is manifested in the anxiety occasioned by separation or loss. The despair stage involves the grief and mourning caused by the separation, while the last stage, denial or detachment, is manifested through the repression of anxiety caused by separation or loss (Bretherton, 1992). Natural selection facilitates attachment behaviors whereby infants, when alarmed or distressed, exhibit various social behaviors (Bowlby, 1969/1982b). For example, when the mother or attachment figure is unavailable, infants express distress and protest by crying, clinging, and frantically searching for the caregiver. This is done either to avert separation or to reestablish proximity with the caregiver, who provides protection from predators and other dangers (Kirkpatrick, 1997; Cassidy, 1999). Thus, proximity-seeking behavior has been found to have a survival value and to be an innate or fixed behavior in humans.

Excessive separation anxiety relates to the phase of despair and, consequently, to detachment, which could be due to unpleasant family experiences, such as frequent fear of rejection by parents (Bowlby, 1969/1982b). It can also be due to a caregiver's ill health or to the death of the mother figure, for which the child feels liable (Bowlby, 1969/1982b). An infant's expression of separation anxiety can either be very low or completely unexpressed which could result in a misleading notion of independence (Bowlby & Ainsworth, 1991). This has been shown as not only false independence but also as the unloved child's defensive attitude, whereas a loved child will likely grieve separation from the mother but in time develop desired self-reliance (Bowlby & Ainsworth, 1991).

Bereavement in infancy and early childhood impacts children and adults whenever attachment needs arise and the attachment figure is absent (Bowlby, 1969/1982b). This may result in the failure of the child to form close relationships with the mother and caregiver. The inability to form close relationships can also happen when a succession of attachment substitutes is recurrent. The child's ability to form a close relationship with the mother or caregiver is attributed to a behavioral system of nearness to the mother that is consistently reliable (Bowlby, 1969/1982b). Attachment can be described as a reflection of an individual's affectionate bond and psychological states with the attachment figure. Psychopathological emotions may be associated largely with disaffection resulting from the individual's relationship bond with significant others (Bowlby, 1969/1982b).

The result of cumulative or repeated attachment experiences or interactions becomes internalized by the infant. The repeated interactions with the attachment figure are represented in the mental representation of self and others. These models influence the individual's worldview and behaviors through his or her lifespan (Bowlby, 1973, 1980, 1969/1982b; Fraley & Shaver, 2000). The internal working models help the infant to develop a set of expectations about self, others, and the larger world (Ainsworth et al.1978). These working models determine how children organize experiences and regulate emotions and behaviors when the attachment system is activated. The working models and the resultant attachment styles have been found to remain consistent throughout the individual's lifespan and guide behavior in interpersonal relationships during adulthood (Bartholomew, 1990; Bowlby, 1998). The respective internal working model developed in early childhood leads to the categorization of the three-dimensional attachment model of secure, anxious-resistant, and anxious-avoidant patterns of attachment (Ainsworth et al., 1978; Bowlby, (1998). An individual's internal working model provides an important system for evaluating the part that early relationships play in determining adult relationships (Collins & Read, 2012. The individual's internal working model, therefore, directs behavior and suggests the action plan. It informs the individuals in romantic relationships to envisage certain responses from partners, to anticipate certain reactions, to read the meaning of other's behavior, and to be able to understand the social world (Collins & Read, 2012). Based on early childhood social interactions, Hazan and Shaver (1987) supported the relevance of attachment style to romantic love.

Secure attachment pattern is consistent with healthy development and the child's confident expectation that the attachment figure will be available, responsive, and sensitive to the child's need for protection especially in a threatening situation (Bowlby, 1969/1982b, 1998). Anxious attachment pattern is characterized by the uncertainty of the mother's or caregiver's availability, responsiveness, or helpfulness toward the child (Bowlby, 1998). This attachment style is maintained when the mother or caregiver uses inconsistent availability and helpfulness, separations, or abandonment of the child (Bowlby, 1969/1982b). Individuals with anxious resistant attachment pattern are said to be preoccupied with a negative view of self as not worthy of love, thereby creating a lack of confidence. They constantly worry about being rejected by others and view their attachment figure as unsupportive.

Avoidant attachment pattern is characterized by lack of confidence in the mother's or caregiver's ability to be available, responsive, or helpful to a child when needed. This group of children often experiences deprivation of love and a support system. It is an attachment system maintained by constant rebuffing, repeated rejection, and ill-treatment of the child, especially when the child needs comfort and protection. This attachment style can result in a variety of personality disorders and behavioral problems (Bowlby, 1998). The individuals with this attachment pattern seem to have a positive view of self while treating their attachment figure as nonexistent. These individuals shield themselves against disappointment and hurt by avoiding their attachment figure.

The anxious and avoidant attachment styles are considered unhealthy and are dimensions of insecure attachment patterns (Bowlby, 1998). Thus, attachment is considered to be more than a mere passive relationship between the infant and the mother or caregiver; rather, it is a cordial relationship between the infant and the mother or caregiver with far reaching consequences. Again, empirical investigation of the ethological notion of infant-mother attachment was further validated with similar three-dimensional attachment patterns found from experiential observation of caretaker-infant interactions (Ainsworth et al., 1978).

Infants with secure attachment style had caregivers who were consistently sensitive and promptly responsive to the infant's material and emotional needs and provided a reliable safe haven in times of distress or perceived threat (Ainsworth et al., 1978). This style of attachment is considered the most healthy and adaptive, and develops in children who are able to use their caregivers as a secure base of comfort and security. In repeated experiments carried out in laboratory and home settings, Ainsworth et al. (1978) found that approximately 60% of the secure infants observed sought to reestablish contact with their attachment figures upon the figure's return. The infants readily approached and maintained contact and sought comfort from parents upon reunion and then left to explore freely in their parents' presence (exploration from a secure base).

Infants who are high on the dimension of anxiety are referred to as having an anxious attachment style. This situation develops primarily from the slow and inconsistent manner in which caregivers respond to infants' needs and interference with their activities (Hazan & Shaver, 1987). These children make inconsistent attempts to receive emotional support from caregivers because they are unable to trust the caregivers' availability and supportiveness (Simpson et al., 1996). These categories of insecurely attached infants seek closeness and then squirm angrily to get away. They simultaneously display contact seeking and resistance to interaction with the attachment figure (Ainsworth et al., 1978; Crittenden, 1985; Main & Solomon, 1990; Main & Weston, 1981; Stroufe & Waters, 1977). Infants with such attachment dimensions tend to "cry more than usual, explore less than usual, (even in the presence of the mother or caregiver), mingle attachment behaviors with overt expressions of anger, and seem generally anxious" (Hazan & Shaver, 1987, p. 512). These behaviors portray infants who were rejected, abandoned, or viewed themselves as unlovable, unacceptable, or unworthy and viewed the mother or others as being available only occasionally. The researchers found anxiously attached infants to be chronically vigilant of strangers and to exhibit exaggerated emotional displays (Ainsworth et al., 1978).

Finally, the insecure-avoidant infants in the observation study constituted 25% of the sample (Ainsworth *et al.,* 1978). These infants showed very little or no distress when the mother left the room and treated strangers in the same manner as their parents. This is a result of mother-infant or caregiver infant interactions characterized by frequent rejection and rebuffing (Hazan & Shaver, 1987). Such infants generally become disinterested in the comings and goings of their parent but focus instead on their toys. At this stage, these infants showed no more distress at parent leave-taking and treated strangers in the same manner as their parents. Avoidant infants had caregivers who were aloof and distant; instead of seeking support from their caregivers, the infants controlled and regulated negative feelings in a highly self-reliant manner (Simpson, Rholes, & Phillips, 1996). The avoidant infant does not seek closeness or contact with the mother. The anxious-avoidant attachment pattern is identifiable by the lack of assurance in the mother's or caregiver's ability to be available, responsive, or helpful when needed.

This group of children often experiences a deprivation of love and of a support system. It is an attachment system maintained by constant rebuffing, repeated rejection, and ill treatment of the child especially when the child needs comfort and protection. Bowlby (1998) noted that such an attachment style could result in a variety of personality disorders and behavioral problems. In fact, a positive correlation between resistant or anxious/ambivalent and anxious/avoidant attachment in childhood and the appearance of personality disorders later in life is supported in the literature (Ling & Qian, 2010).

ADULT ATTACHMENT

Similar to the mother-infant or caregiver-infant attachment relationship, adult relationship and romantic love have been conceptualized as an attachment process in which the basic needs for comfort, closeness, and security are met through an intimate and committed relationship (Hazan & Shaver, 1987; Main, Kaplan, & Cassidy, 1985). Care giving has been described as a process that is not only evident in parent-child interactions but also an integral component of the adult attachment system (Berman & Sperling, 1994). This is because care giving and receiving are considered crucial both in childhood and adult attachment formation. Although some commonalities exist between childhood and adult attachment relationships, adult attachment relationships differ in the sense that there is giving and receiving of care among adults (Hazan & Shaver, 1987). Whereas infants and children require physical contact with the mother or care giver to feel a sense of security whenever in distress, adults depend on the mental representation of their partner for comfort in times of need (Hazan & Shaver, 1987). The perception of the quality of the relationship of parents with their infants and the quality of the parents' relationship with each other has been described as one of the best indicators of the quality of adult attachment (Miller & Hoicowitz, 2004).

For example, research has found that adolescents still use their parents as a secure base for exploration and frequently seek support from them when distressed (Hazan & Shaver, 1987). Although adolescents gradually transfer dependence on parents to mutually reciprocal relationships such as relationships with romantic partners, they do not necessarily detach from partners. The complete transfer of attachment functions does not happen until adulthood following the formation of stable, romantic relationships (Hazan & Zeifman, 1994). Studies on mother-infant interaction and adult romantic relationship as an attachment process provide important insight into the relationship between secure attachment pattern and satisfactory outcome in romantic relationships (Hazan & Shaver, 1987; Mikulincer & Shaver, 2007). On this basis, Bowlby (1979) noted that "there is a strong causal relationship between an individual's experiences with his parents and his later capacity to make affectional bonds" (p. 135). The influence of attachment history is believed to be manifested in romantic relationships. In adult attachment, romantic partners normally play the role of the primary attachment figures (Fraley, 2004; Fraley & Shaver, 2000).

The working model resulting from attachment styles is found to remain consistent throughout the lifespan and guides interpersonal behavior in intimate relationships (Bartholomew, 1990; Feeney, 1998). According to Bowlby (1973), infants form a mental representation of the quality of their early attachment interaction with the mother or caregiver which, over time, impacts their future relationships. Thus, attachment patterns develop in early childhood as a result of the caregiver's responsiveness and support, or lack thereof (Bowlby, 1973). This assumption represents the view of many decades of research in attachment theory that posited that the childhood bond with the mother or caretaker predicts one's adult attachment style in romantic relationship functioning over time (Hazan & Shaver, 1987). Several similarities are found between infant-caregiver relationship and adult romantic attachment relationship. Hazan & Shaver (1987) found that

> Adults and infants participate in close, intimate bodily contact with the attachment figure; both adults and infants feel safe when the partner or caregiver is in close proximity and responsive; both groups engage in "baby talk" with the attachment figure; adults and infants feel insecure when the attachment figure is inaccessible and nonresponsive; adults and infants share discoveries with the caregiver or partner; both adults and infants play with the attachment figure's facial features and exhibit mutual fascination and preoccupation with one another (p. 731).

Hence, the representations developed in early childhood determine how adults organize experiences and regulate emotions, behavior, expectations, and defenses when attachment systems are activated. The attachment system could be activated in adulthood when there is a distressing separation from the attachment figure (e.g., threat of attack) and distressing external stimuli (e.g., pain), (Gick & Sirois, 2010).

Basic to Fraley's (2004) study was that infants' attachment differences impact their interpersonal relationship in adulthood. These differences result from the quality of the primary caregiver's responsiveness to the child's needs. The quality of caregiver-infant interactions culminates in the development of a mental view of self and the caregiver (Bowlby as cited in Bretherton, 1992). When the caregiver meets the needs of the infant, the child forms a secure model of self as accepted and loved. If the internal models are predominantly negative due to the insensitivity of the caregiver to the infant's needs, such an infant would be at greater risk of maladaptive views, actions, and expectations from others in his or her adult intimate relationships (Lawson & Bossart, 2009). In an early study, Main et al. (1985) described adult attachment as a state of mind and observed that adult attachment representations reflected the residue of the infant's relationship history with parents and influenced the way siblings interacted with each other and perceived support in adult relationships (Main et al., 1985). These findings are consistent with the view that early experiences with parents remain salient in the context of adult relationships (Fortuna, Roisman, Haydon, Groh & Holland, 2011).

EARLY CHILDHOOD ATTACHMENT IMPACT ON ADULT ROMANTIC RELATIONSHIPS

Attachment theory has been applied to several adult attachment processes and outcomes. Literature is replete with the suggestion that adult relationships, as an attachment system, mirror the infant's attachment style with the mother or primary caregiver. Thus, childhood attachment style has been found to have a far-reaching effect on all future relationships of the individual (Feeney & Noller, 1990; Mikulincer & Shaver, 2007). Rholes and Simpson (2004) applied attachment theory in a study with adults in romantic relationships. The result of this research suggests that as individuals mature, they develop an orientation toward attachment figures that are a function of their early and unique experiences with primary attachment figures (Rholes & Simpson, 2004). The enduring pattern serves to inform the interactions and relationships individuals maintain with significant others throughout their life (Rholes & Simpson, 2004).

The experienced feelings of romantic love have been demonstrated to be predictable and markedly different between attachment groups (Hazan & Shaver, 1987). This is because attachment styles are related to mental modes, or internal working models, which, according to Bowlby (1969/1982b), show a strong continuity in adulthood. For example, studies with adults who identified either as secure, ambivalent or avoidant in relation to significant others reported similar styles with respect to their mother-child attachment relationship patterns earlier in life (Hazan & Shaver, 1987). Researchers asserted that the attachment patterns in childhood are consistent with adult attachment styles (Ainsworth et al., 1978; Griffin & Bartholomew, 1994b). Bowlby (1969/1982b) commented that

> When interaction between a couple runs smoothly, each party manifests intense pleasure in the other's company and especially in the other's expression of affection. Conversely, whenever interaction results in persistent conflict, each party is likely on occasion to exhibit intense anxiety, or unhappiness, especially when the other is rejecting.... Proximity and affectionate interchange are appraised and felt as pleasurable by both, whereas distance and expressions of rejection are appraised as disagreeable or painful by both (p. 242).

Most studies on the significance of early attachment on later adult relationships (Bowlby, 1973, 1980, 1969/1982b) rely on the difference between secure and insecure attachment experiences (G. I. Roisman, personal communication, April 13, 2006; Roisman, Collins, Stroufe, & Engeland, 2005; Waters & Cummings, 2000). A primary implication in adult attachment is that individual differences in attachment would impact interpersonal relationship in adulthood in the same way as in childhood (Fraley, 2004; Fraley & Shaver, 2000; Hazan & Shaver, 1987). Kobak and Sceery (1988) reasoned that

> Secure attachment in adults should be organized by rules that allow for acknowledgment of distress and turning to others for support, avoidant attachment by rules that restrict acknowledgment of distress and the associated attachment attempts to seek comfort and support, and ambivalent attachment by rules that direct attention toward distress and attachment figures in a hyper vigilant manner that inhibits the development of autonomy and self-confidence (p. 142).

Therefore, adult intimate relationships as attachment process are governed by the same emotions as in the infant-caregiver relationships (Ainsworth et al., 1978; Fraley, 2004; Fraley & Shaver, 2000; Hazan & Shaver, 1987). Adult secure attachment is a bond marked by proximity with the attachment figure, the subject for maintaining close contact. The partner is used as a safe haven for protection and support in times of danger, illness and stress. In this way the partner is used to establish the required sense of safety, security, and confidence, thereby promoting undistracted and uninhibited exploration (Fraley & Shaver, 2000). It is also expected that the characteristics infants find desirable in their attachment figure are similarly desirable in adult romantic partners (Hazan & Shaver, 1987). Thus, the same factors that facilitate exploration in children such as proximity, consistency, and responsive care equally facilitate similar exploration in adulthood (Fraley, 2004; Fraley & Shaver, 2000; Hazan & Shaver, 1987).

The contrast with infant-mother relationships is that in adult relationships either partner could be described as being more helpful, supportive, or protective (Fraley & Shaver, 2000). Either one of the partners could also be characterized as being more helpless, stressed or threatened and needing more responsiveness and supportive care from the other partner. Thus, adult romantic relationships are reciprocal in nature whereas the infant-mother relationship is complementary because infants seek and receive protection but do not provide support to the caregivers (Fraley & Shaver, 2000). Attachment systems are not to be understood as adaptable and changing, but rather that individuals' attachment behavior results from their childhood foundations and experiences. Attachment theorists (Waters et al., 2002) conceptualized that attachment styles should not be characterized as personality traits but as cognitive constructs which define behavioral patterns of relating to others (Waters et al., 2002).

This finding supports other philosophical thoughts of earlier researchers that childhood foreshadows the quality of romantic relationship behavior in adulthood (Crowell, Fraley, & Shaver, 1999). Recent theorists posit that individuals with different attachment patterns are thought to seek "different strategies for regulating their internal feeling states and interpersonal relations" (Cooper et al., 2006, p. 243). The different strategies result from the internal working model, which originates from infant-mother earlier interactions and are responsible for the different attachment patterns exhibited by adults in romantic relationships (Cooper et al., 2006). These patterns of attachment, as earlier noted, have implications for the quality of romantic relationship satisfaction (Collins et al., 2006; Hazan & Shaver, 1987; Lawson & Brossart, 2009). For example, secure attachment style is conceived as an aspect of an individual's positive perception of self as unique, appreciated, and worthy of best care from a sensitive significant other (Shaver & Mikulincer, 2007). Lele (2008) found that securely attached individuals describe their romantic relationship as happy, friendly, trusting and generally satisfactory. Brassard, Shaver and Lussier (2007) observed that there is a strong correlation between a secure attachment style and high relationship satisfaction.

However, insecurely attached individuals have a tendency to resort to defense mechanisms when attachment need arises in order to contain their partner's unpredictable response (Mikulincer & Shaver, 2003). Persons with subcategories of attachment insecurity would adopt differing strategies in a relationship. For example, researchers found that individuals who identified anxious attachment style lack confidence in their significant others to be readily available to meet their needs during distressing events (Simpson, Collins, Tran, & Haydon, 2007). Such a state of uncertainty aggravates anxiety and sustains their attachment systems on alert, resulting in the adoption of emotion-focused coping strategies, such as hyper-vigilance (Simpson et al., 2007).

In helpless situations, avoidant attachment individuals tend to deny their attachment need by inhibiting and controlling their emotions by deploying avoidant coping mechanisms (Mikulincer & Shaver, 2003). Individuals who are classified as avoidant-attached expect interpersonal rejection and so avoid relationships (Cassidy & Kobak, 1989; Kobak & Sceery, 1988). Such persons are also found to be compulsively self-reliant and report few long-term intimate relationships. They do not trust others, are uncomfortable with intimacy, avoid self-disclosure and express hostility towards others (Bartholomew & Horowitz, 1991; Collins & Read, 1990; Feeney & Noller, 1990).

Each mode of attachment coping plays both personal and interpersonal roles in relationships. Mikulincer and Shaver (2005) found that the secure attachment individuals were concerned with developing greater intimacy with attachment figures, the anxiously attached longed to achieve a greater sense of security and the avoidantly attached strived to maintain interpersonal autonomy and control. In another study, Zimmermann, Maier, Winter and Grossmann (2001) found that individuals who identified secure attachment in the Adult Attachment Inventory used a better social skill approach when they encountered partners whose behaviors were less than desirable or insecure (as cited in Simpson, Rholes & Nelligan, 1992). Thus, securely attached individuals in romantic relationships display desirable behaviors and have a disposition for proximity and sensitivity. In contrast, insecure attachment individuals are ill-disposed to such positive attitudes towards their partners (Simpson et al., 2007). Collins et al. (2006) found that women with high attachment security were more likely to regulate their emotions by turning to their romantic partners as a secure base and for reassurance when in distress, which is consistent with findings that secure individuals are low on both anxiety and avoidance (Collins et al. 2006).

Attachment style is believed to be constant and resistant to change (Hollist & Miller, 2005). However, if it does change, the change usually occurs over a long period of time, culminating in the alteration of a mental model of self and others developed in infancy (Klohnen & Bera, 1998). Thompson (1999) noted that these internalized beliefs should not be conceived of as static but as an experience that processes and informs the individual's future adult relationships throughout his or her life span. Therefore, various mediating factors in the environmental, relational and internal domains of the developing person influence their increasingly sophisticated attachment representations. The psychosocial and biological natures of attachment make change on the individual's view of self and others a difficult and gradual process, which supports its global effect on romantic relationships in adulthood (Sibley & Liu, 2006; Sibley & Overall, 2008). Parent-child attachment, which is formed from the earliest mother-infant interaction and parenting, is seen to play a crucial role in the kind of attachment style or the earliest behavior the child forms and how he or she views himself or herself and others in the world of human relationships. The following chapter leads us to how knowledge of attachment theory can facilitate authentic and successful parenting and to its consequences in the future adult relationships.

CHAPTER 4

Attachment And Adolescent Emotional Development

PARENTS WHO HAVE an understanding of the effects of attachment patterns from infancy across the life span are in a better position to be the best parent they can be to the child from birth. Attachment theory provides insight into the nature/nurture debate for an individual's behavioral patterns. Childhood attachment style has been found to mirror adulthood attachment style, a phenomenon instrumental in the development of an internal working model to explain thoughts, behaviors, and social development throughout the lifespan (Fraley, 2004; Mikulincer & Shaver, 2007). The mother-infant interaction, as an attachment process, provides significant insight into the relationship between secure attachment and the positive impacts on romantic relationships (Hazan & Shaver, 1987; Mikulincer & Shaver, 2007).

Previous research demonstrated that married adults with loving parents and secure attachments were more likely to interact more satisfactorily, enjoy lasting relationships, and have more positive attitudes about their relationships (Berlin & Cassidy, 1999). In addition, the experienced feeling of romantic love has been demonstrated to be predictable and markedly different between attachment groups (Hazan & Shaver, 1987). This is because attachment styles are related to mental modes, or internal working models, which, according to Bowlby (1969/1982b), show a strong continuity in adulthood. Studies with adults who described themselves as having a secure, ambivalent, or avoidant attachment style in romantic relationships reported similar styles of interaction with their primary caregiver in early childhood (Bretherton, 1992; Hazan & Shaver, 1987).

IMPLICATIONS

These results of attachment study have a number of implications for parenting, marriage and family. For example, there are several family and social problems that are entrenched in many communities. These family and social problems include relationship conflicts, absent parents, and limited or no employment. Critical to reversing these social problems is teaching healthy parenting styles that are responsive and attentive to the infant's needs. This practice can be encouraged through prenatal and postnatal coaching that emphasizes a caring and loving interaction between parents and their children or between mother/caregiver and child. Such interaction should be encouraged so that infants can develop the securely attached internal working model that would define their behavioral patterns of relating to significant others throughout their lifespan. Clinicians and marriage and family therapists can gain more insights into their clients' complaints by attending to their styles of attachment in infancy and adulthood.

Development of a secure attachment style is important as studies speculate that unsatisfactory relationships among the insecurely attached individuals may spill over to school, therapeutic or work relationships (Powers et al., 2006) and impact the individual's ability to function in a team environment. Exploring the underlying issues that promote dysfunctional and unsatisfactory romantic relationships can be better addressed by focusing on attachment patterns. Moreover, reinforcement of secure attachment styles can buffer against the adverse effect of social forces on the quality of romantic relationships among African-American adults.

The mother-infant styles of interaction have been shown to affect the individual's adult attachment relationships over time. Stroufe and Fleeson (1986) observed that in an adult attachment relationship, people endeavor to maintain or relive relationships that were compatible with their previous relationships so as to maintain coherence and consistency within the self (Bowlby, 1973). In his study, Ugoagwu (2012), found that individuals with secure attachment patterns scored significantly higher on quality of relationship support as compared to the preoccupied, dismissing-avoidant, and fearful attachment patterns; significantly higher on quality of relationship depth when compared to the preoccupied, dismissing-avoidant, and fearful attachment patterns; and significantly lower on quality of relationship conflict when compared to the fearful attachment patterns but not as compared to the preoccupied and dismissing-avoidant attachment patterns. The fearful attachment group scored a significantly lower mean in the quality of romantic relationship support when compared to the secure, but not as compared to the preoccupied and dismissing-avoidant attachment groups. In a similar trend, the fearful attachment group scored a significantly lower mean in the quality of relationship depth when compared to the secure attachment group but not as compared to the preoccupied and the dismissing-avoidant attachment groups, and significantly higher on quality of relationship conflict when compared to the secure attachment group but not as compared to the preoccupied and dismissing-avoidant attachment groups.

The study also found that secure attachment predicts a higher quality of relationship support and depth and fewer romantic relationship conflicts among African-American adults which determine their overall satisfaction. On the other hand, individuals who were identified as preoccupied, dismissing-avoidant, or fearful indicated a lower quality of relationship support and depth but a higher quality of relationship conflict when compared with their secure counterparts. These results are consistent with the literature on attachment style.

Given the result of the above study, it is imperative that parents and guardians are aware of how insecure attachment styles and poor parenting skills may impact negatively on the psychosocial development of the child which could result in poor interpersonal relationships and unsuccessful romantic relationships in adulthood. Besides the method of parenting and style of early mother-infant interaction as discussed in the previous chapters, a child's future could also be impacted negatively if the child is exposed to abuse either physically or sexually by a family or non-family member. This body of information adds to the tools required by parents to ensure the psychological health and safety of children inside and outside of home.

The chapter that follows brings us back to the adolescent period of development as a key stage of child development when parenting skills are put to final trials by adolescent stress and storm. This stage of development offers parents the peculiar signs of adolescence which will enable them to use this last opportunity to right any wrongs in their attachment style and parenting skill before the child leaves their nest.

UNDERSTANDING ADOLESCENT EMOTIONAL DEVELOPMENT

The adolescent period (10-15 years old) is the most misunderstood period of the child's developmental stage. This stage is characterized by an apparent development of physical features due to puberty with its attendant biological, emotional, cognitive, social, and behavioral changes on the child. While the physical changes are very apparent, the emotional and social changes that puberty brings are not easily interpreted and understood by parents and teachers. This chapter will be devoted to providing more practical insights to parents and teachers who have to grapple with this enigmatic stage of psychosocial development. The central nervous system and endocrinal gland that produces hormones are responsible for the physical and sexual development observed during puberty. The factors that could affect the changes include age, weight, height, genes, race, nutrition and an increase in body metabolism resulting from endocrines glands which produce the hormones released into the blood stream.

The body hormones are responsible for regulating growth. The chemical imbalance hormone causes the display of intense emotions and unstable change of moods found in early adolescent age. The nature of these factors determines an early or late development of puberty in both genders. However, girls reach the age of puberty earlier than boys, and the process is completed in about four years among boys and girls with all the body changes and new features which includes acne, menstrual period in girls, more oily hair, more sweat, facial hair, growth of underarm hair, pubic hair, stretch marks and voice change in both boys and girls. Although there may be variations according to individual differences and circumstances, these features are the common noticeable physical appearances of the stage of adolescence culminating in young adulthood.

IMPACT OF PHYSIOLOGICAL CHANGES ON ADOLESCENTS

The physiological and sexual development that occurs in early adolescence brings with it some concerns that require the understanding of parents and teachers. This is critical because children do not understand what is causing their bodies to change and why their bodies have grown taller and bigger with disproportionate body parts and all the features mentioned earlier taking place. Their first impression is amazement, resulting in their asking their peers, who do not know any better, if parents are careless enough not to educate them on why such changes are occurring in their body. Parents are responsible as the first teachers of their children to discuss each developmental stage, especially from the onset of puberty. The important information to impart to children is the reassurance that such changes are normal and expected. Calm your child's anxiety by discussing your own experience when you were at that stage of your life and your reaction or your parents' reaction to it. As a mother, you should tell your daughter to ask you any questions she has about the changes and transformations that her body will be undergoing in the next few years. The father who is model for the son, should equally do the same for his boys. Single parents who have both boys and girls play both gender roles or may ask another family member of the same gender to do so. Parents who are not comfortable at all discussing sex education with their children should ask another trusted knowledgeable adult to do so. Parents can also teach the child indirectly, giving them the gifts of good books with accurate information for their age instead of allowing them to find out from peers or by themselves. The idea that one's parents did not discuss it with them while growing up should never be an excuse to allow the child to wallow in ignorance of his or her body development. Parental understanding and assistance to their teenagers at this stage will not only help the teen to cope with the challenges of transition to young adulthood but will also assist the child to avoid making wrong choices and mistakes that he or she will regret later in life.

Although every child will undergo the adolescent stage process, the way each child experiences it may be different since each child is different and will have to undergo the process in his or her own way, at his or her own pace, and in his or her time frame. In any case, early puberty or late puberty can cause elevated anxiety for the child. While in early puberty, the girl may face embarrassment from boys in the classroom for being different due to such noticeable body changes and features that are not seen among her peers. She may feel ashamed to the extent she wants to hide these features by wearing baggy or oversize clothes to school and other places. At the same time, early maturity may attract appreciation and respect from the child's female peers who may consider her to be more mature and treat her more like an adult. The growth that occurs during this stage of development affects all parts of the body disproportionately. Whether your teenager has early or late puberty, parents are to reassure their children that they are normal whether they develop physically earlier or behind their peers, since no two individuals could ever be genetically the same. Parental support and encouragement for late developers will help minimize the anxiety and embarrassment such children may experience at this stage of development.

ADJUSTING TO PHYSICAL CHANGES DURING PUBERTY

The physical changes that occur at this period are an important centerpiece of this developmental stage. It remains an important aspect of the discussion due to the emotional problems that arise from the new body parts that puberty brings. The changes that children experience from the ages of one to nine are not as dramatic as what they see happening to the body they have been used to at ten and above. Preparing the child's mind for this great initiation into early adolescence should begin at the threshold of puberty or the age of nine. This is because some children can have problem adjusting to their body growth and changes once the process begins. For instance, certain physical actions that were easy to accomplish may be problematic with increases in weight, chest size, hips, larger hands and legs. It is common to notice the adolescent at this period become a bit sloppy, manifested in his or her tripping over objects, spilling drinks at the dinner table or bumping things as he or she moves around the house. The rapid physical growth he or she experiences at this period makes it difficult for him or her to find a matching shirt or pants in his or her closet from month to month due to these changes in body size. Parents should be aware of this spurt period when deciding on the sizes of clothes or shoes they buy for their children.

These features require that the individual adjust to his or her new situation in order to function better in athletics or at work, for often adolescents do not understand that their body changes could be responsible for their inability to perform at the same level they had earlier been performing, which often leads to anxiety and frustrations in sporting competitions. It might be better to discourage late maturing adolescents from competitive sports because competition with much bigger and more developed peers can expose them to the ridicule of their peers possibly affecting their self-esteem. However, self-competing sports like track and field events, golf, and gymnastics should be encouraged by parents and teachers as such activities enhance the desired development, personal performance, and effective coordination of the rapidly developing body parts. Moreover, it provides an avenue for adolescents to ease their restiveness and to help the heart, which is slower in development, to pump blood fast enough throughout the body to meet the needs of the super active early adolescent life (Caissy, 1994).

Adolescents also display a voracious appetite for all kinds of food, including those that have less nutritional values. While this practice may be excused by parents in the short-term, the habit should not be encouraged because it can lead to obesity and its health consequences. As adolescents become more aware of their bodies they begin to visualize how they want to look; while boys may want to eat more food to build muscles like Superman, girls want to eat less to look like a Barbie doll or a Hollywood celebrity idol. Experimenting on dieting may be good in the short-term, but may become harmful in the long run if the adolescent is obsessed with being thin. This practice can become addictive if a girl is preoccupied with a model's body figure, resulting in denying one's body the necessary nutrients for a healthy development leading to the eating disorder of anorexia nervosa. This is a mental illness where the individual is mortally afraid of becoming fat and would always choose to starve, even at the risk of death. This mental disease, although not an adolescent disease, has been found to begin at the adolescent age. A positively responsive parent should be aware of the rapid growth and surge of energy that characterize adolescence and should be adequately informed of its presenting challenges to both the child and the parents.

How are parents and others in the family supposed to respond to physical changes in the adolescent members of the family? It is noteworthy that the adolescent child is self-aware of the various parts of his or her body. Some of these new features may be admirable while some may not be so admirable to the adolescent. It is not uncommon for them to point to the body parts they like and those they do not like, or which are a bit abnormal, comparing their body parts to those of their peers. It could be a bigger nose, head, ears, toes, or eyes that they feel is out of proportion to other parts of the body. For this reason parents should be aware of the adolescent's sensitivity to his or her body image. Some parents have opted to finance early adolescent plastic surgery in response to the child's complaint about the body part they do not like for fear of the child being bullied by their peers. While this may not be a norm or solution to the problem, parents should ensure their children that no one will make fun of them due to any form of real or suspected change in physical qualities. Parents should preferably reassure their adolescents that they are not different from other people as such changes are only normal and temporary. Moreover, parents should tell their adolescents that inner qualities are preferable to physical appearances, and no one is physically perfect, including models. Parents should be sensitive to the adolescent's feelings and realize why they do not allow anyone to see them nude or even want to go to the doctors' office for any kind of physical examination especially refusing to be seen by physicians of the opposite sex. These various physical changes cause a number of emotional and behavioral changes among adolescents. In the following chapter the child's cognitive and moral development are discussed. The knowledge of the capacity of the child's intellectual and moral ability will help parents to properly weigh their expectations of the child during this given period of development.

SEX EDUCATION

Adolescents are considered intellectually capable of understanding the biological and physical changes their bodies undergo at this period. The various signs of sexual maturation begin by the time the child is in middle school. Although adolescents may have a basic knowledge of human reproduction, they still lack sexual maturity. It is for this reason that sex education is advocated during this stage of child development. Although parents have the primary duty to educate their children on this sensitive matter, it has become necessary that such education is complemented through formal education. Sex education in the middle school also helps those children where parents permit children to sit in such classes. Parents who are opposed to sex education do not allow their children to sit in such classes in school which exposes the child to learn by trial and error or from peers. The danger of leaving such an important part of knowledge to the child's whims can have far reaching effects if the child makes a bad decision on matters relating to his or her sex life. Early adolescents will gain tremendously if parents and teachers expose them to knowledge on sexual development as it relates to fertility, child conception and birth, contraception, sexually transmitted diseases including HIV/AIDS, teen pregnancy and its consequences, peer pressure regarding sexual activity, responsible decision making on their sex life, responsible sexual behavior, and sexual assault or abuse. Such a comprehensive curriculum will enable adolescents to equip themselves with proper knowledge of sexual development and responsible sexual behaviors so as to avoid bad sexual behavior as they begin to engage in relationships with the opposite sex. In this way, prevention of catastrophic consequences can easily be avoided for both the child and his or her parents.

This information is vital especially today when the society is ever bombarded through print and electronic media with information saturated with sexual innuendos. Early adolescents should be helped to process their own sexual development and to accept it as a part of normal human growth and development. Although all adolescents will pass through this stage of development, parents and teachers should help them to understand that sexual development can occur at different times. Therefore, the fact that some adolescents will experience sexual maturation before their peers is quite normal and should not lead to anxiety. The middle school age, therefore, presents the most wonderful opportunity to teach adolescents who are beginning to experience sexual development, as they are more likely to retain such knowledge than children who are yet to begin the sexual maturation process.

EXPERIMENTING WITH ALCOHOL AND SUBSTANCE ABUSE

The anxieties and stresses that follow the early adolescent's biological and sexual development and the peer pressure they experience can lead them to experiment with alcohol and drugs. Studies have shown that most underage drinking begins at the adolescent age, just as most addicts have been found to have started their alcohol and drug abuse at 14 and 16 years of age. It is for this reason that parents and teachers will be tremendously helpful to their children if they teach them the dangers of experimenting with cigarettes, drugs, and alcohol. This stage of development in the early adolescent's age is critical as it is generally known as the experimental time when adolescents feel it is "cool" to drink, smoke, and use drugs. Discouraging any form of alcohol and substance use at this period is crucial because studies have suggested that individuals who begin to use alcohol and drugs during adolescence will be more likely to continue to a level of abuse and addiction than individuals who initiate the use of alcohol and drugs in adulthood. Thus, the age of onset of alcohol and drug use remains a significant variable in determining possible future abuse of alcohol and drugs. Early prevention of alcohol and drug use among adolescents can be achieved by parents and teachers through education on the dangerous health issues associated with their use and addiction. Such topics as why some people use alcohol and drugs, its effects on behavior, and social problems arising from abuse of alcohol and drugs, such as domestic violence, crime, and unemployment and poverty are among pertinent information that can dissuade early adolescents from becoming victims of substance abuse. While teachers may be instrumental in imparting such knowledge where it is provided in the middle school educational curriculum, parents have the responsibility as well to home-school their adolescents when such education is lacking in a school curriculum. Parents should also ensure that the triggers which start the use of alcohol and experimenting with drugs, *e.g.* peer pressure and the anxieties associated with biological and physical changes in early adolescents, are reduced to the barest minimum. Parents may also seek the help of school counselors and professional clinical counselors for the child if the need arises. It is very important to ensure that early adolescent anxieties and worries do not degenerate into addiction or depression which has been found to result in suicide, now known be the third highest cause of death among teenagers in the United States.

CHAPTER 5

Stages Of Child Cognitive And Moral Development

ANOTHER COMPONENT TO human development derives from Jean Piaget's (1965) cognitive development theory which was influenced by Jean-Jacques Rousseau's (1762-1948) position that the stages of reasoning and understanding in children naturally evolve in stages. Piaget advocated that parents and educators could be of immense help in children's mental development if they could provide children with the freedom to explore their environment and with learning experiences that are commensurate with their learning ability. This is because while adults are capable of logical and abstract thinking, this capacity in childhood is slow and evolves in four stages of the sensorimotor intelligence characterized by nonrepresentational thought, preoperational thought – characterized by the ability to think, though not yet logically. This is followed by concrete operational stage – characterized by the child's ability to understand and use logical processes such as addition of numbers (3 + 3 = 6), and finally, formal operational stages when adolescents become more capable of abstract reasoning. If parents can understand how a child approaches one kind of task, they will be able to determine how that child will tackle other future tasks. However, children develop cognitive abilities in different capacities.

Generally these stages could be fairly long or short depending on many individual contextual variables and can evolve in an invariant method despite individual differences. It is imperative that parents have a fair idea of the cognitive stages of development of their children so as to follow-up in their academic performance whether they are home-schooled, private or parochial school or in a public school system. This is important because of the assumption that some behavioral developments take place within a certain time frame or "critical period." Although a second language, for instance, can be learned at another point in the life cycle, it is never learned as effortlessly as it is learned at the critical period from age 1 to 5 (Pinker, 1994). It is necessary, therefore, that each developmental task be accomplished during its appropriate time frame as the critical period of learning ends with changes in the brain which makes learning more difficult afterwards.

SOCIAL LEARNING AND EARLY GENDER ROLE IN CHILDHOOD

Social learning and gender role conditioning is part of cognitive development in early childhood. Girls learn how to be feminine while boys learn how to be masculine. Children are found to develop cognitively by actively observing, interpreting, and judging the world around them. Through interaction and imitation of others with whom they share the same gender, children process the information in such a way that they create rules governing appropriate behaviors for boys and girls. This information helps them to form gender schemas of how they should act. This is why little boys' preference for fire trucks and building blocks is often reinforced and approved through the parents' smile at his choice as appropriate masculine toys. By so doing, the child realizes he is a boy and has learned that boys should prefer fire trucks to dishes and dolls "appropriate" for girls. Thus by the age of two children are aware of gender roles. They recognize that boys should act in certain ways different from girls. The gender role expectations learned in childhood apparently influence us throughout our lifespan.

Given the role of nature and nurture on the child's development and gender role expectations, the question will be whether gender change surgery, along with appropriate hormones and gender role expectations of the parents, would be enough to create a stable gender identity. Would a child accept sex reassignment and identity as determined by the parents without his or her consent? What about sex reassignment by parents' even caused by an accident? Is it possible that our sense of ourselves as men or women develops primarily from how our parents or others treat us? Or is biology the best predictor? Huffman (2008) told a compelling story of a tragic accident that led to a dire decision by the victim's parents to surgically alter the nature and gender of the victim.

THE TRAGIC TALE OF "JOHN/JOAN": A CASE STUDY

Bruce and Brian were born identical twins. They were already eight months old when their parents took them to the doctor to be circumcised. For many years in the United States most male babies have had the foreskin of their penis removed during their first week of life. This is done for religious and presumed hygienic reasons. It is also assumed that newborns will experience less pain when the procedure is done at this early age. The most common procedure is cutting or pinching off the foreskin tissue. In this case, however, the doctor used an electro cauterizing device, which is typically used to burn off moles or small skin growths.

The electrical current used for the first twin was too high, and the entire penis was accidentally removed. (The parent cancelled the circumcision of the other twin.)

In anguish over the tragic accident, the parents sought advice from medical experts. Following discussions with John Money and other specialists at John Hopkins University, the parents and doctors made an unusual decision they would turn the infant with the destroyed penis into a girl. (Reconstructive surgery was too primitive at the time to restore the child's penis.)

The first step in the reassignment process occurred at age seventeen months when the child's name was changed. Bruce became "Brenda" (Colapino, 2000). Brenda was dressed in pink pants and frilly blouses and "her" hair was allowed to grow long. At twenty-two months, surgery was performed. The child's testes were removed and external female genitals and an internal, "preliminary" vagina were created. Further surgery to complete the vagina was planned for the beginning of adolescence when the child's physical growth would be nearly complete. At this time she would also begin to take female hormones to complete the boy-to-girl transformation.

According to John Money (1972), Bruce/Brenda moved easily into her new identity. By age three, Brenda wore nightgowns and dresses almost exclusively and liked bracelets and hair ribbons. She also reportedly preferred playing with "girl-type" toys and asked for a doll and carriage for Christmas. But her brother Brian asked for a garage with cars, gas pumps, and tools. By age six, Brian was accustomed to defending his sister if he thought someone was threatening her. The daughter copied the mother in tidying and cleaning up the kitchen, whereas the boy did not. The mother agreed that she encouraged her daughter when she helped with the housework and expected the boy to be uninterested.

During their childhood, both Brenda/Bruce and her brother Brian were brought to John Hopkins each year for physical and psychological evaluation. The case was heralded as a complete success. It also became the model for training infants born with ambiguous genitalia. The story of "John/Joan" (the name used by John Hopkins) was heralded as proof that gender is made, not born.

What first looked like a success was, in fact, a dismal failure. Follow-up studies report that Brenda never really adjusted to her assigned gender (Colapinto, 2004). Despite being raised from infancy as a girl, she did not feel like a girl and avoided most female activities and interests. As she entered adolescence, her appearance and masculine way of walking led classmates to tease her and call her "cave woman." At this age, she also expressed thoughts of becoming a mechanic, and her fantasies reflected discomfort with her female role. She even tried urinating in a standing position and insisted she wanted to live as a boy (Diamond & Sigmundson, 1997).

By age fourteen, she was so unhappy that she contemplated suicide. The father tearfully explained what had happened earlier, and for Brenda, "All of a sudden everything clicked. For the first time things made sense, and I understood who and what I was" (Thompson, 1997, p. 83).

After the truth came out, "Brenda" reclaimed his male gender identity and renamed himself David. Following a double mastectomy (removal of both breasts) and construction of an artificial penis, he married a woman and adopted her children. David, his parents, and twin brother Brian all suffered enormously from the tragic accident and the no less tragic solution. David said, "I don't blame my parents." But they still felt extremely guilty about their participation in the reassignment. The family members later reconciled. But David remained angry with the doctors who "interfered with nature" and ruined his adulthood.

Sadly, there's even more tragedy to tell. On May 4, 2004, thirty-eight-year old David committed suicide. Why? No one knows what went through his mind when he decided to end his life. But he had just lost his job, a big investment had failed, he was separated from his wife, and his twin brother had committed suicide shortly before (Walker, 2004). "Most suicides, experts say, have multiple motives, which come together in a perfect storm of misery" (Colapinto, 2004). Parenting responsibilities include making decisions that promote the wellbeing of the infant who at the time cannot make decisions for himself or herself.

This story is told here to create awareness as to how parents' good intentions can go wrong when they try to manipulate nature or fail to share the truth with their children. Gender is genetic and our genes elicit the responses that shape our development and affect human behavior (Berger, 2011). Any attempt to surgically or artificially change an individual's sexual orientation, especially when it is not by the individual's choice, would amount to extraordinary epigenetic intervention with unpleasant psychosocial consequences. It was bad enough that David in our story happened to be a victim of such a bad accident, but to reassign him a different sexual orientation made the experience even more traumatic. Parents will do well to share significant experiences surrounding the child's birth when it is age appropriate for the child to understand. It is better that children are told such stories by their parents than to hear it from other family members or outsiders. A typical example would be the need to tell a child when she or he is of the age of understanding that he or she is an adopted child and that his or her parents are not the biological parents than for the child to learn of such important information from other members of the family or outsiders. Although parents might think such information may erode the child's love and allegiance to them, it would actually enhance the parent-child relationship and help build trust in the family. Parents who conceal such information from the child will be doing no less harm than the parents of David's who changed his gender and hid the information of the accident that led them to the change of David's gender.

STAGES OF MORAL DEVELOPMENT IN CHILDREN

Moral development is part and parcel of good parenting which enhances human dignity. The human person is very relational, and establishment of moral behavior is vital to human relationships. It is in the search for a relationship that human sexuality, as we discovered in last chapter, finds a fuller meaning. Because life is larger than sex, this chapter will discuss child and adolescent moral development, sense of values, beliefs, and sexuality.

Parents have often struggled with the duty of teaching their children the act of doing what is right. It has been observed that newborns cry when they hear another baby cry and by the age two some children use words like "good" or "bad" to evaluate actions that might endanger their own or other's welfare (Kochanska, Casey & Fukumoto, 1995). Again, why would a five year old think that breaking twelve cups is worse, and deserving of more punishment, than intentionally breaking one cup? This early life observation in infants has led to the speculation that morality might be prewired or evolutionary (Haidt, 2001). Evolution may provide us with the biological basis for these early moral acts in infants with the purpose of helping the species to survive. However, this is only a part of the biopsychosocial model of moral development. We shall, at this point, examine the psychological and social factors and how they elucidate the child's moral thoughts, feelings and actions that change over time.

The first stage of moral reasoning is described by Kohlberg (1976) as the pre-conventional stage. This refers to the period of one to two years when children's moral judgment is self-centered and based on what satisfies or what the child can do without punishment or other consequences. The child's moral understanding at this stage is based on rewards, exchange of favors, and punishments because children at this period have not accepted society's conventional rule-making processes. Parents cannot, therefore, expect the child to make morally sound judgments. Instead of using punishment as a way for training in moral understanding, they may prefer exchange of favors to reinforce good behaviors.

The second stage of moral development, described as instrumental-exchange orientation, refers to that period when children become aware of other people's perspectives. Still at this period, the child's moral judgment is based on reciprocity or equal exchange of favors for good behavior. Their moral judgment is based on the guiding philosophy that "good begets good."

The third stage is described as the conventional level which is when the adolescent shifts moral judgment from a self-centered one to that of other-centered. At this stage, he or she accepts conventional societal rules because it ensures social order; hence, the individual begins to judge morality in terms of compliance with societal rules and values. The moral reasoning at this period is based on obeying the rules and getting rewarded or thus, children's concern at this time is in being nice and gaining approval of parents and peers. Intentions and motives which are considered for evaluating what constitutes a moral act do not necessarily come to play in children's moral judgment.

Stage four of moral development is a law and order orientation period. The individual considers the larger community or society at this level of development. It is understood at this time that if one violates the societal law, even with good intentions, it will be considered disorderly conduct; thus performing one's duty and respect for law and order is paramount at this period of development. Kohlberg considered this stage as the highest level most adolescents and adults could attain in moral development.

The post conventional level is a level in adulthood when individuals develop personal standards for right and wrong. What is morally right at this level is understood in terms of abstract principles and values that are generally applicable to all situations and societies. For example, a twenty-year- old who considered the discovery and occupation of North America by Europeans as immoral because it involved the theft of land from native peoples is thinking in post conventional terms (Huffman, 2008).

The fifth stage of moral reasoning is social-contract orientation which is the stage when individuals appreciate the purposes of law. When laws serve the good of the greater majority, they are kept by citizens because of the social contract. Laws can also be morally disobeyed if they run against the good of the majority or fail to enhance social welfare.

The sixth stage of moral development is the universal-ethics orientation which states that "right" is determined by universal ethical principles that all religions or moral authorities consider as fair or compelling. The universal principles include nonviolence, human dignity, freedom, and equality. At this stage of moral reasoning, adults understand that these principles will apply whether or not they conform to existing laws. Thus, people like Nelson Mandela, Martin Luther King, and Mohandas Gandhi would be counted among people who intentionally broke the laws that violated universal principles such as freedom and equality. Kohlberg (1981) found that few persons can achieve this sixth stage of moral reasoning. This contributed to Kohlberg's combination of the fifth and sixth stages of moral development. Although it was found that most children from different cultural backgrounds develop moral reasoning along Kohlberg's theory, the post-conventional level of moral development among adults is mostly criticized because it cannot be applied to all societies. For example, people do not choose between individual rights and societal rights, but would seek a compromise that favors both interests (Miller & Bersoff, 1998). Kohlberg's standard of measuring the highest level of morality may not apply in all cultures, especially cultures that value individualism over community. However, the contribution of Lawrence Kohlberg's (1987) theory of moral reasoning and development from infancy to adulthood cannot be overemphasized. This theory is useful as both one of the tools of parenting and for individual assessment of moral development in adulthood.

RIGHT AND WRONG SENSE IN CHILDREN

Early in their development, infants are as sensitive to the mother or caregiver's smile as they are to their frowns. Ethical sense in the early development of the child is often emphasized because various cultures have moral norms which must be transmitted from generation to generation if the civilization of that cultural group will survive. Every culture, then, has precepts that border on virtue and sin, duty, discipline, punishment, justice, mercy, guilt, expiation, retribution, salvation, and transgression (Gesel, Ilg, & Ames, 1977). The growth of the art of good conduct in the child advances and matures by natural progression from ages five to ten. A child is born with some ethical dispositions and potentials which grow from infancy as early as the sixth week of age when the child smiles by himself or herself. By the eighth week, this egocentric smile transforms to a spontaneous and reciprocal one, such that at the age of twelve weeks the child can smile back at the smiling face of her mother.

Early in his or her development, the child is said to have developed sensitivity to smiles of approval and will soon be sensitive to frowns of disapproval. Hence, as early as the age of thirty-six weeks, the infant heeds a monitory "No! No!" a nursery game and as well as a serious command. In this way he or she learns self-inhibition and social disapproval, and by the first year, the child is already socialized to know how to please others, although he or she would still repeat actions that are comical to others. At the age of thirteen months, the child develops a will of his or her own, such that he or she no longer heeds "No! No!" and so becomes self-assertive. He or she feels the sense of independence like an adolescent doing anything he or she likes, such as throwing toys. The child could also be excessive in his or her insistence in doing what he or she wants. Parents feel children are too young to behave in such a strong, self-willed manner and are amazed at their little baby becoming an authority of his or her own. Many parents are able to tolerate and understand the significant behavioral changes that are taking place, while some parents may, as well, misunderstand the behavioral changes by a rigid application of standards of right and wrong.

As the child advances to the second year, more is expected. For example, toilet behavior may become an object of emphatic approbation and disapproval. The child may feel ashamed by the age of one and a half if he or she is reprimanded for doing anything considered as a wrong and may claim an alibi by accusing someone else. By the age of two, a child who is sensitive may blush if reproved for any wrongdoing, which Darwin described as the most human of all emotional expression.

At the age of three the child no longer tries out two alternatives where there is a choice to make, but is able to make choices and likes to please. He or she, thereby, presents as a moral agent and assumes suitable responsibilities. In the fourth year, he or she is less anxious to please others, praise or blame, and so needs new kinds of motivation to be obedient. The child at this age tends to become somewhat undisciplined, but when wisely managed by knowledgeable parents, he or she would be conforming again at the age of five. At this age, the child would like and accepts supervision by parents and asks questions even from strangers. He or she behaves as an obedient child. However, obedience is not a fixed trait; thus, the context and occasions of obedience change with the age of the child. At six, he or she is ethically inept and yields to the temptation of cheating, which is learned by being cheated. The child may possess a good sense of possession but may have a poorly organized relationship to her possessions and so will easily lose things. The child may not be capable of losing at a game honorably and so may cheat on occasion. The child will both deny his or her guilt and worry at the thought of cheating. By the age of seven, the child declines in the behavior of cheating and insists that others should not cheat either thus supporting social condemnation of dishonesty. Thus, children help as parents try to ceaselessly weave the thread of the fabric of morals. As the child grows in the sense of the good, bad and ugly, the child begins to lose his or her home ties. He or she begins to develop a more universal standard of conduct and becomes ethically more self-aware.

At eight years of age, the child is more aware of himself or herself and others, has clearer ethical and moral sense, is sensitive, is not overly competitive, and is fairly tolerant of associates' behaviors. At ten years of age, the child advances further along the line of working out his or her relationship with others without assistance. This is the most important period for parents to work on the child to prevent juvenile delinquency. The child is now better aware of how to apply rules and regulations and follows leadership. He or she shows discipline by waiting for his or her turn to contribute to a discussion instead of speaking over someone because she has outgrown the eight-year squabble, the six-year quarrel, and the five-year compliance. At this time she has also developed a sense of humor and so could make a joke of herself which portrays her emerging ethical sense.

The "normal" ten year old is not all around "good." Hence the child can sometimes become selfish, destructive, and deceitful. Despite the virtues we find in the ten-year-old, he or she could use his or her ethical abilities to spite play mates, gang up against them or disrupt their games. It would not be proper for parents to impose standards of moral behavior on the child at this age of transition, since the child is likely to fall back to his or her poor manners. The use of corporal punishment by parents to enforce imbibing moral values by the child would be counterproductive to the child's behaviors. As Gesell, Ilg and Ames (1977) observed "when an adult pits himself against a child for the mere sake of preserving authority, no good follows." (p.392) An apology as a kind of expiation must be demanded with caution since it is meant to set any differences right between child and child or between a child and an adult. A forceful demand of apology from the child would lead to disingenuousness and resentment by the child who may altogether show protest by "a sit-down strike." Worse still, any physical punishment meted out to the child to right a wrong-doing by the child is hardly beneficial. Thus, in times of crisis, parents would do better to control their anger toward the child.

In disciplining the child, parents should be mindful not just of themselves but of the child's good too. They must ensure that they are not asking or demanding too much from a child who is still developing moral responsibility. Every stage of development in the child has its own crisis; parents should be aware of the gradients of growth, should not confuse manners with morals, and should keep an eye on the long term goal, which is to ensure the mental health of the child. Parents should use skills like a sense of humor and face-saving banter, as these could work to defuse emotional tensions in case of breaches in the realms of manner or morals. Parents should therefore pay more attention to emotional equilibrium and less to gloomier use of expiatory punishment and retributive justice since, over the long and challenging years of child rearing that begin at birth, affection and mutual respect between the parent and the child are most stabilizing. Mutual respect is the foundation of morals, and reciprocity leads to reason, then equity, both of which differentiate a mature ethical sense (Gesell, Ilg and Ames, 1977). With background knowledge of the divine origin of the human person and the various child developmental stages and expectations discussed so far, a parent stands a better chance of choosing a parenting style that will facilitate the fullest development of the human person from childhood to adulthood. Whatever parenting technique a parent chooses will enhance the healthy growth and development of the child positively or negatively.

CHAPTER 6

Types Of Parenting Styles

PARENTING IS AN onerous task and yet the irony is that, as difficult as it can be, few lessons are given to would-be parents as to how best to rear their children. It is, therefore, often presumed that every man or woman could be a good parent or know what it takes to raise a psychosocially healthy child. If we take lectures on how best to raise our animal pets, how much more imperative should it be for any parent to know the "nitty gritty" of parenting or even being a guardian of growing children. This is critical because an individual's personality, whether we know it or not, could be affected by the way we were treated or raised by our parents. This has been evident from the many studies carried out to determine how the different ways of child-rearing have impacted children's behavior, as well as their mental health. In a study, Baumrind (1980, 1995) classified parenting into three styles permissive, authoritarian, and authoritative.

PERMISSIVE PARENTING STYLE

The permissive style of parenting is further divided into permissive-indifferent and permissive-indulgent. Permissive-indifferent refers to a kind of parenting where parents set few limits and provide very little in terms of attention, interest, or emotional support. In this kind of parenting, there is little or no commitment on the part of parents to the child, as the child and parents live in two different worlds that have little or no chance of meeting or interaction. Children of permissive-indifferent parents are often known to have poor self-control, poor social skills, and are demanding and disobedient.

On the other hand, the permissive-indulgent kind of parenting refers to a situation where parents are highly involved in the life of the child with little control over what the child does from day to day. The children of permissive-indulgent parents are found to be disrespectful to others, impulsive, immature, and out of control.

AUTHORITARIAN PARENTING STYLE

This style of parenting refers to parents who are rigid and punitive in their child-rearing style. They demand blind obedience and mature responsibility from the child, while keeping a distance or remaining detached from the child. Such parents would instruct the child thus: "Don't ask questions; just do what you are told or else." Children raised by authoritarian parents are easily upset, moody, aggressive, and often have poor communication skills.

AUTHORITATIVE PARENTING STYLE

Authoritative parents are found to be close, tender, caring, and sensitive to the child's needs. At the same time, the parent sets firm limits for the child and ensures their enforcement, in this way encouraging increased responsibility in the child. It is found that children who are raised by authoritative parents are the best behaved and the most responsible. Children reared by authoritative parents are also found to demonstrate a greater sense of self-reliance, and self-control. They are high achievers and are more content, focused, friendly, and socially competent in interpersonal relationships (Parke & Buriel; Holbein & Quilter, 2002).

Although children who are raised by parents who do not use the authoritative parenting style can also turn out to become successful children, it will depend on the child's temperament, expectations, and the warmth he or she enjoyed from the parents. Thus, how successful a child may be depends on the child's temperament, parenting style, and response to the parent's effort. Parents of competent and mature children may develop an authoritative style of child rearing as a result of the child's behavior rather than by the parents' deliberate choice.

OTHER FACTORS TO FACILITATE POSITIVE PARENTING

Another determinant factor for competent and successful child rearing other than parental rearing style is the child's expectations. A child's expectations of how parents should behave towards children from the cultural perspective also play a role as to how the child develops. For example, in most parts of Asia and Africa, such as South Korea and Nigeria, adolescents expect a strong parental control which they interpret as a sign of love and care from their parents, whereas in some other societies that emphasize individualism, like the United States of America, adolescents would interpret similar attitudes by parents to mean a sign of hostility and rejection by parents.

The degree of parental warmth or rejection for the child has been found in cross-cultural studies as the most important predictor in parenting styles and child development. Findings from about one hundred societies demonstrated that parental rejection negatively impacts children from all cultures (Rohner, 1986; Rohner & Britner, 2002). This was evident in the positive correlation found between parental neglect and indifference with hostility and aggression in children who also had problems establishing and maintaining close relationships with family and peers. Children with this psychosocial background were prone to a psychological breakdown that might require psychological intervention to heal. Contrary to Baumrind's (1980, 1995) findings that a competent and successful child must be a result of authoritative parenting style, factors such as child temperament, expectations, and parental warmth have been found to play a critical role in predicting the competence and success of the child through his or her lifespan.

According to Mary Ainsworth (1979), the specifics of parenting practices may not be the most important consideration in the child's development over time. For instance, breastfeeding versus bottle feeding may not be significant for later emotional adjustment of the child. Rather what matters is the relationship context within which such parenting practices occur. This is because while some parenting practices may be described as more consistent and responsive caregiving, others are not. For example, when a mother breast feeds, she holds the baby close to her body and, in this way, provides the contact comfort which soothes the baby. Similarly, when she bottle feeds the baby, the mother could also hold the baby close providing effective and equally soothing comfort for the baby.

However, it is also possible that the mother could hold the baby away from her body during bottle feeding and so fail to provide comfort contact; thus, both breastfeeding and bottle feeding can be good ways of feeding the baby if practiced in a way that ensures close and comfort contact. However, breastfeeding remains the choice method because it is conducive to mother-infant interaction and enhances both physical and cognitive development (Broderick & Blewitt, 2010), which bottle feeding does not provide (American Academy of Pediatrics, 1997). The significance of the mother-infant interaction in the later emotion regulation and social relationship development of the child culminated in attachment theory. Attachment theory explains how this early mother-infant interaction informs how the infant constructs a framework for interacting with the world using both tools from nature and the childhood interaction experience with the mother or caregiver. Further, the impact of attachment styles on the quality of romantic relationships as measured by support, depth, and conflict will be explored in this book so as to ascertain the effect of attachment from childhood through adulthood and adult relationships.

PARENTING ACCORDING TO THE CHILD'S TRUE NATURE

Most of the parenting styles suggest the "if/then" scenarios: in which case if a child does A then parent should discipline in a specific way. This style is not only reactionary and conditional but ineffective. It teaches reacting to behavior instead of the parent understanding and honoring the root of the child's behavior. It is the traditional and hierarchical parenting method the older generation was raised under, where the child has to do what the parents had said because they were older and knew what was best for the child. That method helped parents and guardians to get away with lots of poor parenting skills and left them making less effort to instruct and truly know who their children were trying to become. The millennials or the present day children no longer give in to their parents and are coming into this world more fully expressive and committed to living their natures and not that of their parents or guardians. They are less willing to be repressed and wounded by parents, grandparents, and other adults in their lives. The best parenting style should therefore seek to understand and honor your child's true nature otherwise any other parenting approach will likely result in unpleasant, frustrating and possibly painful interaction with the child. It will be most rewarding for parents to seek to discover children's specific motivations, allow them to show you exactly what they need; this in turn allows parents to raise a child who feels more capable, confident, and valuable in the world.

It's pertinent that parents realize their own unique nature and that of their children. It calls for parents to adopt approaches that honor just their own true nature rather their children's true nature. Parents can be unintentionally hurting the child when a parent ignores, judges, or squashes that which is true to the nature of that child. When parents and children understand each other's nature, there is better understanding, appreciation, and less conflict. There is a more loving relationship in the family.

I have purposely added childhood trauma in this book because some parents have unintentionally hurt their children and those children today are still struggling in life and trying different kinds of solutions to heal from past wounds and lack of self-understanding. Even those who seemed to have a good childhood often feel insecure or feel as if something is standing on their way from living their true selves. I can identify with that group because I was raised in a culture and parenting hierarchical parenting system where all that mattered was what my father or mother said was right for me to do. This parenting system can be injurious because it neglects the true nature of the child and convinces the child that he or she is incapable of doing anything right. Due to this lack of validation and acknowledgement of their values, they would probably develop a personality that is not congruent with who they really are. Children resist such a parenting approach, resulting in power struggle and frustration for the parents who feel their parenting style is right and therefore resort to discipline to enforce their way of conceiving life on their children. Such parents may succeed in the short run but will distort the child's self-confidence. This can be observed when the child withdraws from parents physically or emotionally, does not listen to or respect the parents, appears distant, or throws tantrums frequently. Parenting does not need to be a frustrating or daunting experience when parents learn to encourage and support the best character which is true to the child. This helps their children to be happier, more successful and cooperative with their parents.

THE PHILOSOPHY OF CHILD WHISPERING

The term "whisperer" became popular in the 1998 movie "The Horse Whisperer" which showed horse keepers how horses think and communicate. The idea was to teach both the human keeper and the horse how to accept each other and to work responsively together. The main objective of the horse whisperer is to make the animal feel secure around humans so that horse and rider can achieve union and increased cooperation (Tuttle, 2012). This same idea was also used by Cesar Milan in his work in rehabilitating problem dogs on his popular television show, "The Dog Whisperer." The philosophy here is that if the dog owners could intuitively read their animal's needs and respond correctly, the animals would cooperate. This is equally same for humans as I discussed previously which dealt with attachment theory. Though children are not animals and we do not own them in the strictest sense, the same principle applies in raising children. When a parent knows how to read the cues and messages that the child gives even before the child begins to talk, and the parent responds to the child with love and compassion, the child will then respond with mutual love and respect.

"Child Whispering" as a model of working with children uses an Energy Profiling assessment as a tool to evaluate the child's body language, communication, learning processes, personality, and physical characteristics among other observable qualities the child may exhibit. Children see the world through these various lenses and innately express them; parents who are familiar with child whispering should be able to intuitively understand how their child conceives the world. When a parent is able to identify the child's true type based on the energy profiling system, that parent becomes his or her child's whisperer. The parent will clearly understand the child's pattern of thoughts, feelings, social interactions, motivations, and priorities. Through their observations, they will learn what they are naturally gifted to express, experience, and what supports or honors them. This creates a symbiotic relationship that enables them to parent in a way that creates a greater degree of mutual cooperation and deep bonding with their child which in turn decreases the need for discipline. Although most parents have been brought up with the idea that disciplining children is the only way to get a child to cooperate, the child whispering model is the other side of the coin. Thus, training to obey rules or a code of behavior by using punishment to correct disobedience is not the best way; child whispering is. Children can learn appropriate behavior through means of understanding and communication and not through punishment or coercion.

Every child is different even if they are identical twins. Every child should be raised in a way mindful of their true nature and primary needs; one size cannot fit all when it comes to bringing up a child. These unique natures can be expressed in their thoughts, feelings, communication, learning style, body language and even facial features. What a child expresses is motivated by the child's particular needs. When those needs are met there is a remarkable increase in cooperation and harmony in the parent-child relationship. The child will also respond to the adult who loves, honors, understands and respects his or her true self. When a parent possesses such a knowledge of their children, the children want to be around the parents because they feel understood and at ease.

To be a child whisperer requires that parents define their ultimate goal as a parent. The ultimate goal of every child whisperer is to raise children who are true to their nature so they can grow up feeling honored, confident, and free to be themselves. Tuttle (2012) outlined the purpose of parenting as a child whisperer to be that of raising children to be true to their natures so they can grow up feeling honored, confident, and free to be themselves. To know whether a parent has succeeded in achieving their parenting goal, one will need to answer such questions as: "Do my children know who they are and accept themselves?" What matters is what the child thinks of himself or herself and not what others think, otherwise the child will not be able to maximize their potential gifts and future happiness if they do not feel their inner natures are worthwhile and valuable. The child's little steps and accomplishments no matter how small should be appreciated and acknowledged rather than judging them for every mistake. Tuttle (2012) noted that the most powerful gift a parent can give to the child is the permission to be their best self.

The second question is: "Do my children use their natural gifts and trust them?" This will require that parents help their children to develop and optimize their natural gifts to best serve them as they take up responsibilities and face the challenges of life. Children should be given tasks at home that help them to develop their natural gifts and talents and prepare for life.

The third question would be: "Are the things that I think are important in fact really important? This all-important question helps us to put our love for our children in perspective. We want them to succeed whatever that might mean for the individual parent. But focusing on success before you focus on the true root of success will invariably undermine all your efforts. Most parents' expectations of their children are self-serving. Even if they define success as your child's happiness, can they say their happiness was measured in a way that honors the child or the parent? When the parents try to change them from who they are, they are only saying to the child, you need to please others to be loved. This may have an adverse effect on children, causing them to withdraw into themselves or grow up with poor self-worth and unable to look people in the eye as adults for shame of who they were as children. Allowing children be in their own space will build more self-confidence and ability to interact by expressing trust in them to make the right choice when they are ready.

This does not mean that I am advocating that children should be allowed to do whatever they want or should not be taught appropriate social skills by their parents. The message here is to emphasize the need to reevaluate the expectations behind our guidance and our teaching, especially in social situations. Do we want to look like good parents or do we want to actually be good parents? Genuine support for our children as they grow up will naturally help them express themselves in ways that are congruent with their true talents and expression, which will result in the child's future happiness and personal success.

PARENTING FOR THE CHILD'S TRUE SUCCESS

A recent book in parenting entitled, *"Battle Hymn of Tiger Mom"*, by Amy Chua, has been discussed extensively due to the attention it has brought to the question about parents who raise children to be high-performing, high-achieving adults. There is nothing that can cause high anxiety for both parents and children than such a purposeful endeavor. The world is saturated with so many individuals who know how to do things. They function mechanically but do they know how to be? They are the worst of professionals if they are in human services as caregivers or healthcare providers. No patient likes them no matter how much medicine they know, because they cannot relate to or talk to their patients but talk over them with no feeling at all. Such can only be the result when we train our children to base their self-worth and value on performance. This can result in raising a child who turns out to be an over-achiever or workaholic in adulthood. They over-exhaust themselves to please others and not themselves. This is due to the belief that high performance is the standard of success for both the child and the parents. We could be encouraging such values when they are conditioned that way to believe that their achievement should be their ultimate value rather than be who they are in nature and in essence. At a point in their adulthood such an individual would realize the truth and face the reality of undoing the lie in order to find and appreciate that their true worth is not based on their accomplishments but on their unique nature.

They need to be loved for who they are and not because of what they have done. Success as a good parent is not to be measured by the child's achievement but on how a parent helps the child to develop the abilities true to their nature. In this way, high achievements flow effortlessly without causing stress over the achievement of success. Whatever is done to the child must be what really has value for the child's development and personal happiness and not for the parent's satisfaction. Parent conflict can be avoided when a parent seeks to encourage and support that which is true to the child's true nature and not centered on the parent's happiness. The child is not responsible for protecting the parent from uncomfortable emotions (Tuttle, 2012). The aim and objective of a good parenting style must be based on the need for the parent to help the child to be happy just by being who he or she is. This needs to be reinforced always by saying to the child: "I love you just the way you are." That is what it means to be a child whisperer. It means that you do not need to wait for the child to begin to throw a tantrum, become rebellious, or get out of control. To avoid getting to this point know your child's natural motivations and honor and support them so that crises do not occur. All children, no matter their energy type, have some basic traits and needs in common. Every child is active and innocent, they have childlike curiosity, imagination, and a desire to explore. Most importantly, every child needs to be validated, loved and accepted by their parents for what they are and not necessarily for what the parents want them to be. Meeting that need is the reason why you need to read this book for both yourself and your child and know your child's type as to know how best to respond to their behavior and true nature.

WHAT IS YOUR CHILD'S TYPE?

There are four known types of children a parent should be familiar with in order to raise a happy and successful child. These are Type I– the fun-loving child; Type II–the sensitive child, Type III–the determined child; and Type IV– the more serious child. Every child will have some level of each kind but will eventually be dominant in one of these types.

The Type I child is described as a fun-loving, social, bouncy, spontaneous, cheerful child; primary need of the Type I child is to have happy parents and to have fun. Children who have this dominant energy type will have the most natural disposition of all the types of energies. These children are characterized by their animated nature: bubbly, brilliant, light-hearted, and unstructured. Among adults, such children are described as a "ray of sunshine." This is because they always have a twinkle in their eye and a sparkle in their infectious energy. Their aim is to keep life light and fun. Some cultures value this kind of energy in children but expect them to grow up and stop playing games at some point or face the backlash. But treating a Type I out-going, playful movement as a strength will give them powerful permission to live true to themselves. When such children are supported by their parents and family, they live to be true to their nature which maintains their youthful energy and love of fun straight through to their adulthood.

One of the outstanding characteristics of this type is that they are naturally gifted with new ideas and the hope that these ideas are achievable. Their vibrant nature brings energy and new life to everything they do. However, this natural gift of being light-hearted and carefree can also mean that they do not naturally follow through. Given their natural flow of new ideas and experiences, such children may face the challenge of choosing an idea and following it through to the end. In their role as guides, parents are not required to follow through all the ideas that their type one child may have; nor encourage them to carry them to the end because they are not necessarily realistic. They are only required to acknowledge their child's ideas as good and fun. Sometimes that is all a Type I child needs to feel validated and enable them to move on to the next new thing (Tuttle, 2012). As socially oriented, this type children being naturally optimistic, make friends easily with everyone as they grow. They are often devoted friends whose energy and carefree nature draw other children to them. They excel in cheering others up because life is meant to be fun and happy. Parents know that in life everything does not need to be a game, but for a parent who knows the characteristics of a Type I child, everything is a game. These children have a natural orientation to be playful, animated; they love surprises, games, and pretending. This is a good thing and so the parent of a type one child should validate and honor the child's orientation to keeping things light and playful, by making little games out of ordinary tasks like cleaning their room, getting dressed, grocery shopping, getting mail and doing their hair or getting a haircut. Such validation brightens the type one child up. So as a parent think of how you can make your daily family activities a little more fun for your Type I child.

TYPE I PERSONALITY TRAITS

Children with a Type I personality exhibit cheerful, friendly, charismatic, outgoing, funny and cute traits. These characteristics are seen in everything they do. Their fun-loving, entertaining personality makes them the center of attention. Others may describe them as little social butterflies, even as babies or toddlers. This quality makes them likable and helps them make friends easily throughout their entire lives. Some may judge their personality negatively as a weakness, as if they were flighty, hyperactive, and irresponsible. Since the Type I child is not naturally structured or serious to wonder aloud what he or she will become will only make the children doubt their natural spontaneity and cheerfulness. It is better to validate and acknowledge their natural tendencies as strengths before teaching them how to manage it better for their happiness.

The thought processes and feelings of Type I children tend to be quick and random. Their spontaneous way of reacting makes them seem as if they were acting without thinking things through. But they think too quickly for anyone even their parents to notice. They juggle many things at once even when it makes them look childish in the presence of others. They long to be respected as they grow older. In order to be taken seriously, they commonly tend to slow down. They have hyped-up emotions. What gives others a bit of joy presents huge delights for them; conversely, hurt feelings can result in emotional outbursts. As toddlers, Type I children would scream in delight or frustration. They feel their emotions quickly and move on. Although their emotions may seem disorganized or disconnected, it does not make their feelings any less valid or real.

It is always better to give such a child permission to express their emotions before they turn into explosive expressions. This is because the child may shy away from expressing the emotion when they perceive that it may cause their family stress or sadness. To repress their emotions may result in depression and emotional overload for this type child. Parents should encourage expression of the child's emotions and show patience with any outburst or emotional expression. Type I children make their parents happy and will try to cheer their parents up when they are perceived to be sad, especially if the sadness is directed at them. While it is not the child's duty to make the parent happy, it is advisable to let the child know that everyone is sad sometimes and reassure the child that you, the parent, will be happy again. It is best for the parents not to manipulate the child with their sadness. If the parents are not emotionally connected with such a child, they must realize that the child may feel like the parents are not having fun with him or her. If everything is heavy and serious when the children are with parents, they may feel controlled and have no room to express their random nature. In addition, they may feel judged or unimportant because of their light and airy nature. The child might feel confused because their true expression is in conflict with what has been judged as improper or weak. When parents honor the Type I child's true nature, they become happier and emotionally connected to the parent.

Where communication is concerned, the Type I child is chatty from a young age. He or she are verbal, motivated to engage in social interaction and friendly. Such children can interrupt you in a conversation as soon as a new idea comes to their mind. To shush them may not be the right approach in correcting them; on the other hand, acknowledge their spontaneous nature. Let them know that you will listen to them in a moment or that they must not interrupt you before they could be heard, but that you know what they have to say is important to them. Do not let them wait for too long before they are given opportunity to say what they want to say or else they may lose it and disconnect from the idea. Communication for type one personality is loud, animated, characterized by movement of hands and bodies in gestures to convey their mind and make it fun. They are people pleasers or helpers who may compromise their true nature or needs in order to please others.

People might take advantage of them because of their willingness to help. If the spontaneous and random type one child is getting on the nerves of a more structured child in the family, shutting him down may not be advisable. It will be more honoring if the more structured child leaves the space rather than criticizing or shaming the Type I child as childish and crazy. Because of their random nature, parents should help them to meet children of like nature, since they easily make friends with whoever is available and so not feel isolated. Their spontaneous nature can also affect punctuality to school or appointments, so parents should help them make even getting to an appointment fun.

Transform work and house chores into play to keep them engaged as they would rather choose to play than clean up. For example, "Cinderella, mop the floor!" or "Quick! Let's see if we can make all the toys in the front room fly into their box!" (Tuttle. 2012). Every young Type I child likes to join the fun and likes helping when it is fun to do so. They also like to spend money on what seems most fun to them. They are naturally generous with money and like buying little gifts to make others happy. Their generosity is something that parents should encourage. However, at the same time, the parents need to help them understand that money is not the best or only means to make someone happy. They derive fun by sharing their gifts. They equally enjoy recreational activities like dancing, pretending, running, jumping, riding bikes, playing sports or games outside. They enjoy activities that allow for creativity and imagination. As naturally socially-oriented, the type of children should be engaged in high-energy activities that allow for significant amounts of interaction with peers and friends, rather than as isolated events. These children are happier when that which is true to their nature is encouraged and supported by their parents. It is worthy to note that they love new ideas which make them jump from one activity to the other. Thus they could start working on something only to be distracted about the next new thing, get excited and abandon it for a new idea. Demanding that they stick with one activity or sport or talent for extended periods of time will make that activity an ordeal for such children. They will stay with one idea if it is important to them and it allows them to express their true nature, so before signing them up for a long program help them to identify what holds the most meaning for them.

    Other traits associated with Type I children are their preference for a learning style that is visual rather than one that involves listening to spoken instructions. When they are given supportive teachers, their classroom behavior could be very pleasant. They are often regarded as the teacher's pet or the class clown; they are described as happy, confident, and always willing to participate especially when activities are not too structured. Such activities could easily distract and bore them, causing the child to become loud, disruptive, bad or taking on the role of the teacher's pet to make him or her happy. Due to their random movements, many have been labeled hyperactive or victims of ADHD. In actual fact, they are just highly energetic, brilliant and creative children who may not have been given the opportunity to learn to move according to their nature. Physical development of Type I children should not be hastened. For instance, give them time to crawl and engage in that way. Studies show that crawling helps such children to connect the right and the left brain hemispheres, which they sorely need. When they are encouraged to walk too early, it could pose a problem for them in the future solving problems in reading and math. As noted earlier, they love to talk and interact early in life, making up words and talking to imaginary friends. They enjoy potty training when it is made fun. The training may be accompanied with occasional accidents when they get distracted or do not want to stop playing. They may also have a tough time falling asleep. They do not like being put to sleep alone in their own room, as that will make them feel socially cut off. To assist them go to bed and sleep, keep the noise low in the home, turn the TV off, disengage from noisy activities that may be going on outside their room. Pre-school may be fun for such a child as they see all the fun everyone is having in school and separation anxiety from parent does not last long as long as the parent does not make parting or saying goodbye a serious event. They enjoy having babysitters as it offers another opportunity for a playmate. In the teenage stage Type I children have lots of love possibilities. They are prone to change girlfriends or boyfriends in order to experience lots of different options which is true to their way of experiencing life. The teenagers enjoy the social aspect of high school. Care, however, must be taken so that they do not fall into the trap of peer pressure or imitate the negative energy of their new friends or become weighed down with the effort to please everyone and being unable to be themselves. Such children excel in school when they engage in activities whether academic or sports that feel fun to them. Parents should support them in finding a way to make the subject they find boring, more entertaining for them.

The reason most Type I children do not perform well in subjects likes math, science and history is because of a lack of fun in the more left-brain subjects. In addition, the style of teaching these left-brain subjects may cause the child to lose interest. Understanding their learning style and creating ways of making the subjects more interesting will make a significant change in their performance in academic areas. Since Type I children are quick in thinking and reacting, they could be easily distracted in driving. In order to help them concentrate when learning to drive, extra distractions such as car radio and cell phones should be kept away and side conversations kept to the minimum to keep them from getting distracted and help them keep their eyes and attention on the road. One of the greatest challenges as the parent of a Type I child, is keeping a the child focused, or on task. These children can get distracted easily and do not follow through on anything they begin. Parents often think that the solution to this is to provide structure in their life. Structure is not natural for them because spontaneity and randomness are their natural way of expression. To try to change them by the use of discipline will only wound them or cause them to act more randomly to the point of increasing the stress and storms characteristic of adolescent life. Parents should not demand that their Type I child focus on one thing at a time as he or she will not and if the child tries to do so in order to please you, he or she will feel flawed, inadequate, frustrated and conflicted.

Instead, parents should help them to decide on the idea that they value most and support them to remain socially engaged all the way through the experience. The responsibility of the parents of the Type I child is to encourage and support the child's natural gifts and traits even when the parent is not a fun-loving individual. The parents are not responsible for creating all the fun for them but need to support them and not shut them down when they are creating their fun ideas. Supporting and encouraging the Type I daughter to feel recognized for her brilliant ideas and talents as she grows into a young woman will help her embrace her cuteness as something she will not grow out of. The energy of these children is not gender specific as both genders can be Type I. Though the male child may start to question his nature as he begins to mature and may begin to alter his true nature due to the cultural belief of what is male energy: something stronger, bolder, and more serious and not fun and spontaneous. Parents of a Type I teenage boy may find themselves using the cultural cliché "It's time to grow up and be a man." This could cause such young men to become conflicted and to think that they can never be successful if they live true to their nature. Experience has shown that many Type I men have contributed immensely to humankind's progress through their ideas and optimism. Martin Luther King Jr. and Nelson Mandela are just two examples of such persons in human history. Therefore, do not send the message to the young Type I son that he needs to "grow up and be a man!" Help him to love and cherish living a life true to himself and honor his random, buoyant nature as he grows. When supported in this way, he will turn out to be a happy, accomplished, and successful man. It is never too late for the parents who have this type child who is 16 years old or even 40 years old to validate and affirm all their previous stages of development. The information that has been shared here should help in recognizing and healing from some of your own inner child's unmet needs to assist in feeling much happier now.

Every parent of a Type I child should always remember that their child wants and needs them to be happy always. He or she will always try to help the parents smile a lot more about life. Let him or her realize that they are not responsible for the happiness of others. They need freedom to move, create, explore, to interact and to adapt. Too much structure boxes them in and restrains their true nature. Praise them for their ideas and creativity. Help them to follow through on ones they feel are most important to them. Encourage them to live true to their nature since they easily adapt to family and friends. Change is another name for

Type I children. They grow tired of things being the same; give them freedom to change things up in their life, like their room, hairstyle, toys, friends, and respect them when they change their mind about things. Schedule time to have fun and let your hair down, even with adult Type I children. Engage these children to reminisce about funny memories that help everyone to laugh. Take the Type I child seriously in their light and animated nature. Acknowledge it without having to become serious. Do not try to get them to take life more seriously, by becoming more serious. Parents may easily get upset with them for dropping the ball on things, being late, letting their rooms get messy, or not turning in homework. For you as parents pick and choose that which you need to discipline them, as well as how to discipline them. It will be necessary to make adjustments so they can create success consistently in their own natural way. Avoid using phrases such as "settle down," "grow up," "you're too silly," "when are you going to become responsible?" "Okay, that's enough fun; everything doesn't have to be a game," and so forth.

THE TYPE II CHILD

The Type two child connects with the world through his or her emotions, being subtle and flowing in movement. Their primary need is to have their feelings honored and for everyone in the family to feel loved and connected. The Type II child's expression is derived from the element of water and oxygen which has a natural, fluid and flowing movement. Children with such a nature will be naturally calming, subdued, and sensitive. They maintain a medium to medium-low level of movement and strive to keep life comfortable for themselves and others emotionally and physically. The flow of energy in the Type II child could also be described as soft, steady, easy-going, relaxed, and tender. Parents often value the lower energy of these children because they are generally quieter, and have the capacity to sit still for longer periods of time. Given their calm nature, they are often told to "Talk louder!" "Hurry up!" Recognizing and honoring their lower energy and their need to take their time will be validating and encouraging for them to live true to their life. In this way they grow up to know that their steady pace and need for comfort are strengths. Type II children are naturally talented with the ability to use details they gather to make life peaceful for all. Their catchphrase is: "What do we need to know and plan to make the idea possible?" They move like a deep steady river. Given the time they need, Type II children are deliberate and methodical in whatever they do in life. They ask detailed questions and "Father, I don't understand what it' is," comes easily to them and works hard to find answers to them.

Parents of such children should encourage them when they face the challenge of moving from the question phase of a problem to actually putting their plan into action. They are prone to questioning themselves after making a decision and starting to act on it. An informed parent should help them to understand that shutting down their natural tendency to ask questions will go against their nature. Parents may not have the answers to the questions the Type II child may ask. So instead of asking them to stop asking questions, direct them to resources where they can find answers to their questions such as, the library, online resources, or family members whom they feel comfortable to ask such questions, like their grandparents, uncles and aunts. A Type II child will use all they have learned to make life flow comfortably for others. For example a toddler will gather all the supplies, new diaper, wipes, and blanket to lie on, then would go to the mother who immediately seeing those supplies will know what he or she wants. They pay attention to details and put together a plan to make it easier for the parent to do the job. That is how they can be thoughtful and make plans in advance that they think will please others. They are naturally sensitive to other people's feelings and they empathize readily with anyone they feel is unhappy. They are equally very sensitive to themselves, and can easily be offended or feel hurt. They can also take too much emotional responsibility for those they love, especially their parents. To meet their emotional needs, parents should maintain physical connection with the Type II child. They enjoy frequent touching especially as babies; they enjoy cuddling, hugging, and need to be held and comforted. Due to the personality they exhibit, others describe them as being responsive, sensitive, concerned, low-key, gentle and emotionally aware.

People are naturally drawn to them. They tend to hold back if they feel pushed too hard by others. They would rather blame themselves when their plans go wrong than blame anyone else. Planning together with your Type II child will help him or her to lower their anxiety level due to upcoming changes like changing school, moving to a new town, or meeting new people. They need time to think through any change in order to enter into such new situation comfortably and safely. Despite their strong emotional orientation the Type II child needs to be encouraged to share his or her feelings as they would not ordinarily share their feelings unless asked. When this group of children is not supported in experiencing their feelings and working through them, they develop into children and teens who lack self-confidence. If parents do not feel emotionally connected to their Type II child, it may well be that they do not feel they can speak up around in the parents' presence. They may feel rushed or pushed if asked to speak up when in public or with their parents. This will make them feel as if the details that matter to them have been dismissed. This can also cause the child to lose confidence in their parents and feel that he or she cannot count on them to follow through with their plans. They may feel required to take emotional responsibility for the parents, and they may also be confused about who they are, because their naturally emotional expression has been judged by their parents as weakness. When a Type II child's needs are met they will become more peaceful and emotionally responsive. Their lower level of movement shows in their communication style. They are soft-spoken and emotionally aware. They prefer a comfortable conversation and may withdraw, worry, or cry when things get heated up. They are slow to speak their mind or ask for what they need and so parents should not neglect them because they do not express their needs adequately. Parents should tell their Type II kids that they can come to them if they need help with anything.

Type two children enjoy activities that entail details; gathering detailed information is central to their learning style. They are good in doing research or engaging in games and activities that involve detailed planning as long as it remains interesting. Teachers love this type of children because they are quiet in the classroom and follow directions. They can be sensitive to their emotional environment, especially the classroom. They are sensitive to how the teacher feels about them or how their peers feel about them or how the school children treat each other. If a Type II child refuses to go to school it will be necessary for the parent to ask the child how comfortable they feel at school or how they feel about his or her peers. Because of their tendency to be detail-oriented they may be late in completing their school assignments or wait till the last minute or stay up all night to complete a big project. Ask how you can help them move into the action phase and not delay any longer over the details. They are hesitant to go to school and need some time to acclimate and observe before getting involved in any activity. Although they have difficulty making decisions when they do not know what to expect parents should do something to help them. Ask questions that encourage them to move forward, for example: "I noticed that you have been meaning to complete your project for some time now, but have not done it. What will help you to complete it?" Type II children are not slow but need time for both planning and breaks. And when they are engaged in their work, their pace is strong and steady. At each developmental age, every child has a specific emotional need. Parents must ensure that those needs are met. Consider how to express the phrases in action to help the child feel loved and wanted in every stage of their life.

When the child is emotionally supported to live true to his nature he will grow to adulthood able to maintain a healthy relationship. Parents can do this by always inviting them to share their feelings since they find it difficult to do so and do not have the best communication skills to convey exactly what they want as children. Such interaction will lay the foundation for trust and openness. In general, parents who have a Type II child should always remember the importance of comfort for them in areas of clothing with soft materials, supportive beddings, study areas, food and so forth. and provide conditions that support a peaceful and comfortable home environment. Given their tendency to worry, they should be corrected gently when they make mistakes. Let them know that it's okay to feel sad when one makes a mistake. Validating the feelings expressed helps them to feel supported and to stay emotionally balanced and stable. In all their developmental stages they should be encouraged to live true to who they are. Throughout their childhood, support their inquisitive spirit by supporting their questioning nature which is their process of making meaning and success through all their developmental stages. Physical connection is an important way of being with your Type II child. A hug or a pat on their back, even though their teenage years, ensures that they will continue to cuddle and sit close to you. In other words, they desire an equal amount of attention like the rest of their siblings who are more outspoken in their needs. They want to be heard, so encourage them to share their feelings, interests, hopes, dreams and plans as they grow up. Do not show frustration over their endless questions, or slow energy to complete a project. Rather focus on the calming energy they create when their nature is honored and validated. Therefore phrases such as "hurry up," "you're too slow," "you're too quiet," "stop worrying so much," "don't be shy," "you're too picky," "you're a little awkward," or "when will you finally finish," should be avoided as much as possible. And know that their strengths are greater than their weaknesses. Avoid negative labels like cry-baby, overly sensitive, pouty or shy.

THE TYPE THREE CHILD

The Type III child is described as the determined one. Their primary way of connecting with the world is physical; their primary movement is to push forward and remain determined whereas their primary need is to be challenged and have new experiences with parental support. The Type III child can be compared to the elements of hydrogen and fire, active and reactive. They are naturally determined, purposeful and persistent. They show the intensity needed to create new things in the world and express medium to medium-high level of movement in relation to the other three types (Tuttle, 2012). The Type III dominant energy is remarkably turned towards being independent, adventurous, and self-motivated. They are busy and always need to get things done. Their huge priority is to physically explore their world; their incessant quest to explore may get parents irritated or have them judge it as a weakness. In such a case an uninformed parent may tell the child to calm down and stop being too demanding but if a parent recognizes the Type III child's swift, determined energy as his or her strength, the parent will support it and so give the child the permission to live true to him or herself. Type III children who get the encouragement and support they need early in life grow up to be more confident and determined to make big things happen. Many Type III children have grown up to be very talented and successful athletes. Their courage and determination to create results, encourages everyone around them. The cycle of energy being examined here so far points to the fact that the Type I energy initiates the cycle with new ideas and hope. The Type II energy gathers the details by asking questions and making plans and the Type III energy moves those ideas and plans into action. The natural energy of the Type III child to push forward and to create results starts from their childhood. The result they create may not be the kind parents may expect but will be honored if parents recognize this gift and help them set their course appropriately and permit them to live true to their natural gifts.

Whatever a Type III child sets their mind to accomplish they will go out of their way to get done at any age. As an infant he or she may crawl early so that they can reach the toy they want. I can identify with this energy because as an infant, my mother would tease me by narrating how I used a sickle to cut the corn-maize I wanted when she had not plucked it for me. The catchphrase for this energy type is "Let's get to work and get it done!" This type may start a business on the front lawn to raise money for something they want to buy. The possibilities of what they can accomplish are endless; they always have an end in mind–action/reaction. They think big and aim big, and when encouraged and supported to pursue the goals that they value, they are naturally driven to achieve them. They do not like to feel blocked or thwarted from the goals they want to achieve and any attempt to block them will run contrary to their true nature. If your Type III child is pushing for results that may harm them, for example running toward a busy road, the parent may not need to stop the child but redirect the child where he can run. If they are pushing for results bigger than what the parents can handle, consider the possibility of letting them go for it rather than interfering. Their extrovert energy enables them to connect easily with people of various age groups and size does not matter to them in relating to those older than them. Their sense of confidence comes naturally to them and helps them to lead or take charge when they are playing games with their peers. Encourage them to take charge of some household gatherings or a dinner. In this way their natural gifts are being acknowledged and honored and their confidence will help them to accomplish great things.

The personality of the Type III child is passionate, determined, and confident. Their passionate disposition fires those around them into action. When they are encouraged to pursue what they are passionate about, others around them experience their contagious and fiery energy as encouraging rather than pushy. They would pursue a result confidently and swiftly before they realize all the details of what they want to do. Their personality is naturally big and loud but they do not perform to impress others or consider so much what others may say. Others may see their personality negatively as pushy, aggressive, demanding, or out of control, which may suggest that their natural energy is too big or too much. If this is a consistent message, they may get the erroneous impression that their personality is flawed. As a consequence, they may try to alter their natural energy or shut down altogether. When confronted with being so shamed or confused into living a life contrary to their nature, that forceful natural energy will need somewhere to go or be exhibited in lots of fiery frustration which can quickly get out of control. Parents of Type III energy children should endeavor to help them balance their outward energy and fiery personality by recognizing and honoring them as their natural strength that encourages anyone that knows them. This type child will be happier as a parent provides the support and encouragement they need to actively pursue their dreams no matter how big. Get out of their way, cheer them on, and trust that they can do it. Their thought pattern may indeed seem impulsive, taking action when they should have thought more about it. This is because they are more action-oriented than descriptive. It is important to know that despite fiery personality their actions are well-intended. To discipline a Type III child because of their impulsive tendency will only cause them more frustration.

On the contrary, encourage or honor their self-confidence to accomplish a task without parental guidance or permission. However, if the child's choice is one that could cause harm to the child or someone else, the parent will do well to admire the child's adventurous nature and add that parents need to be informed the next time the child wants to leave the house for somewhere else. Disciplining the child should only be considered if the child leaves home again without telling the mom or dad. Their impulsive and abrupt actions and reactions could get them into trouble. It will be a sign of understanding if the parents receive their thoughts and actions without immediate negative reaction. Instead, the parents should look into their eyes and assure them of understanding that he or she needs attention and will have it in a moment. You probably may never wonder how your Type III child feels because they will tell you whether they are happy, sad, excited, or upset and they will do so in all their intensity. Although this child is confident, they still need expressions of reassurance and love like the other types of children. If the parent does not feel emotionally connected with the child, it may be that the child feels that you always tell him or her "No!" or that he or she feels too restricted when he or she is around you, or does not experience enough physical activities together with the parents. They may also feel that parents talk about what they will do, but never do it. The Type III child may be confused about who he or she is because his natural physical expression has been judged by their parents as a weakness. The Type three child needs physical outlets for their energy. Telling such a child to stop moving is like telling fire to just cool down a little bit. Do not be surprised at their outbursts and persistent loud reaction especially when they feel they are not being listened to. They are compassionate and kind and will be the first to help someone who needs help. On the other hand, they may try to boss everyone in the family around, make decisions for their siblings, or tell everyone what to do. The best action a parent can take in such situations is to redirect the child's energy to more productive activity. Do not expect them to be punctual in every activity.

The messages that parents need to persistently send to this child is: "You are smart and brilliant; you learn quickly; you are able to move at whatever pace feels best to you. You can succeed in doing whatever feels right and honors who you are. Trust your intuition, you deserve to succeed. Follow your heart, be true to yourself and you can change whatever you're doing at any time without apologies. Remember it is not your duty to be in charge of pushing the family to be at its best or responsible for our happiness. We are proud of you for being active and understanding so you do not need to change yourself because of anyone. You have the right to set your boundaries and pursue what is important to you."

Your young teenage Type III child may push back against structures he or she may find at school. They may be reprimanded for being too loud or not sitting still in the classroom. Often termed as rowdy, this does not mean that they will not do well at school. If shown the purpose for those structures they will obey and work with them and not go against them. Though their movement is active, it is not explosive but purposeful provided they are not heavily pressured. Experience of conflict in any form at school may mean that a Type III child may need more physical activity or more academic activity. The child should be given opportunity during the day to explore and engage in experiments and to play. When such children have not been raised to live true to their natural energy and movement, you will notice some level of stress in their behavior and feelings of anger and rebellion. The parent can begin to make a difference and help the child begin to live true to himself or herself by saying to the child, "I know that you always have things you want to do. What would be the most important thing I could help you to do now? As a young teenager, this child is very easy to support because of their confident nature. They can easily separate and easily create their own independence from the family. Friends become very important in this stage of their development. They should be encouraged to relate with their friends as they feel best. Tell them they do not need to please others to make them love you. Show them you they can take all the time you need to grow up; that it is acceptable to make mistakes and to correct them and then move forward with the things that are important to them. Assure them that you the parents will always be here to help them. They do not need to do anything to be loved, just be themselves. Point out to them that it will be good for them to think for a moment before committing to a project. Children should be encouraged to develop their own interest and relationships. They should also be taught about sex and be responsible for their needs, feelings and behaviors. Even when you have not raised your Type III child in these principles, it is never late to begin and when the parents gain their children's trust, they can turn things around for their child and themselves. In whatever stage of development we maybe, we still carry our unmet emotional needs over to the next stage. So all the parents need to do is validate and acknowledge all the previous stages in their development that they were unable to validate and support that which was true to them. In working with the field of Energy Psychology, parents as adults heal their inner child's unmet emotional needs. One of the parents when she was reading this manuscript once commented, "I wish I had this book before I raised my children". There is no doubt she could relate to the wisdom shared here and may have taken something out of it for her personal growth and inner child healing. It is never too late to become a better parent to your child whose energy type you never understood and so wanted him or her to be like you and not be who they were made to be.

In summary the parents of Type III children should endeavor to remember these points in parenting which are supportive of all these children. Physical activity is necessary for these children to thrive. Make sure they are getting outside and are adequately engaged in physical activities that correspond to their nature and help them connect to the world. Parents should also keep close to their children by making physical contact, like hugging and holding hands or putting an arm around their shoulders. To prevent them from feeling bored, provide them with projects without a lot of details or learning to keep them engaged. Remember that the Type III child is thrilled with embarking on work that will yield a result they can admire. Praise them and make a big deal of their hard work and the results. They need to be encouraged, validated, and supported to live true to their nature.

Parents should also create times when they can do things together with the children, spend time engaging in physical activity or a challenging game with their child and all their different energy type children. Teach them craft works, how to cook, how to mow the lawn, and many more things they may like to do. Parents need to tell the Type III child how impressed they are with his or her accomplishments and results from whatever project they may engage in and consequently achieve with determination. Remember that when they begin to do aggravating things the Type III child is seeking attention. This is their way of communicating their need for attention. Parents should not respond negatively to them but with understanding, let the child know that they noticed that he needs their attention, and then give positive attention instead of reprimanding the child for acting out. Parents should not also over-stress their mistakes or get frustrated over their intense and determined energy type. Finally, avoid phrases such as: "Shush, you're too loud, you think too big, calm down, stop being pushy, settle down or when are you going to grow up and so forth." Parents should formulate their own phrases as to how to encourage and motivate these children to be their best and avoid those phrases and words that demoralize or do dishonor to those children.

THE TYPE IV CHILD

Type IV child-energy is described as the more serious child. The elements that represent this type is carbon and earth whereas their natural movement is constant, still, and reflective. This group of children have dominant energy to be independent, focused, and bold. Their personality is introverted and holds low level movement hence they can hold still for much longer than other children. They are described as mature, reserved, authoritative, logical, and respectful. Some adults refer to the them as serious and older than their age. They are more reserved when meeting new friends or people. They are motivated in perfecting their own world and being their own authority. Many adults may misinterpret them as being critical. As the Type IV child grows up, he or she is likely to be told by family and friends to lighten up, loosen up, and stop being judgmental. When parents know and support their Type IV child to live true to his or her natural reflective movement as strength, that child will grow into adulthood with less tendency to criticize, have a healthy relationship with their family, and respect and honor their gifts.

Respect and efficiency comes very natural to them. They possess a keen eye for the big picture of a perfect world. The Type IV energy brings to a full cycle the energy type wholeness. Type IV provided ideas and optimism. Type II is noted for gathering of details and planning. Type III moves ideas and plans into action, whereas Type IV looks at what has been made or created and naturally identifies inefficiencies that can be perfected to improve the final result. The phrase often associated with the Type IV child is "This is how we can make it better" or "this is the way it should look." All children are playful but the Type IV child expresses their playful nature in a more exact and straightforward way. They can be misjudged as inflexible. This type of children is in control of their own lives and the things they care about. They are focused and precise, organized and intentional. They believe their way of doing things is the best and possess natural ability to step back and see things in its totality and are able to determine how things work best. Whatever you show them how to do, they will find a better way to do it. The Type IV child's way of seeing the world may sound critical but to stop them from being a perfectionist would amount to stopping them from being who they are. Such action may make them see themselves as flawed which could lead to inner criticism later in their adult life for being accused as a child of being too critical. Parents should embrace them and their critical mind. Instead of dreading their criticism, you might ask your child to tell you what could make any work you are doing better or to suggest a better way doing a particular project. They will feel honored to be asked and more so because they value their own opinion highly. When parents are open to their Type IV child's feedback the less critical they become because they know that they will not be shot down whenever they want to express their views.

The introverted nature of the Type IV children makes them appear reserved, private, and independent. This disposition make them seem more mature than their chronological age. They begin to honor their own movement very early in childhood to the surprise of parents who do not yet understand the energy type of the child. While they are reflective and connect intellectually with the world, they are also deeply emotional. Parent should not make the mistake of thinking that they have everything under control and neglect their needs for emotional support in difficult times. The Type IV child may appear more serious in dealing with themselves and others. Their reflective, structured and more contemplative energies make them look more like adults in their young age. When parents consider their insistence on being their own authority, they can better appreciate their immature behavior and remain patient with them as they grow in knowledge. Since their view of the world is that of serious business, and some of their actions may not be as mature as they feel, parents should understand that the title of being mature is meant to honor their natural gifts and disposition to life. Parents should not worry that their six-year old or five-year old is not child-like enough when they behave in a more serious manner like older adults. It could be frustrating at times when you hear your Type IV child at the early stage of their life say "I want to do it myself" or "I do not need help to do it." How do you handle such a child who wants to be in charge of his or her life from the earliest moments of life? This type of child wants you to be a partner of authority in their life. When you understand their nature and modus operandi they need you to be there both to set boundaries and validate the age-appropriate decisions that you permit them to make. You need to believe that he or she will be able to do all of the grown-up things and are capable of doing more than you might think. Although they have a natural structured movement, as parent they still need you to provide some solid parental presence to thrive and to form a sense of security in the world. When their true nature is so honored and respected, they will highly respect you as their parent and form a close lifelong bond with you. The Type IV child's qualities of being serious, structured, discerning, picky, and so forth. should be seen not as a weakness but a strength. When they are seen as tendencies to be honored rather than flaws to be fixed they will naturally feel more confident to manage their natural dispositions with greater success.

Their thought and feeling process is straightforward, white or black, all or nothing. Their method of connecting with the world is their intellect; they think things through, and try to understand the process that was used to create things and to understand how everything fits together. Since these kind of children are thinkers and connect with the world intellectually, there may be a tendency to think that they relate only with their heads and not with their hearts as well. But they feel their emotions deeply and can only allow people who honor and respect their nature to see their emotional side. It is okay to allow them their emotional boundaries. Try not to break it down since that will only make them keep building it higher and stronger. The key to connecting with them is to first connect with them mentally before emotional connection can be possible; discuss with them on a mental level before getting to an emotional level.

Though the Type IV child may not connect very easily with his or her feelings like the rest, when supported at a younger age in learning how to connect with their feelings, how to connect with their feelings will come naturally as they grow. Some older children who have not learned to connect with their feelings may express their frustration by presenting the emotion of anger. Instead of disciplining them for that, understand it as a teaching moment to help them make an emotional connection by helping them to connect with their deeper feelings of sadness or any other deeply held emotion. You can help the child by saying: "I notice that you are angry. What is upsetting you?" "You are really mad. What is troubling you?" When your Type IV child knows that you really care and that you look out for his or her best interest, the child will open up and begin to share their deepest feelings and allow you into the most sensitive part of their nature. These children do not fake their emotions and while other types may readily adapt to expectations placed on them, the Type IVs do not. Their structured nature makes it difficult for them to put on a face and pretend they feel a certain way when they do not.

If a parent does not feel emotionally connected with his or her Type IV child, it could be that the child may have had one of the following experiences with you. They think you do not respect their opinions; you talk down to them or treat them like a baby; you do not trust them to make their own decisions,; the Type IV child feels like you put him or her on the spot or embarrass them, you do not keep their issues confidential when talking to others, or they feel confused that their parent judged their natural structure as flawed. The Type IV child does not just appreciate respect, they need it as part of their nature. Once they feel safe with their parent, their relationships will flourish. Type IV children express the lowest level of movement of all the four Types. It does not mean that they cannot be fast, run, and jump but means that they are reflective and maintain an inner stillness that has to be respected in the activities they pursue. They need time to prepare and to feel well grounded in demonstrating their talents and abilities either in competitive sports or dance. They set high standards for themselves and they hesitate to engage in a new activity if they feel they cannot meet the standard. They hate being embarrassed or put on the spot. They can excel in any sport if allowed to approach it in their own way. Individual sports that require precision and repetition are usually a good fit for the Type IV child. When they love a game they will play all the way to the end. Their one-track mind helps them to focus well on the one thing that they tend to overdo or overwork. Once completed the may lose interest and move on to something else.

Their learning style is primarily through observation. They have the gift of understanding a process or concept by seeing how it works and the ability to duplicate and improve upon what they have seen. Once they master an idea they want to jump in and do it without anyone's supervision. They feel bad if they make a mistake in the process of executing a project in which they have a mastery. For them it is all or nothing and if they do not master it all, they will see their learning as a failure. They perform very well in the traditional school system due to their keen tendency to be thorough and aware of their responsibility. They value fairness, structure, routine, time to focus, and just being themselves. However, some Type IV children could be resistant to go to school and rebel boldly against any move by parents to make them comply. This attitude may be necessitated by their resistance and respect for authority. Some do not feel respected at school or may have a reason to resist authority of the teachers that teach them. Parents should not only try to convince them to go to school but endeavor to find out the root cause of their resistance. Ask the child about his or her concerns about school and listen for cues like 'stupid', which points to their frustration due to lack of understanding by their teachers and classmates. Then be their advocate if their teachers and classmates do not understand them. Their study habits favor repetition and study routines. Some will like to do their homework immediately when they return from school; some others will prefer to decompress after school before doing their homework. Some may be resistant to homework they do not like or think is boring, which might be a red flag to you that they do not like or understand the subject and may need help. Parents should not be offended if they do not consider them as an authority in their schoolwork. Some Type IV children do not like to be reminded to do their homework since they are very aware of their responsibilities and take measures to manage their time well. Instead, parents should simply comment when they do not see them doing homework by saying, "I know you have a plan to do your homework or do you want any help with your homework"?

Generally Type IV children, like the adults they mimic, try to do things for themselves. They try to walk fairly early as toddlers. They pay attention to language and then try to duplicate it accurately and so do not babble as other children do. They may wait a bit longer to speak and when they do, they are very articulate and may feel frustrated if they feel you do not understand what they are trying to communicate. In potty training, they are more tidy and efficient. They dislike mess and lack of control over their bladder and so let him or her hear about the process in matter-of-fact terms and they will be motivated to try using the toilet like the adults. Let them be their own authority and choose between the big toilet and a shorter potty seat. They also prefer a bedtime routine and stick with a particular sleep pattern and repeat the same time of wakefulness and length of naps for a long time. It serves them best when their need for predictability and repetition is honored. In pre-school and school age, Type IV children need time to observe and feel safe before engaging in school activities and interacting with other children. Early school experience could be difficult for them; they need to know that they can be respected as they interact at their own pace. They do not want to feel anxious at being unprepared or caught off guard. For this same reason they need advance notice before being taken to a babysitter. They may initially feel uncomfortable with being left with someone unfamiliar and in an unfamiliar place. It takes them time to come to trust a new person coming into their space. So prepare them in advance for what is coming up. Communicate the big picture, who is coming and for how long and allow them to prepare themselves mentally before the fact. The IVs because they are reserved and for their nature of all-or-nothing, will either love dating or feel no need for it. They are therefore likely to wait until they feel comfortable to date in their late teenage years unlike the other three types of children. When eventually they are ready, some may be deeply connected with a boyfriend or girlfriend for the sake of sharing their deeper thoughts and feelings with someone. Rather than stop them, try to build trust and respect so that you can win them over to value your guidance and wisdom as parents. During this stage and high school age, they are likely to keep few friends and belong to smaller groups; they do not need to be pushed to be more social against their nature of movement and energy. They need parental support to have friends over and do things in small groups. They are not comfortable going to birthday parties where they do not know anyone and should not be forced to attend such parties.

Among the top tips every parent of a Type IV child should know is to support them in being their own authority. Parents should acknowledge their Type IV child's need to be their own authority from the earliest of their life. This will help to avoid power struggles and frustration and help parents and child to experience cooperation and a life-long bond. Show respect for the child's sense of authority, logical nature, and bold stance in their opinions. Privacy is important to them and so parents should respect their need for space and time they could call their own. Allow them to pick and choose what they want don't want to share with the public and what they do not. Encourage them to be who they are and not what others want them to be. Validate and encourage your Type IV child to live true to his or her nature throughout all the phases of their childhood. They take time to reflect and so may not give you answers to questions you ask them immediately. They prefer to take time to think through every situation. Let them observe first without pushing to size up a situation and to engage or disengage. Encourage to take time to be alone and reflect on things as often as necessary. They require undivided attention when communicating. Look them in the eye to show your attention and listen to their answer and not make them repeat themselves. They need advance notice for family daily plans, weekly plans, and family vacation in order to mentally organize and move forward with ease. It will be of great help to your Type IV child if you find him or her one best friend who shares similar interests and abilities. While it may not be necessary to push them to make many friends, parents should encourage them to stay in contact with their best friends even when they move to a different town. Although the child may cause the parent much frustrations through their criticisms and perfectionist tendencies, parents should learn to let go of such frustrations and continue to show respect to the child. By so doing parents create mutual respect between child and parent. Finally, parents should stop using phrases such as: "You are a loner," "stop being so picky," "what a know-it-all," "smile more," "lighten up," "you're uptight," "or quit being so critical." Parents can identify their child's energy type from the earliest time of their birth.

In summary parents should remember that Type I energy moves upward and outward, unstructured, more carefree, finds delight in simple pleasures, and demonstrates a major characteristic of randomness and loving fun. Type II energy moves downward with a steady flow; they enjoy whatever creates comfort, the key characteristics are and sensitivity and gentleness. Type III moves forward with a push, and focuses on the end result with swift determination. Key characteristics are determination and adventurous. Meanwhile the Type IV child remains constant, still, reflective, straightforward, concise, and knows precisely where they stand with themselves and others. Their key characteristics are exact and particular. It will be of great advantage if parents are able to identify their child's energy type early in the life so as to have the insight into the unique nature of the child and be able to intuitively make decisions in order to support them in feeling safe, loved and cared for adequately as they begin to know the world they are getting into. When you know your child's type everyday events such as bedtime, homework, friendship, and house chores become effortless because you will know how to respond to the child's behavior and support what is true to their nature. Parents should endeavor to live true to their own nature. Your own childhood wounds should not be getting in the way of allowing your child to live their truth. Parenting style should be one that is consistent with the child's true nature rather than the parent as the child will be resistant to such an approach thereby causing friction between parent and the child and then respond with disciplinary action. You may be punishing your child for behaviors and attitudes that are true to the child's nature, which may send a wrong message to them that "It is not right to be you." Children who feel judged, punished, or belittled for who they are in their family often grow up as wounded or repressed adults.

CHAPTER 7

Parenting And Adolescent Views On Values

IN THE FOURTH psychosexual developmental stage, children develop a sense of industry as they gear all their energies to work and play. In this period between the ages of six and twelve, children also begin to develop a sense of the value of right and wrong. This is a period in which they ask many questions and begin to approve or disapprove of their own actions and those of others. Children are started in a Christian Religious Education program to prepare them for the sacraments, first Penance and Eucharist, because it is the beginning of the age of reasoning and knowledge of right and wrong. This stage prior to early adolescence is when children judge things by the way such things affect them. Children believe adults know everything and so believe whatever their parents tell them without question. Children do not care about things in the outside world that do not impact them. This kind of thinking changes during the period of puberty when children begin to think in the abstract terms of adults. With this emerging adolescent competence, children begin to look at life differently. The adolescent begins to depend less on the opinion and knowledge of adults as he or she begins to find out that the world is not really as he or she had thought. The previous idea of good and evil or right and wrong are now challenged, as the good no longer triumphs over evil as the child was made to understand. For example, finding out that bad people or those who do evil are not always caught and punished confuses the child as his or her belief is turned upside down and he or she does not know what to think. The adolescent may begin to question how drugs, for example, can be bad when often he or she hears on television that many celebrities, some of whom are idolized, are using drugs. They see them looking attractive on television and performing very well. How can drugs be bad or destroy their life as they were made to believe by their parents. Situations like this make adolescents begin to question the values parents have to instill in them.

Children who have been brought up in religious homes and have been taught to believe in God, religion, and church may begin to question the reality of God when they meet good and happy people who neither believe in God nor are churchgoers. Since the child cannot see God physically anywhere, he or she may begin to think that the individuals who do not believe in God are right in believing that God does not exist and they may not want to go to church anymore. Another example that might make the child question his or her parents' advice is when the parent tells the child to study hard in school to make good grades, go to college, and get a good paying job in order to enjoy life. This accepted value will be questioned when the child hears of some baseball stars or entertainers who make millions even though they never went to college, or some salesman who became a millionaire and does not know how to read and write. Examples like this may make the child begin to think that education is not the ultimate means to earning a good living. Such experiences make adolescents begin to rethink what they have been taught by adults and lead them to think that adults may not be as knowledgeable as they thought. Early adolescents question what their parents and other adults have taught them because they are only beginning to think like adults. They do not have enough experience, so they cannot see the whole picture of life which leads them to erroneous conclusions about life and adults. Adolescents question everything adults say including their values and upbringing. They strive to determine if the values they were taught as a child are valid when compared to their own limited life experiences. However, the point here is not to discredit talents in athletics, music, and art but to emphasize the importance of acquiring basic education before pursuing one's dream.

Early adolescents are fond of displaying a know-it-all attitude in their attempt to clarify their view of the world. As they mature they begin to see the world from an adult prism which reveals a complex range of problems they never knew of before. They present a simplistic solution to complex problems and feel adults are not as smart enough as they thought to figure out simple solutions to problems. Due to the younger's simplistic approach to complex problems, adults might find it frustrating to deal with the early adolescent's presumption to have answers to life's complex problems. While this attitude gives early adolescents a momentary sense of superiority, it also exposes the adolescent to disappointment and frustration upon the realization that he or she does not, after all, have a realistic solution to life's complex problems. This search for true values continues until the adolescent reaches full adulthood.

WHAT IS IN THE MIND OF THE EARLY ADOLESCENT?

There is excitement in the early adolescent's first attempt in thinking about life and his or her search for wisdom and the truth about life. Early adolescence is the beginning of critical thinking, asking of questions, and conceptualizing what the adolescent thinks life is all about. From their observation of life they are able to conceptualize or idealize their future plans and envisage the outcome of such plans according to their belief. However, ideas do not often turn out the same way in the real world. Early adolescents are confounded when their elaborate, idealistic plans do not materialize as they expect, leading to disappointment and disillusionment.

Early adolescents appear selfless in their search and so envisage a perfect and happy world rid of all wrongs. They enjoy debating and discussing philosophical issues on human life and the world. They identify with masses and want to be counted among those who fight oppression of the poor by the rich and powerful of the society. For example, the large number of young men and women who enlist in our armed forces each year demonstrate the deep-seated value this age group places in fighting to right all the wrongs in the world. They show great enthusiasm and interest in whatever they put their mind to accomplish which may not often be sanctioned by adults or parents The early adolescents' new ability to analyze events and identify faults makes them become critical of the world, adults, and anything that is not the way it is supposed to be from their own worldview. Generally, adolescents are critical of others, including their parents. They are not bothered only by the ideas people hold, but also by how they look, dress or talk. While they criticize everyone, they do not like to be criticized because they think they are wiser than those who may want to criticize them. This inability to accept criticism demonstrates the early adolescent insecurity and lack of self-confidence which make them feel frustrated when criticized. The self-discovery and discovery of the world that occur at this time of development and the effort adolescents make to adjust and behave in a socially acceptable way make them feel frustrated when criticized by parents or other adults. This situation makes them feel less confident and secure about anything; this is why it is common to hear them say "It's no use. No matter what I do, it's never right" (Caissy, 1994, p. 49).

THE EARLY ADOLESCENT'S VIEW OF HUMAN SEXUALITY

Early adolescent understanding of human sexuality is completely different from what has been earlier observed in the chapter on the theology of human body and sexuality. The early adolescent's view on sexuality is neither based on truth nor reality. Rather, it is distorted. Most of the information adolescents have about human sexuality is learned from the electronic and print media which constantly target adolescents with materials that are replete with sexual language, behaviors, and innuendos. The media use television, music, and videos to push sexually explicit materials on young people in the name of marketing and advertising goods and services. The media try very hard to sell the idea that sex is not sacred. Rather, it is to be viewed like any other material goods and services that can be bought with money for the ultimate means of pleasure and fulfillment of the individual. Furthermore, like any other material goods, it can also be abused by the users. Adolescents are drawn to believe what the media present to them as the meaning of human sexuality and its purpose because of the constant exposure to sexual behaviors. Consequently, it appears more real to them than what their parents and their religion teach about sex and human sexuality.

This idea of sexuality is made more appealing to adolescents by the media when, in the romantic movie scenes, adults passionately fall into each other's arms and into sexual activity without considering the implication a casual sexual activity will have for morality, pregnancy, and sexually transmitted diseases. The fantasy the media associates with sexual encounters can be misleading for early adolescents who are yet to distinguish between reality and fantasy, fact and fiction. Parents have the responsibility to help their adolescent children reject the media impression that because they are sexually mature they should be sexually active, that when they go out on a date, sex is expected, or that sex is an adult activity and since they are young adults it is acceptable to be sexually active. In addition, parents must help their adolescent children reject the notion that because "everyone" is doing it they will be labeled as "prudes" by their peers if they are not sexually active at a young age. If they do not dress in a "sexy" manner and act seductively in order to be attractive to the opposite sex, or if they do not buy into the erroneous belief that sex and affection are the same. It may be necessary for parents to discuss and debunk some of these common media-peddled ideas for their adolescent children who are yet to be emotionally mature. It will enable them to avoid any abuse of the gift of human sexuality, as well as infatuation or the costly mistakes that often lead to children begetting children, abortion and the contracting of STDs or HIV/AIDS. A good parenting technique will facilitate imparting the parents' shared values and morals. The following chapter will examine the adolescent's various temperaments so as to prepare parents to respond to them in a most helpful manner.

CHAPTER 8

Infant And Adolescent Temperament

THE PSYCHOSOCIAL DEVELOPMENT of the child is often reflected in the child's temperament. To assess a child's temperament parents should observe whether the child lies quietly and seems unperturbed even when there is loud noise in the environment, or kicks, screams and responds spontaneously to every sound. Does the child respond warmly to visitors or does she fret, fuss, and withdraw? Answers to these questions will determine the type of temperament the child may have. Temperament is the totality of the individual's innate, biological behavioral disposition and emotional response style. A study by Thomas and Chess (1977, 1987 & 1991) found that sixty-five percent of the babies studied could be categorized into three groups, easy, difficult, and slow-to-warm-up children.

The easy children were often found to be happy, relaxed, agreeable, and easily adaptable to new situations. Difficult children were often moody, easily frustrated, tense, and irritable to most situations. Slow-to-warm-up children were noted for mild responses, were somewhat shy, withdrawn, and took time to adjust to changes. Some studies have found that some children can consistently maintain a temperament from childhood through adulthood (Stams, Juffer & Van Ijzendoorn, 2002). However, there would be many children who may shed their childhood temperamental disposition before they reach adulthood due to other psychosocial transformations that take place during the critical period of development. The greatest factor for such changes could be attributed to the good fit between a child's nature, parental behaviors, and the social and environmental conditions (Lindhal & Obstbaum, 2004; Realmuto, August, & Egan, 2004). A temperamental child can develop a healthy personality if parents provide him or her opportunity to grow out of it. For instance, a slow-to-warm-up child can grow out of the temperament if parents give him or her time to adjust to new situations without fussing. So also could a difficult child overcome his or her shortcomings if brought up in a structured and understanding environment rather than an inconsistent and intolerant household. Hence, Alexander Thomas, a pioneer researcher in child temperament, observed that a child may develop a socially good personality when parents work with their child's temperament rather than when they work to alter or change it. This implies that nature could be transformed through nurture if the necessary and desirable nurturing environment is provided by parents. Thus a child could develop to the fullest potential if parents could create an environment of unconditional positive regard as proposed by Carl Rogers (1987). This implies a setting where a child, despite his or her natural endowment and temperament, realizes that he or she is loved and accepted with no conditions or strings attached. It is a condition which Gordon (1975) described thus: Acceptance is like the fertile soil that permits a tiny seed to develop into the lovely flower it is capable of becoming. The soil only enables the seed to become the flower. It releases the capacity of the seed to grow, but the capacity is entirely within the seed. As with the seed, a child contains entirely within the organism the capacity to develop. Acceptance is like the soil–it merely enables the child to actualize his potential (p.31).

Unconditional positive regard and acceptance in parenting does not mean that children should be allowed to do whatever they like. Good parents, like humanists, would accept and reinforce the child's positive nature and basic worth and discourage destructive or bad attitudes and behaviors. Hitting or yelling at a child is contrary to the child's positive nature as well as offensive to adults. Hence, parents will do well to engage in a good parenting style that would enable the child to develop a healthy self-concept and healthy relationship with others since the child-parent relationship affects the child's lifespan interrelationships.

ADOLESCENT EMOTIONAL STATES

The child's rapid biological and sexual development to adolescence presents an adolescent with various emotions as he or she grapples to adjust and make sense of the physical changes. The adolescent releases unequal amounts of hormones into the blood stream, leading to a temporary chemical imbalance manifested in rapid change of moods during this period of development. Some of the common moods displayed by adolescents at this period of development are moodiness, anger, fear, worry, anxiety, instability, extreme feelings of inferiority, doubts about self-esteem, and questioning of values.

MOODINESS AND HAPPINESS

The uneven release of hormones during adolescence results in mood swings. This is why an adolescent, in a moment, will be found giggling and laughing and all of sudden will be found moody, unhappy and intensely angry for little or no known reason at all. This unstable mood is a result of the secretion of various levels of hormones into the blood stream during this stage of development. A swing in mood is very common in early adolescence. In their moodiness, adolescents could display rude and sarcastic behavior because they are preoccupied with themselves and care less about hurting other people's feelings. They could display excessive anger or show no emotion, even when it is desirable to be emotional. This is why some adolescents often seem to show no emotion, and appear cold faced as if they do not give heed to parental scolding or parental-advice on matters that parents consider as important. It is important that parents and teachers are aware of the prevalence of emotional highs and lows in early adolescents so as not to misunderstand or misjudge them, especially when they try to hide it, as often the case. Another behavior that characterizes early adolescence is the tendency to ignore or not acknowledge the presence of adult guests who visit their parents' home. They either stay in their rooms unconcerned by who comes into their house or, when they do come out, they say nothing to acknowledge the guests. Often parents have to tell them to say hello to their visitors which they may perfunctorily do, and then rush out without further conversation. This behavior may be embarrassing to both parents and their guests who may judge the parents as raising a rude and thoughtless child.

ANGER

The early adolescent period is fraught with difficulty and frustration associated with the reality of growing up to a young adulthood and its challenges. Adolescents are provoked to anger when others make fun of them, when they are being cheated by older siblings, when parents pry through their doors, or when things generally are not going their way. They exhibit their anger by leaving the environment or situation, by causing a scene manifested by slamming of doors, and by storming out of the room or house to display their anger and outrage at a situation or condition that hurt their feelings. The sudden outburst of anger is often unleashed at those who have nothing to do with the cause of the anger. Adolescents might release on their parents the anger caused by friends who made fun of them at school. This occurs because they cannot afford to vent their anger or lose their friends and peers whom they consider important in their life at this time as they progress in the process of individuation and separation from their parents. Thus, siblings are the most common targets of venting their anger and frustrations, shown by getting into a fight with their brothers and sisters. Parents should not get too worried at this behavior in early adolescence. The adolescent will eventually learn to control his or her emotions rather than displaying them carelessly because his peers, with whom he will share such experiences, will eventually begin to criticize and frown at such behaviors. More so, as the old adage says, "children learn what they live." If the parents have been mature in handling their own anger in the home by modeling anger management, there will be no doubt that the adolescents will equally begin to imitate the way their parents and other adults handle similar actions. Parents should also bear in mind those issues that early adolescents worry about and be ready to demonstrate empathy as they deal with the early adolescent stress.

CHAPTER 9

Early Adolescent Anxieties

THE ADOLESCENT PERIOD is filled with all kinds of anxieties and worries especially between the ages of thirteen and fourteen. The worries and fears often experienced at this period of development are related to the adolescent's changing social roles and new identity. Above all, adolescents are overly conscious of their physical appearance. They take time to choose what hair style to wear and are concerned if they are not complimented for their appearance. They feel bad if their friends ridicule or feel indifferent to their style of dressing in school or at social function, as that would amount to a disapproval of their fashion tastes and choices. Adolescents also worry about school and performance on school tests; they feel good if they perform academically well and worry if they do not. They are also worried about how best to interact with their opposite sex peers at school, what to say and how to behave like adults and engage in a good conversation.

Adolescent anxieties are related to the emotions of fear and worry about physical development that occurs during this period. A number of issues that can result in the anxiety adolescents experience during this time include physical size, lack of sexual development, muscular strength, obesity, acne and perspiration among others. The differences in ages at which boys and girls experience puberty also contribute to early adolescence anxiety. It should be noted that boys grow bigger and stronger than the girls in childhood, while the girls develop faster, bigger and stronger than the boys during puberty, and this situation contributes to anxiety among adolescents. Early development among the girls is often rebuffed by their male peers leading the girls to turn to older boys instead of waiting for their "immature" male peers. However, early adolescent development among girls contributes to their anxiety because of their lack of self- confidence, their insecurity, and their concerns about how they look and what other people think of their new physical appearance.

UNSTABLE EMOTIONS AND INTERESTS

Constant change in both emotions and interests or goals characterizes the early adolescent period. As an experimenting period, adolescents try their hands in all kinds of games, hobbies, and work. It is not uncommon to observe enthusiasm for a particular kind of activity, work, or game and then all of a sudden see frustration and hear how the adolescent hates the activity. Although things may change very quickly for this age group, this does not mean that they never enjoyed the activity at a point. Parents should be aware of these constant changes in their likes and dislikes. This may often be costly for parents, especially when the adolescent requests something and, after it has been bought for him, rejects it because it is no longer the favorite. It could be a color or style of clothes he wants or some musical instrument he wants to learn. It is almost impossible to determine what will interest adolescents at this period of their development. For reasons that border on their instability, their decisions are always changing, so whatever they say they hate or like should be left for time to tell. Early adolescent life is full of drama in their emotions and expressions.

BEING COMFORTABLE IN THEIR OWN SKIN

Early adolescents find it difficult to accept their bodies' appearance due to the various physical and biological changes that have taken place. Transitioning from a comfortable childhood body to a more complex and bigger body makes it uncomfortable for adolescents to accept this reality. However, adolescents who are well informed by their parents about these imminent biological changes are less uncomfortable than those who were uneducated about the developmental process in early adolescence. Noting that their bodies are taking an adult form remains a source of worry because they do not know for sure what they will look like. Even though they know that they will inherit most of their parents' traits in adulthood, adolescents have role models and stereotypes of masculinity and femininity in their mind that they wish they could emulate as adults. They become critical of themselves upon realizing that their physical appearance runs short of the media ideal for beauty and sexy physique. Upon this realization, adolescents want to try out every advertised product, exercise, diet or power drink and food supplement to change their appearance to match the media model for the "ideal" body. Although obsession with physical appearance is not pronounced in early adolescents, it becomes a major source of concern as they progress in this stage of development. However, once the child has completed this stage of physical development and has come to adjust to or accept his or her physical appearance, the craze to always appear fashionable begins to wane.

ADOLESCENT BODY IMAGE AND SELF-ESTEEM

The body image the adolescent forms at the end of the adolescent stage of development determines his or her self-esteem which implies how good or bad the adolescent feels about herself or himself. When he or she is happy with physical appearance, the individual's self-esteem is positive and healthy. If the individual feels unhappy about his or her physical appearance, the individual may have an inferiority complex; this is a feeling of self-pity and of being unacceptable to one's self and others. An inferiority complex in adolescents may result from thinking themselves unattractive, having few friends or perceiving themselves as being unintelligent, reinforced when their peers call them "dummy." Early adolescents who are attractive and intelligent are always admired by many and this boosts the child's positive self-concept, whereas children who are overweight or have not developed to full adolescence are often ignored, less popular, generally have low self-esteem and feel inferior before their peers who are popular.

Early adolescents grapple with the difficulty of changing appearance and the identity crisis it presents. This sense of insecurity and vulnerability leaves them with a poor self-concept. Self-concept is how one views one's self. Parents can be very instrumental in helping their adolescents at the ages of twelve to fifteen to form a good self-concept and positive self-esteem which are fundamental to their mental health and happiness. This is because positive self-esteem promotes self-confidence, success at work and school, less peer pressure, and happiness in their own skin. Children with positive self-esteem demonstrate a better sense of responsibility to family, peers, and community. There is need for parents to have a clear knowledge of what their roles are in promoting the desired good self-concept and positive self-esteem for their children given their importance in the early adolescent life and beyond.

Positive self-esteem and good self-concept are built from the parent and child interaction beginning from infancy, as we shall further explore under the attachment theory. Parents who are sensitive to the needs of the child make them feel valued and loved. This quality of sensitive care instills in the child a sense of good self-concept and positive self-esteem. Parents can help the child to build up this positive feeling through direction, guidance, support, encouragement and, above all, through what the parent says and does to the child. The love, support, and encouragement that parents give to their adolescents as a part of their day to day interactions go a long way to reinforce and to help them to feel good about themselves and to believe in themselves. Self-esteem is a feeling that comes from within the child and continues to develop as the child continues to grow in self-competence. Such self-esteem is derived from learning to do things by themselves successfully without the help of the parents, such as shopping, cooking, sewing, playing a musical instrument, operating household machineries like washing machines or driving.

Acquiring the skills to do these things very well from parents, instructors and teachers makes the child happy and increases his or her sense of satisfaction, pride, and independence. This is why parents at some point in the child's development will have to allow the child to take initiatives and learn to do things by himself or herself and so create his or her own happiness and depend less on the parents for needs and happiness. For a parent to be overly protective of the adolescent child for fear of failure and sadness is retrogressive and unrealistic in a real world. The child achieves the desired good self-concept and positive self-esteem by creating his or her own happiness through self-competence in knowing and doing the basic things expected of his or her age group. When parents, family, and friends compliment the child on his or her achievements, he or she feels a sense of pride and fulfillment which energizes the adolescent to achieve greater heights. The child will continue to grow in his or her self-competence and self-esteem as he or she is continually helped to discover and develop abilities in different areas of endeavor through the support, recognition, encouragement and praise of the parents.

While parents are instrumental in helping the child to acquire the necessary tools and skills required to achieve competence and self-esteem, there is also need for them to teach the adolescent how to solve problems and deal with disappointments or failure whenever one arises. As Oprah Winfrey told Harvard graduates in a commencement speech recently, failure is an invitation to look at life differently. Parents should be bold enough to tell the adolescent child that it is acceptable to make mistakes as long as such mistakes are not intentional. The parent's unconditional love and acceptance of the child even in his or her failure gives the child encouragement to try harder and to realize that the parent's love is not lost by his or her mistakes and failure. This assurance helps the child to be confident and encourages her to build trust that the parent will act for his or her best interest whenever the adolescent turns to the parent for help. The child should always be told that all that he or she is required to do is his or her best. Pushing the child beyond his or her abilities, as some parents tend to do, will be counterproductive as that will hinder the development of positive self-esteem and will force the child to view himself or herself as a non-achiever, at least as far as the parents are concerned. To achieve a positive self-esteem is an ongoing process which adolescents who enjoy the love, support, and praise of parents and friends attain through a continual reinforcement. The child's total development is a challenge both to parents and children. Awareness of the challenges of childhood and especially the early adolescent period, as discussed here and in the following chapter, gives parents a special vantage point so that they will not leave anything to chance and will not take adolescent stress and storm personally.

CHAPTER 10

Adolescent Storm And Stress

PARENT-ADOLESCENT STRESS REFERS to conflict or intense and frequent verbal arguments that are rarely resolved in a mutually satisfactory manner (Robin & Foster, 1984). Adolescence, or the stage of puberty, is one marked by the task of identity and the crisis of isolation. Some of the noticeable stresses and storms of the adolescent age are conflict with parents, mood disruption-swings from one extreme to the other and risky behavior, like norm-breaking and so forth. (Arnett, 2000). Boderick, & Blewitt, (2010), noted in their illustration with Rebecca how adolescent conflict with a parental figures manifests itself. Rebecca was upset that she was asked to leave the adult company of her aunt and mother and study for her test. An adolescent stands between childhood and adulthood in developmental stages, and therefore, the tendency for an adolescent not reckoned with as a child and not regarded as an adult could create a special anxiety for him or her when he or she is excluded from adult circles. This leads the adolescent to seek the company and dependence of peers with whom he or she has more in common and in this way he or she begins a struggle for independence from parental control and identity.

Many studies focused on the adolescent stage have found this stage of child's development as more challenging than other stages. Adolescent difficult behavior could be considered as a part of the storm and stress of the adolescent stage (Hall, 1904). For Hall (1904), adolescent stress and storm in his time was aggravated by the failure of homes, schools, and religious organizations to recognize the nature and potential self-destruction of adolescents and to adjust their institutions accordingly (Eccles et al.1993). Both the earlier psychoanalytic school and the moderate psychoanalysts assume that the conflict that arises between parents and adolescents is a normal way of adolescent expression for emotional and affective detachment from parents and autonomy and dependence on peer group and age-mates for identity (Broderick, & Blewitt, 2010). In like manner, Erikson (1968) described the adolescent stage as a time characterized by the crisis that ensues as the adolescent struggles to pull away from her parents and differentiate herself. Buchanam *et al.* (1998) also posited that adolescence is a difficult time of life for children, parents and teachers. They also confirm in their later studies that adolescents are more likely to have symptoms of internalizing disorders and risk-taking behaviors. The study of Holmbeck and Hill (1988) equally supported adolescent-parent conflicts.

The commonality among researchers is the agreement that parent-adolescent conflict is normal and expected. However, much later studies did not support the view that adolescent storm and stress is a universal phenomenon among adolescents. The observed storm and stress origin in adolescent age was only partially supported biologically, while affirming this stage as the most difficult developmental stage in the child's development (Arnett, 1999). Hence, parenting style at this time should take into consideration the need to show restraint in policing the child, and the letting go in the child's quest for autonomy and independence. However, Collins & Lauren (2004) noted that emotional detachment of adolescents does not presuppose independence of the child and personal responsibility. It therefore means that adolescents will still need the guidance of parents to attain a responsible adulthood.

Despite the popular view, most parents and adolescents report that they rarely argue. It goes on to say that parent-adolescent storm and stress is not common in most families contrary to some theorists with psychoanalytic background who posit that parent-adolescent relations would be inevitably and fundamentally stressful (Adelson & Doehrman, 1980). Literature reveals that parent-adolescent conflict varies as a function of family social status, family structure, characteristics of parents and adolescents and, above all, the style of parent-adolescent interaction (Montemayor, 1986). This implies that parent-adolescent relations would vary in degree of interpersonal discord depending on the above factors. The point which parents should bear in mind is that most families' relations would usually be harmonious if the parents adopted positive parenting style, while other parent-adolescent interactions could be discordant and acrimonious especially when the parents adopt a less than desirable parenting style. In this light, parent-adolescent conflict is to be understood as symptomatic of many adolescent and family problems (Montemayor, 1986). Persistent conflict and stress affect the parent-adolescent relationship in many ways. They can lead to spending less time together with parents and more with peers. It increases the risk of involvement in deviant and criminal activities, and it can also be predictive of adolescent externalizing behaviors, such as delinquency, marijuana and alcohol use, running away from home, and premarital sexual relations (Patterson, 1982; Adams, Gullotta, & Clancy, 1985; Inazu & Fox, 1980). In some cases of parent-adolescent conflict, the child may develop problems of low self-esteem and suicide attempts (Tishler, McKnery, & Morgan, 1981). There is a probability that these problems can either be causes or consequences of parent-adolescent relationship conflict. As earlier noted, variation in parent-adolescent conflict could depend on variables such as family context, family structure, characteristics of parents and adolescents, and style of parent-adolescent interaction.

FAMILY SOCIAL CONTEXT

The social contexts in which families find themselves impact their relationships. Some societal changes such as industrialization and urbanization, for example, resulted in the decline of parental authority and democratization of family life. This period equally brought about a longer period of adolescent financial dependence on parents and an increased importance of peers which increased parent-adolescent friction. The mass unemployment of the Great Depression that led to family economic crisis and hardship equally reduced parental control over adolescents but varied across cultures. On the other hand, in some cultures where a strong sense of intergenerational loyalty or social organization is the norm and parents have control over their adolescents; conflict decreases and harmony increases. While there has not been any proven evidence of a relationship between socioeconomic status or poverty and parent-adolescent conflict, social conditions of poverty can lead to a variation in parent-adolescent strife. Low economic status has been found to positively affect child and adolescent abuse (Garbarino & Gillian, 1980; Montemayor, 1986). The social condition of poverty and unemployment results in "insularity" which is a way of interaction that is characterized by coercion. Insularity arises more often among the poor than with the middle class. Studies with mothers and children have demonstrated that insularity is positively associated with aversive interactions between mothers and their children (Montemayor, 1986).

FAMILY STRUCTURE

There are three basic family structures: nuclear family, single-parent family, and extended family. Other family structures include stepparent family, adoptive family, grandparents alone, two same-sex parents, and polygamous family. A nuclear family consists of a father, a mother, and their biological children under age eighteen. Single-parent family consists of only one parent and his or her biological children under age eighteen. An extended family is a family of three or more generations living in one household, as practiced in many African, South American, and Asian countries. The legal and genetic connection among related people living in the same household is less important than the functionality of the family. A functional family structure refers to how a family cares for its members. Therefore, function is more important than structure in every developmental period as observed in child-parent attachment style. No matter the family structure, children need family love and encouragement which varies as the child develops. For example, infants need responsive care giving and social interaction; teenagers need freedom and guidance; young adults need peace and privacy; the aged need respect and appreciation (Berger, 2013). Children need families to provide basic material necessities such as food, clothing, and shelter. Families can support, encourage, and guide education during the child's school-age. When children become self-critical and socially aware, as is always the case, families can provide opportunities for success. The harmony that children require at this time can be provided by protective families who have predictable routines. Although no family functions perfectly, children worldwide do better in families than in other structures such as group homes or foster homes which often lack stability, especially during middle-childhood when children resist change.

Family structure moderately affects the nature of the relationship between parent and adolescent. While the size of a family does not significantly account for the quality of the parent-adolescent relationship, it positively correlates with parental punitiveness, rejection, and control (Bell & Avery, 1985). It is known that increased parent-adolescent conflict occurs in divorced, single parent, and stepparent families than it does in families with both parents present. Children and adolescents have also been found to adjust better to parental divorce but do have great difficulty coping with remarriage and a stepparent. Studies show that families with two natural parents have a lesser level of parent-adolescent conflict and discord than families with divorced or separated parents. Disciplinary actions are usually problematic for adolescents and stepparents, both male and female (Lutz, 1983).

It has been found too that children raised in one-parent families may have difficulty in establishing intimate relationships as adolescents and adults, in which case, it may be proper for such parents to get married in order to provide a second parent for the child. Situations may get worse rather than better if the parent does so. Better that such parent should make an effort to have friends of both sexes with whom the child can interact, owing to children's difficulty coping with remarriage and a stepparent.

PARENT AND ADOLESCENT CHARACTERISTICS

Again, the characteristics of both parents and adolescents affect their relationship. Montemayor (1982) found that the sex of parents equally plays a role because adolescents of both sexes are likely to argue more with their mothers than with their fathers. This is because adolescents of both sexes spend more time with their mothers than fathers and mothers are more involved in the socialization of their adolescents than fathers are. Where a working mother is involved, she expects the adolescent son to help with household chores. This leads to friction when the adolescent son does not help the mother enough with work around the house while the mother is at work. Mothers who suffer from depressive mood and irritable or low self-esteem are more likely to have problematic relationships than mothers who do not (Patterson, 1982; Montemayor, 1982). Issues relating to unemployment and illness do contribute to the disruption of the mother-adolescent relationship. However, the only characteristic known to lead to adolescent abuse and conflict with the father is alcoholism (Blumberg, 1974). Although mother-adolescent conflict seems to be more frequent due to closeness or the mother's personal problems, it could be alleviated if the mother has a social support systems like family and friends. However, she may risk higher discord if she is isolated from family and friends or lives with a husband who is always absent and unsupportive. According to Montemayor (1982), conflict between mothers and daughters is more frequent than with sons. It is expected that parent-adolescent difficulties will improve as children develop from childhood to early-adolescence due to family relationship reorganizations that will occur as children mature into early-adulthood.

PARENT-ADOLESCENT INTERACTION STYLE

This is the most important factor that can determine the nature of relationships in the family as none of the previous factors provide an answer as to how they influence conflict. Parent-adolescent interaction style presents the process that explains why there would be conflict in some relations and none in others. Literature suggests a variation in parent-adolescent conflict arising from the following:

ROLE OF PARENTS

How can parents carry out their responsibility to their adolescent children at a time when their children are trying to pull away from them to the point of rebellion? To promote a tranquil adolescent –parent relationship, or less conflict with adolescents, parents who are knowledgeable about the need of their adolescent children are open to the needs of the child and gentle in exercising the parenting authority over the child. Research findings have been consistent in that parents who are happily married are more sensitive, responsive, warm, and affectionate toward their children and adolescents (Grych, 2002). Thus marital satisfaction is associated with positive parenting as marital relationship plays a crucial role in how the parents involved also relate to their children. For example, in a situation where a marital relationship is characterized by support and depth, there is an increased level of rapport, intimacy, and better communication between parents and with their children.

Given this scenario, it is easier for parents to remain affectionate and, at the same time, firm in demanding compliance of their adolescent children where issues of risky and immoral peer-pressure activities like stealing, rudeness, justice, safety, and so forth are concerned (Darling et al. 2007). Parents can also be less intrusive in their adolescents' personal concerns like clothing, hair styling, type of music, and so forth. Providing teens with control over some of their personal life is a way of helping them establish the autonomy and identity they most crave at this stage of their development (Smetana, Crean, & Campione-Barr, 2005). The most recommended parenting style is, therefore, an authoritative parenting style, where parents being aware of their children's needs, demonstrate warmness and responsiveness in meeting these needs. This will imply that parents encourage their children's self-acceptance, confidence, and assertiveness by being warm and involved and acknowledging their legitimate needs and feelings (Broderick, & Blewitt, 2010). It will also involve dialogue where parents explain their actions or why they regulate or impose limits to what children may or may not do. In this way, parents can inculcate discipline and expect compliance from their children. Parents' ability to blend the listening skills and empathy of a counselor in relating to their children and wards, coupled with watchful care and a firm sense of discipline, will, no doubt, convince the child of his or her parents' love and concern for the child's well-being and safety, thereby mediating adolescent and parental conflict.

Parents will do well to "let go" of their teenagers, allowing them to be themselves and to be free to explore with their peers, thereby consolidating their identity. This development helps adolescents to become more independent and personally responsible for their actions which results in greater emotional detachment from the parents (Collins & Lauren, 2004). In most cultures both parents and adolescents believe that parents understand certain aspects of parental control as legitimate. Thus, parents are expected to exercise authority over their teens when it comes to matters bordering on morality, for example, sexual behaviors, stealing, and justice or conventional rules on table manners (Darling et al. 2008). Conflicts arise between teenagers and parents when parents impose rules that the teen perceives as personal issues such as what they can wear out, how they wear their hair, what music they listen to, what they say on facebook, what they email to friends etc. Ordinarily teenagers would want to exercise their freedom on these issues to show a gain of control over their personal matters, demonstrating autonomy and gradual gain of independence from parental control.

However, some issues that teens consider as personal or trivial may not be all that unimportant. Such issues as when adolescents should begin to date, whom they date, where they should or should not go, and how late they should stay out may lead to many arguments over even more serious issues like alcohol, substance use, automobile driving safety, and sex (Arnett, 2000). While most parents will consider these issues as important and requiring prudence which may be lacking in adolescence, teenagers would rather also consider them as personal, which may result in conflict when parents suggest potential serious consequences to the teenager's wrong choices. Parents can educate and counsel their teens in order to bring them up as responsible adults.

According to Baumrind (1971, 1978, 1991) two important aspects of parenting behavior towards teens are critical and predictive of teenagers' characteristics. Key to a healthy parent relationship at this stage of development that begins from early childhood parental attachment is parental warmth or responsiveness. Responsiveness of parents to their children's needs does not, therefore, begin and end at early childhood attachment. Responsive parenting requires parents to foster self-acceptance, confidence, and self-assertion in their children by being warm, involved, and accepting of their feelings and providing for the needs of their children. They should consider their children's feelings and expressed needs seriously. They should give reasons for their actions especially when they impose restrictions on the child. Secondly, parents can exercise their control and expectations of their children by encouraging self-discipline and achievement and making mature demands of the children. They should also make and enforce family rules, provide consistent supervision and monitoring, and hold their children accountable when their behavior is below expectation. Thus authoritative parenting style is considered the most effective parenting style because it combines high responsiveness and high expectation (Baumrind, 1991).

The effectiveness of authoritative parenting is dependent on the parent's ability to blend listening skills and empathy like an experienced counselor. The challenge of proper parenting today, as implicated in authoritative parenting, which remains the best and the most effective method of parenting, is how parents can be skillfully warm, responsive, and respectful, yet, at the same time, be democratic on one hand but firmly controlling and watchful on the other. Good parenting cannot be authoritarian, permissive, indulgent, or neglectful of parental responsibility in any form. Good parenting implies that good parents will have to consciously play the role proper to parenting and that they must not minimize it by being friends to their children instead of being parents and models for them. In the chapter that follows, parents will gain insight into ways to deal positively, as well as with grace and resilience, with adolescent storm and stress without abdicating their responsibility to the child.

CHAPTER II

Coping With Adolescent Stress And Storm

MUCH GRACE AND resilience is required by parents and teachers who work with adolescents. As earlier observed, the nature of early adolescence is such that all who have to work with adolescents have to prepare themselves emotionally and spiritually, as best they can to be able to cope with the unpredictable and continual instability of moods, irritability, argumentativeness, and impulsiveness of early adolescents. Foreknowledge of these emotional behaviors puts parents and teachers in a better position to know what to expect and to know why their children behave in such a manner. This helps parents and teachers feel confident to deal with early adolescents' behavioral manifestations.

BEING OBJECTIVE IN DEALING WITH ADOLESCENT EMOTIONS

It is necessary for parents and teachers to be cognizant of adolescent negative emotional behaviors as a background in their relationships. Such knowledge will assist all who work with adolescents not to take personally the often unconscious negative emotions which adolescents will take out on parents and teachers in their frustration with life's demands. Although this anger and frustration may not occur often, parents and teachers who are often with adolescents cannot but experience the adolescent emotional outburst which would seem to be directed at them. Parents' and teachers' common reactions to this might be to feel hurt and frustrated themselves with the child. However, a demonstration of understanding of the source of their anger and dealing with the situation objectively, not taking it personally or feel angry or hurt by the adolescent outburst, will be a better approach and more helpful for both the parent and the child.

To be emotionally removed from early adolescent outbursts would imply that parents can objectively examine what the child is mad about to see if there is a justifiable cause for such negative emotional reaction. If no such cause exists, the parent should know that the child is probably taking out his or her frustration about work, teachers, or peers on the parents who cannot escape such negative emotional outbursts from time to time. This approach to adolescent stress and storm can help parents to feel less angry. More importantly, it can help them to manage the situation or to deal with events that are legitimate and deserving of parental attention.

Another way in which parents and teachers can prepare would be to be predisposed to accept early adolescent stress and storm in the form of moods, hate, likes and dislikes, and annoyances, as part of the normal adolescent development processes. It would also include coming to terms with the reality of early adolescent negative moods and being open to accept as normal for this age group such behaviors as the adolescent's exaggerations, self-centeredness, angry moods, critical know-it-all attitude, adventurous and experimenting inclinations, changing interests, and impulsiveness. To appreciate that one is not the cause of any of these behaviors and while one may not like them, it is the normal process of growth in adolescents to be self-conscious, to feel insecure, and to worry about their looks and what others think of them. As the saying goes, "knowledge is power," and being with this knowledge of what to expect from your adolescent child at home or in the classroom provides the power to deal with it in the most loving and understanding manner that is in accord with the best practice of authoritative parenting.

RESPONDING TO ADOLESCENT STRESS AND STORM

Making sense of the adolescent's difficult behaviors can be possible if parents reflect on their own adolescent years. Some parents may be able to relate with their child's adolescent outbursts if they remember that they were once adolescents and that their own parents probably had problems, dealing with their own out of control behaviors. There is a possibility that a parent may have had similar difficulties in early adolescence and may also have caused his or her parents a great deal of frustration coping with adolescent stress and storm.

Acknowledging and accepting one's own difficulties with one's parents in the early adolescent years helps a parent to realize that adolescent storm and stress is normal. However, it does not imply that all of the adolescent negative behaviors should be permitted or allowed unchecked. Allowing the child to have his or her way could cost the family emotionally. Although parents should show understanding for adolescent negative behaviors, it should also be expected that in exercising their authority they are seen to be firm and caring as they deal with the child's problems. In disapproving of early adolescent negative behaviors, parents should also be clear in letting the child know why such behaviors are unacceptable and why have to change. Children are to be told how their behaviors affect others and are to be taught the adult way of behaving as they grow into adulthood. Give a brief reason for not approving of the behavior, and if the child has his or her own reason for behaving in a particular way, listen to his or her excuse as well. A parent has no obligation to justify every direction given to the child; however, a parent's action should not be seen as arbitrary or imposing on the child who may begin to resent parental advice. The fact is that parents always have to be parents by not engaging in a prolonged argument with the child. Such arguments could lead to resentment. Rather, endeavor to keep the door of communication always open with the child. The child should not be left in doubt as to what he or she is doing wrong. Such knowledge is necessary for the child to know why he or she is being punished. Give directions for best behaviors next time or discuss the necessary house etiquette pertaining to guests or visitors to your home. For example, the child can be counseled that, when guests visit, they should be greeted, and some time should be spent with them. Then the child could go to his or her room for the rest of the time. In this way, the parent has succeeded in letting the child know it is wrong and poor manners to ignore visitors to one's home, as such attitude would be an embarrassment to both the parent and the visitor, who may make the judgment that the child is not being trained in courteous and acceptable home manners.

Parents should also remain calm during the adolescent outbursts, but should find time to ask the child when he or she has calmed down about the source of the anger. The child may deny being angry or may be open to discussing the source of the anger, such as a friend or peers in the school who calls him or her names. This will be an opportunity to help the child to get it out of his or her mind without misdirecting aggression or attacking some innocent person again. Adolescents may accuse parents of only criticizing them; in this case, it is necessary for the parent to let the adolescent know that they are being taught how adults act in such situations since they, too, will soon become young adults. Parents should know that adolescents are neither appreciative of advice nor open to accepting criticisms or reprimands, but that they do keep it in their minds.

HOW CAN YOU BE HELPFUL TO A PROBLEM ADOLESCENT?

Parents can be helpful in calming early adolescent anxieties by being ready to answer their questions, even those that parents think are trivial. If the child is worried because of his or her looks or what his or her peers may think of the adolescent it will be necessary for the parent to assure the child that it is normal for teens to develop such body features and physical changes, therefore, the child should not be worried or feel ashamed of himself or herself. While it may be good to point out any exaggerations of the claimed problem, it may not be a good idea to dismiss the problem as unimportant. Telling a child "Don't worry about it" would be interpreted as the parents' lack of interest in the things that bother the teen. It is also not helpful, to sound accusatory when a child shares his or her problem with the parent, as such attitude would make the child stop sharing his or her problem with the parent in future. On the contrary, the parent can win the child's confidence if the child's question is answered directly as the child might just be curious about the right information on the matter about which she is asking questions. It could also be possible that the child is asking his or her mother a question the child's friend feels too afraid to ask his or her own mother at home. The way parents handle their child's early adolescent questions will determine whether the adolescent will keep asking his or her parents questions and asking for clarifications on their issues when they run into problems in the future.

LISTEN TO YOUR ADOLESCENT

Parents can do substantial good for their adolescents if they can cultivate the habit of listening to their numerous questions. This is because their need at this time is not necessarily advice but a listening ear. The need of adolescents at this time is more of encouragement, especially at a time when things do not seem to be going their way.

Being available to listen to the adolescent provides the space and parental presence needed to vent frustration. Advice on the problem will come later after the child has been relieved of his or her anxieties by a compassionate listener. A parent can be more practical at the appropriate time by sharing with his or her adolescent child similar experiences which the parent had as an adolescent, thereby teaching how such problems were resolved in the parent's own case as an adolescent.

Again, during the early adolescent stage of development, adolescents will question what they have been taught as children. It is often shocking for parents to hear their children questioning their values. It is normal for adolescents to discover those values and beliefs for themselves through personal inquiry before they can make such values their own. Parents should not be alarmed when the child wanders away from the belief systems they had taught them during this stage of development. However, children are the fruit of their parents and, as such, parents remain the source of development of the child's values. In any case, adolescents who were well grounded in the family's values and beliefs at childhood are likely, after a long futile search, to come back and adopt these values through their adulthood. This is why parents should not be troubled or influenced by the changes their adolescents frequently make in their choices.

Although it may seem to be a waste of time talking to an adolescent child who does not listen and seems to be indifferent to whatever is said, as long as the parent do not push the adolescent to the extreme, the adolescent will sooner or later realize the wisdom in the pieces of advice given to him or her. Early adolescents internalize their experiences with parents and such perception often keeps pulling them back after they wander off course. Adolescents often resort to what their parents have taught them when they meet difficult situations. Adolescents may not recognize the fact that their parents were acting in their child's interest until they come to this point in their lives. Furthermore, parents may think that they have not been effective parents or that all the lectures and talking has fallen on deaf ears until the child calls and tells his or her parent that a problem has been solved because he or she applied advice received as a child. The adolescent may not know that the parent is wiser than he or she or that parent is a good parent until this "Ahab!" moment.

APPRECIATING ADOLESCENT POSITIVE BEHAVIORS

Early adolescence is not all about the negative emotions of the developing child but also about the energies and positive side of this age group. As earlier observed, the greatest need of the early adolescent is encouragement. Parents should not hesitate to appreciate and encourage the adolescent when he or she does something good. Adolescents also look forward to being praised when they behave very well or work hard at school or at work. Commend them and tell them how proud of them you are when they show intelligence, or how good they look when they dress well. It is such reinforcement of their positive behavior, as earlier observed, that will help them to develop self-confidence, self-esteem, and a positive self-concept. Commendations will help the child to be confident with his or her accomplishments and life in general. It will also work as a boost to engage in positive behaviors in the future.

On the other hand, adolescents are not quick in expressing their love and emotions towards their parents. This does not mean that they no longer care about their parent, but early adolescents associate affectionate behavior towards parents with babies and childhood, and they do not want to be viewed as a baby or a child anymore. However, some adolescents may be openly affectionate with their parents while some others might consider such behavior as foolishness. Even though adolescents may not feel comfortable expressing their affection physically for the parent, parents need to show affection to reassure them that they are loved.

Such continued parental affection reassures them as they continue to grow out of adolescent insecurity due to the various physical and emotional changes they are undergoing. Parental love and care should be expressed in such a way that the adolescent can regard it as one thing that is constant in their lives while every other thing around them changes. The home and family should be sign and symbol of this constancy in the adolescent's life. That is why it will always be a bad idea, with subsequent negative results, for an adolescent to be pushed to the extreme, causing him or her to run away from home or for parents to divorce at this time. It is vital, therefore, for parents to ensure a stable, secure home and environment for a child at this stage of development. Although parents may think their adolescent child has grown and no longer needs them, the child is to be constantly reassured of his or her worth, abilities, and parental support as he or she undergoes constant adolescent changes. One of the new phases in adolescent development that often confuses parents is adolescent self-assertion and separation from parents and family in favor of attachment to peers and friends. The next chapter deals with this issue in a way that parents can make sense of it as a normal part of the early adolescent developmental stage.

CHAPTER 12

Adolescent Social Development

EARLY ADOLESCENTS' GRADUAL development into adulthood necessitates the quest for acknowledgment as he or she transforms from adolescent to more adult social interaction. This is observed in the adolescent's need to be independent of parents and other adults in his or her life. The need to know who the adolescent is leads to continual separation from the family and more attraction to peers and friends, with whom he or she prefers to spend more time than with parents and family. Often parents are puzzled by this development, asking how a child, who was totally dependent on his or her parents now wants to be independent. Parents have to know that this stage of self-assertion is a vital aspect in child development. Parents should only show understanding as the child undergoes this process of individuation and searching for their place and role in life. Adolescents are excited to grow into adults who they think are free to do whatever they like without parental restrictions. However, they do not see the responsibilities of an adult, which includes getting a job, getting up every morning to go to work, supporting oneself and family. Their idea of adulthood is dominated by how adults are presented by the media, especially on television and movie shows. Early adolescents believe the unrealistic ways adults are presented to be true of adult life. For example, they believe that beautiful women are always popular and happy, that excessive drinking is fun, that girls who dress in a sexy manner are attractive to men, that smoking is sexy and cool or that wearing brand name clothing improves one's look and makes one popular among peers. Early adolescents do not realize that these ideas are not realistic until they grow into adulthood and are more mature in reasoning. However, they try to do the things they observe adults doing on television and movies as a way to disassociate themselves from childhood by exhibiting adult behaviors. Their idealistic tendency makes them object to parents' sound advice from real life experiences even when they are told of the consequences of living in a world of fantasy. Their claim to invincibility makes them feel that nothing bad can ever happen to them. For example, many adolescents think drunk driving cannot lead to an auto crash; however, most national statistics have shown that drunk driving often results in the most fatal motor accidents world over.

Parents and teachers will feel frustrated as they try to convince early adolescents to think realistically. The stress adolescents feel from wanting to keep the childhood safety and security provided by parents but still experiencing the strong desire for freedom and independence from parental control cause fluctuations in their behavior. This struggle between childish and adult behavior confuses parents, too, who are no longer at ease in treating their child as the little baby they used to know. Advice offered to the child during this period may be accepted at one time and, at another, rejected as interfering or nagging by the parent. It will be helpful for parents to exercise resilience and ask for grace to follow patiently this period of early adolescent experimentation which involves everything from harmless things like hairstyle or makeup to those of a more negative nature like smoking or sex.

Parents are to be aware that adolescents are more likely than not to be preoccupied with themselves and to be more selfish and self-centered than ever before. They are often focusing on their own needs and do not care about what others need or think. They do not care about inconveniencing others by spending more time than necessary in the bathroom in the morning or about asking parents and other adults for help when they know they are very busy. Moreover, when they are helped, they show no appreciation. Adolescents may think the parent is old- fashioned because the parent does not permit behavior the adolescents have learned from the media. It should not be strange for parents to notice how their adolescent child is gradually rejecting the parent and family to find their own identity as well as rejecting family values and norms. At this period, early adolescents prefer friends and peers to their parents and family. Becoming aware of their parents' idealize, one whose fault they cannot observe because they are not within the adolescent's immediate environment; consequently, the adolescent may never know this idol enough to observe his or her weaknesses. However, parents should know that teen idol worship does not last and so should not worry about the adolescent's new craze for adult movie stars or rock stars in Hollywood.

It should be noted that the way early adolescents try to establish their independence from parents and adults is by rebelling against them. The boldness to rebel and defy parental authority provides adolescents with signs of their maturity and freedom from parental authority and control. Parents should not, therefore, view this attitude as directed against them or as insult, but as an adolescent's normal process of self-assertion and independence from the controlling authority of adults. Parents may be provoked to anger by the adolescent's criticisms and rebellious attitude whenthey choose to do the opposite of the things the adolescent was advised against, like smoking, hanging out with peers until late at night, and so forth.

This is not a time for parents to ask questions like "What did I do wrong"? Rebellion by the early adolescent is necessary for the adolescent child to develop and establish himself or herself as an individual with his or her own feelings, tastes, opinions, mind, and values, even though it makes the parent feel hopeless and helpless about the fear of losing control of the child. Adolescent rebellion is, therefore, not a result of how a child was raised. It would be abnormal for an adolescent not to follow through this process, and if adolescent rebellion does not occur in early adolescent it may occur later. The consequence of later rebellion when the child is in the mid-twenties might be worse than in early adolescence, as such may be more difficult to reverse (Caissy, 1994). Parents' response to early adolescent rebellion should not be to stop it but to assist the adolescent in confining such behavior to things that will not cause him or her bodily harm but that will allow the adolescent to rebel in safe ways.

Again, the tendency of early adolescents to stop needing their parents at a point in their life must be understood by parents as normal. Parents should learn not to take it personally, not to feel hurt, anger, or bitterness, and not to resent the child as a result. This gradual withdrawal from parental authority and family ways of life is only a sign of maturation in the adolescent. While parents will allow the adolescent some independence, the need to play a supervisory role cannot be abdicated, for early adolescents prefer parents who act like parents, not too old fashioned, not too modern, and conservative. They feel embarrassed before their friends if their parents act like they do, and so are not comfortable with the mothers who dress sexy and too fashionably or fathers who are too far out of fashion (Caissy, 1994). As early adolescents continue to withdraw from parental control and authority, their need for friendship increases. Parents will be doing their adolescent good and providing them with a great deal of understanding by allowing sleepovers with their group of close friends, for it is better that parents know with whom they are associating and what they are doing. Socializing in the parent's presence offers opportunity for supervision of early adolescents.

RESPONDING TO THE INFLUENCE OF PEERS

Friendship plays a more significant role in the adolescent life as he or she disengages from dependence on the parents and engages in freedom and independence. The commonalities adolescents share between the ages of twelve to fourteen attract them to each other and to be allies in their struggle to fight off parental and family domination. They "hang out" together in the malls and on street corners where they prefer to talk and share experiences and support each other. Early adolescents are likely to befriend persons of the same sex and, by the age of thirteen are ready to form friendships with children of the opposite sex who share the same background, interests and values with them. Their behavior at this time is heavily influenced by peers and friends to win their approval and support. Adolescents often change their personalities to please their friends by doing what the friends like because of the desire for social acceptance. They try to please parents, friends and their peer group but often their loyalty is torn among these groups. Eventually early adolescents will transfer their allegiance from the parents to their friends and peer group. The best friend syndrome, especially among adolescent girls, is also pronounced at this period. The adolescent finds this individual a confidant with whom the adolescent shares her experiences every day, expecting complete loyalty from that friend. A betrayal can be emotionally devastating. Parents may be shocked at first when they realize how much friends and peers influence their adolescent child's behavior.

However, this is an age when adolescents find it fashionable to become a member of a peer group. This peer group places on the adolescent a pressure of social compliance. For the child to be socially acceptable and avoid peer rejection, she will have to comply with the norms and accepted behavior shown in the peers' manner of speaking, dressing, and likes. Adolescents cannot afford to be different from their peers at this period and do not like to be criticized by their peers for being different. This fear of being criticized and the tendency to yield to peer pressure is born out of the adolescent's low self-esteem, insecurity, and self-consciousness which can be traced to the early part of their development as explained in the chapter that dealt with styles of child attachment.

Parents should responsibly promote adolescent friendship as a way and means of socializing the child away from the family. Friendship helps adolescents to avoid isolation, which could be devastating. Good friendship should be encouraged, just as bad friendship should be discouraged because friends have as much influence as the family in determining the course of the life of the child, whether negatively or positively. For example, the peer group that evolves into a secret cult should be discouraged as such deviant groups can derail the course of the child's life with devastating long-term effects for the child and the family. On the other hand, associating with the right crowd during early adolescence can play a significant role in the child's life as such groups will help generate positive pressure on the child either to do well academically, learn to play a musical instrument, excel in sports, or live a moral life instead of a life of misconduct associated with deviant peer pressure. The adolescent finds a sense of security, influence, recognition, and power in his or her peer group as he or she continues to be independent of parental authority and control. Every adolescent will try to define his or her status within the peer group, the school circle, and finally, the society at large. The peer group, therefore, provides the child a natural way of initiation and entrance into the adult world of freedom and responsibilities.

All peer pressure is not about negative influences, as earlier observed. Peer pressure can be responsible for keeping a group of adolescents out of trouble when it serves as a means of standardization of adolescent behavior. This is because adolescents want to be similar to their peers in their likes and dislikes, appearance and behavior. The type of peer pressure influence that parents would not encourage is that which can result in either physical harm or negative consequences for the child. It is necessary for parents to discuss adolescent peer pressure as soon as the child begins to form a group of friends. The adolescent should be made aware of the two sides of the coin, to embrace the positive influence of their peers while at the same time avoiding the negative or dangerous and unsafe influences of their peers. Let the child express himself or herself as regards the peer pressure. Listen to their questions, too. The question might be "What should I do if my friends say everyone must use drugs, drink, or smoke Cigarettes?" The adolescent usually would like the input of parents and how they would feel should the adolescent do any of these. This input will be a reference point for them should the matter arise. Neglecting to have dialogue with an adolescent to prepare him or her for this eventuality will leave the child at a greater risk as he or she had not been prepared to face such pressures, to say "No" or to walk away from situations in which he or she does not feel comfortable. Adolescents who have positive self-image and high self-esteem are more likely to resist peer pressure because they are not afraid to disagree with their peers on issues. Those who have a negative sclf-image and low self-esteem are more likely to be influenced by peer pressure. This is because they are in need of other people's acceptance and are afraid of rejection by peers. Parents can minimize the child's tendency to fall to negative peer pressure by establishing a healthy and trusting relationship with the adolescent child in order to boost his or her sense of self-confidence which will serve as a defense against negative peer pressure.

While parents are encouraged to promote their adolescent's socio-psychological health through friendship, they should encourage friendship that fosters positive influence and discourage those that encourage negative behaviors. Parents should take the opportunity, whenever their adolescents bring their friends home, to judge the kind of friend the child keeps. It is advisable, too, for parents to take advantage when it comes, to know the parents of their adolescent friends so as to gain insight into the child's home background. In this way the parent is better placed to make judgment on the company the child keeps. Early adolescents will listen to their parents' instruction to disassociate from a friend who could be a bad influence. However, an adolescent at the rebellious stage is likely to disobey the parents' instruction to stay away from friends who could be a bad influence, thus proving that the parents are wrong in their judgment.

Parents cannot give up on their adolescent child even when he or she is rebellious. The need for parents to raise a self-confident child cannot be overemphasized as doing so remains the best alternative to falling easily for bad peer pressure. However, parents should encourage their early adolescent child to avoid picking on other children who feel insecure for one reason or the other, as bullying behavior promotes the child's tendency to give in to peer pressure and all negative influences from bad friends by whom they feel welcomed and accepted. Apart from school friendships, parents should encourage their adolescents, especially those who are put down by their peers in school, to join other community organizations like the Girl Scouts, Boy Scouts, church youth groups, sports clubs or choral groups made up of children of the same age. Moreover, making friends with other children outside of the school who do not know about his or her rejection experience with other peers will help to form a character devoid of possible negative peer influences. By keeping the child busy with such after-school programs the need to turn to peers will be reduced to the barest minimum.

Parents should always help the bullied child to have self-confidence and to know that there is nothing wrong with him or her. Rather, it is the bully who is in the wrong. The adolescent should be encouraged not to fight or react to the name calling of peers, but to ignore their ridicule as such ridicule is done just to hurt his or her feelings. The child should report such behavior to a teacher. Parents should praise the child's bravery for not responding to the ridicule and show the child that he or she is a good person. They should let the child know that they are proud of his or her behavior and performance at school. Parents can reward such behavior by allowing their adolescent to choose popular brand name clothing as the family budget permits. This allows the adolescent to affirm his or her personality and to exercise influence over his or her peers as well. Parent can also disapprove of any dress choice that does not conform to family ideals such as transparent and very sexy clothing. Parents should explain to the child why he or she should not choose such attire even though the child would like to look like his or her peers. They should be realistic in explaining to adolescents that adult life is not as rosy as they might think, just as the fantasies they see on television are not always authentic in real life. Rather, they serve as an escape from the reality and routine of everyday life. Therefore, it is imperative that parents remind their early adolescent in their fascination for adult life that adult life is often not as fantastic as they think.

Responsible adults are bound to work very hard to meet their needs and those of their dependents. Popular and attractive models and stars may not be as happy as everyone thinks. Everyone is bound to encounter problems and difficulty but has to accept them as part of life. No one is happy all the time. People should not be carried away by television advertisements on alcoholic drinks and cigarettes as a means of happiness and fun. These are merely marketing strategies. While moderate drinking can be good for adults, too much alcohol can be dangerous to health as can smoking cigarettes. Adults also learn to cope with life challenges rather than finding escape through the use of alcohol and cigarettes as a way of venting the anxieties of work and relationships. Helping early adolescents to be aware of the harsh realities of life and the responsible ways of living will help them to avoid living in a fool's paradise and help them to embrace life with the correct knowledge and attitude required for responsible adulthood.

EARLY ADOLESCENT INTELLECTUAL DEVELOPMENT

Early adolescents grow and mature not only biologically, physically, emotionally, and socially, but also intellectually. Most early adolescents develop formal thought processes before the ages of twelve and fourteen and are enrolled in seventh and eighth grade or in the junior secondary school. The brain develops fully between the ages of fourteen to sixteen, during which the early adolescent has developed the formal thinking skills of adults. At this age, children transition from middle school to high school and their intellectual ability continues to grow and fluctuate between a child-like thinking pattern to an adult thinking pattern. As earlier observed, early adolescence is a problematic stage of child development as the adolescent revolts against adult control. Like parents, teachers who teach middle school must be aware of the characteristics of children in this transitional age group and so must teach and instruct like parents, with graceful resilience coupled with adequate disciplinary and management skills. They need to do this in order to positively impact the child's personality. Parents have the responsibility of encouraging their adolescents to be respectful to their teachers and to encourage teachers in their duty since they know what it means to work with early adolescents.

Parents and teachers should be aware that the developmental changes in the early adolescent can affect their academic performance during this period. Adjusting to a new academic curriculum or setting can affect performance. The restlessness of this developmental stage can be a problem for the adolescent getting himself or herself organized and so can affect academic performance. Academic work may be more challenging at this time because the adolescent will have to begin to take responsibility for doing homework without parent's help or other adults. To do it all alone without teacher or parents' help could be difficult at the initial stage of working alone. After this period the child is supposed to perform as before middle school. Otherwise parents should go to the child and work with the school counselor to evaluate the child for the cause of poor academic performance. Lagging behind academically at this period can also be attributed to the slowdown in the learning capacity, shorter attention span, and the ability to concentrate from the age of twelve to fourteen (Caissy, 1994).

Parents and teachers should encourage these children to work hard even though they do not score a high grade at the beginning of middle school. They could be helped to understand the change they are undergoing in their thinking process and problem-solving abilities. It should be noted that mental development varies from one child to another, and that not all adolescents perform on the same level; some could be late mental developers. The physical, emotional, and social changes adolescents undergo during this time could also be very overwhelming, in that they lose concentration in their studies which results in poor performance. They should be helped to understand how not to be preoccupied with the transitional changes they experience at this stage. Adolescents who are distracted and are always worrying about what others think about his or her physical changes or lack thereof may perform poorly. This is not because they do not study but because they neither pay attention in the classroom nor focus on their academic work. Some adolescents could be more interested in the social aspect of school than in academics, which may also affect their performance.

Apart from the above mentioned factors that can affect adolescents' performance in middle school, other factors may result in poor results in academic performance. For example, adolescents may become involved in bad behaviors arising from social and emotional problems which could lead the child to indulge in substance abuse or to engage in crimes which may be a result of negative peer pressure as earlier discussed. This group of students is often rebellious and uncooperative with parents and teachers. Such adolescents are often absent from school. When they do attend, they hardly pay attention in the classroom and do not do their assignments, but instead are preoccupied with their social life.

Adolescents who manifest such disruptive bad behaviors would require the professional intervention of school psychologists, psychiatrists, social workers, or mental health counselors who work with adolescents to deal with the fundamental causes of such bad behavior. These skilled professionals can turn things around in the adolescent's life before the parents and teachers totally lose control. When the adolescent is unable to adjust and perform well in middle school, the problem could be attributed to the factors discussed here rather than a learning disability. Thus, it is believed that any learning disability would have been uncovered and treated before this stage in the child's intellectual development except if it had gone undetected.

Patience is required from parents at this time so as to avoid mounting more pressure on the adolescent should he or she fail to maintain or improve in his or her academic performance. Parents should be conscious of the enormous pressure from the various changes the adolescent is undergoing in addition to peer pressure. It is not right to nag the child or choose a profession for him or her to prepare for in college, for example, with failure to comply resulting in denying him or her monthly monetary allowance. The parent should show concern and encouragement and be a counselor to the child by showing empathy and providing the child with extra academic help if necessary, especially if the child's performance is significantly low. Parents should work with psychologists and counselors to uncover the underlying problem and provide help for the child without pushing him or her to the limits. Unnecessary pressure on a child who is already feeling overwhelmed can make him or her lose hope and give up on everything. Parents should not overreact by blaming school administrators and teachers when they receive a call from their child's school about bad behavior or poor academic performance. Such calls may be very shocking, especially when the child has been known to behave well and has always had good grades in his or her subjects. Such information might be a wakeup call for parents who do not care or who are unaware of the child's changing behavior due to peer pressure.

Such a situation offers parents the opportunity to work with the school for the benefit of the child. During adolescence, children should learn to be responsible for their negligence in their school assignments without reminders and assistance from parents. However, parents might still have to assist the child to study for tests and examinations. The next chapter encourages parents to remain patient, be loving and kind in the face of the early adolescent attitudinal changes and rebelliousness.

CHAPTER 13

Resilience In Parenting

MOST PARENTS FEEL frustrated with the transition from being a happy mom or dad of a baby who was all pleasant, obedient, and compliant to now raising a child who now has a mind of his own. This development challenges parents' patient endurance to love and care for a stubborn child. This is why the period of puberty or early adolescence is said to be the most stressful stage both for the child and for the parents. As earlier observed, the biological, physical, social, and emotional changes that rapidly take place during puberty are responsible for the stress and storm that characterize early adolescent life. The sudden changes in the way the child behaves are the major reason parents feel sad having to deal with a child who is now described as moody, irritable, changeable, impulsive, rebellious, defiant, inconsiderate, smart-mouthed, and critical (Caissy, 1994). It is these attitudes and behaviors observed in early adolescence that make parents question their effort and parenting skills. Rhetorical questions like

"Why is she behaving this way?" "Why doesn't he seem to care about us anymore?" "Why is she doing this to us?" "Where did he learn this?" "Where have I gone wrong?" the shock of adolescent behavior question their ability to parent. All these questions arise in the mind of parents who do not see these attitudinal change as a result of the developmental transformation that the child is undergoing during puberty. Most parents, therefore, seem to think that it is their fault that the child has developed a behavior that is so deviant from what he or she used to be before the age of nine. Awareness of these natural changes during puberty will relieve parents of their frustration and better position them to manage adolescent stress and storm in a more insightful and helpful manner, devoid of self-blame.

Parents of adolescent children should not lose hope in the child when all they observe from the child is lack of gratitude. It is part of the process of adolescent development to be critical of parents and all they do for the child. Parental sacrifices are not going to be appreciated and parents may feel lost because most of the child's actions communicate that the adolescent "hates" the parents as the child continues to withdraw from parent and family. The hurt they feel as parents can be worse if the adolescent is the first child and the parents are first time parents of an adolescent, since the child's behaviors may seem strange to them. Parents might seem to lose the memory of raising a wonderful and loving child. Parents should realize that the responsibility of raising an adolescent child is one that requires hard work without immediate reward. The reward of parenting is often only realized after the age of adolescence. Parents who persevere will surely smile at the result of all the time and sacrifices they made on the child upon seeing him or her succeed in life as an adult. The child will also become appreciative of the parent's sacrifices and fusses with him or her realizing that these things were meant for his or her own good.

The need for resilience and grace, therefore, cannot be overemphasized in parenting an adolescent. Parents must learn to wear patience and persistence in parenting like a maternity robe. They must remain tenacious in the struggle and difficulty of raising an adolescent child. This is because the stress and storm of unappreciative and critical adolescents can bring them to the point that they no longer care to carry on as dedicated parents. They should understand that extra time and effort are required to successfully navigate the child through this difficult period of development. And no one may be able to do it all by one's own power except through the special grace that comes from a higher power. Prayer is good when you reach this point and the cooperation of both husband and wife is imperative where both parents are together. Such collaboration and support for one another when raising an adolescent makes the burden easier. Parents must be conscious of the fact that some adolescents may do things to cause misunderstanding between the parents or try to set one parent against the other, resulting in their not being able to agree on any plan to control the child's behavior. No one who is worthy of the designation "parent" will take sides with the adolescent child against his or her mate for being too hard or being too compassionate with the child. If this happens, the child's behavior will worsen as he or she would have succeeded in pitting one parent against the other. If parents disagree on the kind of disciplinary action to be taken on behalf of the child, it must not be in the presence of the child. Agree to disagree in private. And whatever action is taken to help the child must be reinforced by both parents so that the child does not get the impression that the parent who is enforcing the disciplinary action is the one who "hates" him or her while the other loves the child and feels opposed to his or her punishment. When both parents condemn the early adolescent's bad behavior it has much greater impact on the child. When the child improves by behaving well, both parents should also commend and appreciate the child's efforts. Although the adolescent will not appreciate whatever the parents do now as being in his or her interests, when the child becomes a parent, he or she will understand and appreciate what parents did during the most difficult stage of child development. Then the adolescent will take pride in their parents' perseverance and hard work. That will be a moment of appreciation and happiness for both the parents and the child, especially if he or she now has children of his or her own to raise. The child will now draw from his or her own experience growing up under his or her parents and will be better equipped for dealing with his or her own children.

PRACTICAL PARENTING STYLE

Given the complex and unpredictable nature of early adolescent behavior, it is difficult to prescribe a technique that can apply to all adolescent child Types. However, certain general principles and disciplinary methods have been noted to be successful most of the time in the management of early adolescent stress. The guiding framework parents use in managing the adolescent must take into consideration the child's personality and the family's values and beliefs. This is implied in the authoritative parenting style which has been considered the most acceptable and successful system of parenting. In early adolescence, while parental authority and control remain the general guiding principle, parents may need to adjust their parenting style to be able to manage unstable early adolescent behavior. This is because the adolescent child is no longer compliant with parental authority but is opposed to it, defiant, and rebellious. The early adolescence will quickly change to the manner in which adults think and act. This will necessitate a change in the use of parenting authority because the child will want to be recognized and treated like the adult he or she is becoming. In dealing with the adolescent at this time, parents should be more persuasive than authoritative in their style of parenting. Parents should be less controlling and authoritative and resort more to compromise when dealing with the adolescent child. Parents remain the authority figure in the family but when it comes to the adolescent child, it is more successful to be less bossy and to play more of the role of advisory and negotiator. This means that parents should listen to the adolescent's complaints, discuss whatever issues he or she may have, and compromise where it serves the best interest of the child. Although this approach to early adolescent parenting might be frustrating, patient parents can successfully turn a rebellious and irritable early adolescent behavior around by patiently guiding and showing than by commanding or ordering the child about. For parents to back down, feel frustrated, or become impatient in this responsibility because of the adolescent's rebelliousness would mean abandoning responsible and resilient parenting. As a result, may develop into a wild adult as he or she may no longer be controlled after developing into an adult. Some situations may require that parents use their authority to impress on the child a realization of the seriousness of his or her behavior and to demonstrate their unwillingness to condone such behaviors. In minor cases, parents should be more compromising and less controlling.

Parents should make it a point to listen to their adolescent children when they ask to talk. Instead of turning down the child, listen to the question and if they do not respond with a ready answer, tell the child that you will think about it and give him or her an answer later. The parent should take time to think or to discuss the request with his or her spouse to arrive at a good answer that can be justified. While parents are encouraged to dialogue with their early adolescents, they should know when to say yes or no and remain steadfast in such decisions especially when the decision is in the best interest of the child. When a request is refused, give the child the reason that the request was turned down. It does not put any parent in a good light when he or she refuses the child's request only to change the decision after a short while. The child may capitalize on parental indecision to argue and pressure parents to change their mind each time they say no to the child. If they yield to pressure, the child will not take the parents seriously because they change their decisions frequently. As required in authoritative parenting style, what is needed in early adolescent parenting is for parents to balance between parental warmth and firmness. It is required that parents should listen to their adolescents before saying no. To do so will make the child think they are fair, that they consider the child's requests, needs, feelings, and views and then make a decision that will serve the child's best interest. It is necessary to compromise when possible on less serious issues and to use authority and control on serious matters. Be aware that the child will rebel and become defiant against your authority as expected, but behavior should be kept in check and not allowed to run rampant so as to become dangerous and uncontrollable (Caissy, 1994).

THE IDEAL ATTITUDE TOWARD EARLY ADOLESCENT BEHAVIOR

Many parents often ask what they can do in the face of early adolescent restlessness. There are a number of positive ways to respond to adolescent stress. First, parents should know that early adolescent stress and storm could cause them emotional and mental breakdown if they do not restrain themselves. As earlier observed, it means that parents cannot afford to take personally the bad behaviors of their early adolescents who are only undergoing the normal routine of development. The aim of this book is to avail parents and those who work with adolescents of the opportunity to know and understand the kind of behaviors to expect of this age group and why adolescents behave the way they do. Knowing that neither the child nor the parent is necessarily responsible for such behaviors, parents should accept the adolescent child with the crises and challenges this stage of development brings. The adolescent rebellion, criticisms, or need to separate from parents should be viewed objectively, as part of adolescent developmental needs, without any hard feelings by parents. It is not the parents' fault that the child is behaving a certain way. Parents have to recognize that some behaviors are normal and that they can help the child in this very stormy stage of development to be a man or woman by courageously standing by them, helping the child to control and keep these behaviors under check so that they do not harm themselves or others by making wrong choices.

Even though they may behave as they do, that is as though they do not need their parents during this time, they really do. Parents need to step in by following when and how to intervene to exercise control and authority as earlier recommended.

In order not to allow frustration to stand in the way of playing their role as parents during this period, it is advised that parents "take a deep breath" and remain calm and patient. This is because early adolescent behavior could easily make you resort to anger and pounce on the child in ways that could worsen your stress level and the child's ability to count on your love and understanding. When you consider the adolescent's every day mood changes, hates, loves, challenges, and annoyances as normal, you significantly reduce your stress level. A display of such patience and understanding is what is required of any parent who is aware of the signs and symptoms of puberty which neither the child nor the parents can control or stop no matter how hard they all try. It is natural and must run its course, so parents need to remain calm during early adolescent development and play their role as best they can. This difficult and challenging stage lasts for only a short while. Parents who do not exercise enough patience with early adolescent stress and storm are likely to resort to resentment and use of inappropriate corporal punishment in an attempt to bring the child into compliance. In the next chapter, the use of corporal punishment and its effects will be discussed so that parents are aware of when spanking for example, as a form of corporal punishment, goes beyond being a disciplinary action.

CHAPTER 14

Moral Internalization And Corporal Punishment In Parenting

DISCIPLINE IS OFTEN initiated by parents to achieve immediate compliance by the child and, by so doing, to promote in the child the development of internal control which the child would need in long-term socialization (Golick, Deci, & Ryan, 1997). According to Grusec and Goodnow (1994), moral internalization is defined as "taking over the values and attitudes of society as one's own so that socially acceptable behavior is motivated not by anticipation of external consequences but by intrinsic or internal factors" (p.4). Moral internalization is fundamental to the child's development of social and emotional competence (Kochanska & Thompson, 1997). Parental discipline serves the purpose of helping the child to internalize the necessary societal morals. When it is applied via minimal parental power, it enhances the child's ability to make choices, achieve autonomy, and offer an explanation for desirable behaviors (Kuczynski & Hildebrandt, 1997). Research on attribution defined as an explanation why people think, feel, or act as they do, suggests that power assertive methods such as corporal punishment can promote the child's external attributions for their behavior and reduce attribution to internal motivations (Hoffman, 1983; Leper, 1983).

PARENTING AND CORPORAL PUNISHMENT

Corporal punishment has long been part and parcel of parenting discipline. Corporal punishment includes threats, time-out, withdrawal of privileges, or other techniques (Grusec & Kuczynski, 1980). Despite the fact that in recent times, many countries for example, (Austria, Croatia, Cyprus, Denmark, Finland, Germany, Israel, Italy, Latvia, Norway, Sweden, USA, and so forth), have adopted laws that prohibit parents from the use of corporal punishment as a part of child-rearing strategy, arguments both for and against it still remain strong even in the countries where it is prohibited (Gershoff, 2002). This is in addition to the fact that psychologists and other professionals do not agree on whether the benefits of corporal punishment outweigh any potential hazards it could pose. Some parents and theorists believe that it is both effective and desirable (Larzelere, 1996, 2000). On the other hand, others argue that corporal punishment is ineffective and harmful to the child (McCord, 1997, Straus, 1994a). However, there is limited knowledge on how the child's behaviors and experiences are related to parental corporal punishment.

According to Straus (1994a), "corporal punishment is the use of physical force with the intention of causing a child to experience pain but not injury for the purposes of correction or control of the child's behavior" (p.4). Corporal punishment is often criticized because non-abusive corporal punishment is often mistaken for harmful and abusive behaviors, thereby confounding the effects of child spanking (Larzalere, 2000). For this reason, it is difficult to know where to draw the line between acceptable corporal punishment, like spanking, and dangerous physical abuse in countries like the United States, Denmark, Finland, Germany, Israel, Italy, and so forth. (Hyman, 1997; Gelles & Straus, 1988). Therefore, some state laws that define what constitutes physical abuse would classify corporal punishment as physical abuse or child maltreatment when it is excessive, unlawful, unreasonable, severe, inhuman, extreme or cruel. However physical abuse is defined by the National Clearinghouse on Child Abuse and Neglect Information (2000) as:

> ...characterized by the infliction of physical injury as a result of punching, beating, kicking, biting, burning, shaking, or otherwise harming a child. The parent or caretaker may not have intended to hurt the child, rather the injury may have resulted from over-discipline or physical punishment. (See What the Main Types of Maltreatment Are? Section, paragraph 2)

Thus, behaviors that do not cause any physical injury, such as spanking or slapping, are considered corporal punishment while those that cause physical injury such as punching, kicking, or burning are considered physical abuse (Gershoff, 2002). The primary goal of parents' use of corporal punishment is to immediately stop the child from bad behaviors.

Punishment is understood to act as a kind of conditioning that prevents a behavior from happening again as opposed to reinforcement that strengthens a behavior to reoccur. Punishment could be corporal, verbal, or shaming. Punishment affects behavior reinforcement although with the opposite effect, for punishment decreases the likelihood that the child will repeat the bad behavior. According to Skinner (1953) and Gordon (1989), punishment can be either positive or negative. Punishment would be positive if it adds to the stimulus that decreases or weakens the possibility of the behavior reoccurring. Negative punishment, on the other hand, would take away or weaken the possibility of the behavior occurring again. Thus, parents use negative punishment, for example, when they take the car keys away from the teenager who does not come home on time. In this case, both positive and negative punishment for the behavior of being late coming home is weakened or discouraged (Huffman, 2010).

The use of punishment in parenting refers to the disciplinary actions employed by parents, teachers, and other authority figures to discourage unruly behavior in children. In some countries (United States, Denmark, Finland, Germany, Israel, Italy, and so forth) for example, it is illegal to use corporal punishment. Punishment, as examined here, encompasses much more than a parent giving a child a time-out for misbehavior, because any action that adds or decreases a tendency and affects the behavior to decrease it is punishment. As Huffman (2010) noted, for example, if a parent ignores all the excellent grades in a child's report card and asks questions about the B and C grades, the parent may unintentionally punish the child, thereby weakening the child's likelihood to attain A grades in future courses. Likewise, dog owners who yell or spank their dogs for finally coming to them after being called several times will actually be punishing the desired behavior, that is. coming when called. Similarly, parents who always take away all the change from the teen who did shopping for the family because it was unspent money may be punishing the desired behavior, that is saving money and honesty.

Given this scenario, it is evident that punishment as a way of inculcating discipline is questionable. However, parents who have a basic knowledge of parenting psychology and knowledge in child rearing will fare better in bringing up children who may become the best they could ever be. It is necessary to be mindful of how positive and negative punishment affects the child. Emphasis must be placed on the significance of the positive and inevitable role punishment plays in ensuring an orderly society. This is because reinforcement has been found to be insufficient, as a result, deviants and other dangerous criminals must be stopped or removed from society. Just as parents must stop their small children from running into a busy street and stop their teenagers from drinking and driving, teachers too, must stop disruptive children in the classroom and bullies on the playground (Huffman, 2010). Although punishment may at times be necessary, care must be taken any time punishment is applied (Reie, & Grenyer 2004). Effective use of punishment requires that it must be immediate and consistent. But in the real world, we know this is not possible because, for example, we cannot expect parents to time out a disruptive child in the classroom all the time. The argument here is that when punishment is not meted immediately, the delay can lead to the undesirable behavior being reinforced; consequently, any punishment applied will only act as a partial reinforcement. As a result, the undesirable behavior could become more resistant to change because the recipient may learn what not to do but not learn what she should do. Hence, parents should teach children by showing them examples of correct behaviors because what children see is what they do. That is why positive modeling is critical in parenting.

PUBLIC HUMILIATION AND SHAMING

Whether punishment is meted out physically or verbally, it does not minimize its side effects. The use of public shaming or humiliation as a form of punishment among parents is one that has attracted substantial criticism due to its consequences on the child's psychological health. Karyl McBride, a family therapist, observed that shaming and humiliation cause fear in children which stays with them for a long time. The fear of public shame and humiliation children suffer can be difficult to eradicate and, therefore, can constitute an obstacle to the child's healthy emotional development. A number of these public shaming incidents have been a source of news items on television in recent times. An example was that of the father who became disturbed by his young daughter's habit of stealing at home. To stop his daughter from stealing he made her wear a T-shirt with the inscription "I AM A THIEF" and required that she stand by her school gate so that teachers and students could see her as they entered the school. Similar to this kind of public shaming punishment was the case of a mother who could not stop her young daughter from binge eating and gaining too much weight. To stop her daughter's bad habit, she made her wear a sign around her neck that read "I AM FAT." This is how this kind of punishment is gaining traction today. Both parents complained that they had come to the end of their ropes in trying every persuasive method to help their children to change, and so felt that public shaming might be a way to get the message of their frustration across to these young children. While public shaming as a form of punishment had attracted reprobation from social scientists, some parents have hailed it. Some other commentators noted that humiliation works better as a form of punishment than for a parent to resort to corporal punishment (Belkin, 2012).

However, social scientists do not buy into the idea of public humiliation as a good form of discipline because it leaves a bitter taste for the child, often times for life. Alfie Kohn, in his book **Unconditional Parenting: Moving from Rewards and Punishments to Love and Reason,** noted that humiliation as a form of punishment is counter- productive because "doing to" as a process of parenting is less acceptable when compared to "working with." The former can hardly achieve results beyond temporary compliance, and such compliance comes at a very high cost. This is because the lessons children learn from such an experience are often quite different from what the parents have intended. Children develop a bad impression of the parents as uncaring, unloving, disciplinarians, and as someone who should be avoided. They may learn the wrong lesson; that if you have a problem with what someone else has done, the right thing to do is to use power to force the other person to do what you want. The child may be conditioned to believe that the reason not to steal, lie, or hurt someone is because of the punishment the individual will incur if caught and not because the bad behavior negatively affects others. Such is the lesson children may learn from common discipline techniques even when it is not intended by parents. Alfie (2005), invites parents to rethink their assumptions about raising children, to shift from "doing to" to "working with" parenting. This will involve replacing praise with unconditional support that children need to grow into healthy, caring, responsible people. In other words, no child should be made to think that he or she will be loved only when the child please or impress the parents. Children are not to aspire to earn parental approval but to be loved unconditionally and be raised to know that even if they make mistakes or make wrong choices, they will be accepted and supported to start again.

EMOTIONAL IMPACT OF CORPORAL PUNISHMENT

The emotions arising from the parent-child interaction can predict whether the child will comply with parental control or not. When children experience a positive mood and emotions with parents, they are more likely to be receptive to parental controls than when they experience negative moods (Lay, Waters, & Park, 1989). This underlines the fact that the pain and anger which corporal punishment arouses in children could lead them to resist parental control or even retaliate against parents when parents do not approve of the child's goals. Feelings of fear or distress from such punishment can motivate children to withdraw from interaction with the punisher. Only minimal arousal of emotion in children is actually needed to draw the attention and concern on the part of the child which will facilitate internalization of parental values and morals (Hoffman, 1983; Kochanska, 1993). By contrast, negative emotions from parental corporal punishment will motivate children to ignore the disciplinary message and resent or avoid the punishing parent. Severe or frequent corporal punishment is counterproductive because it arouses emotions that make children focus on themselves rather than helping them understand how their behaviors may adversely affect others in their lives (Eisenberg et al. 1988).

PAIN

Corporal punishment inflicts momentary pain intended to immediately stop a child's misbehavior. The feeling of pain can make the child stop the misbehavior, thereby stopping the painful stimulus and restoring a sense of compliance and security with the parent (Grusec & Goodnow, 1994). Apart from this immediate utility of compliance, the pain can also initiate some other unintended negative effects. Ordinarily, pain provokes motivation to escape the painful stimulus, which, in the case of corporal punishment, is the punishing parent. Children with punishing parents would want to withdraw or avoid interaction with their parents (Parke, 1977). Corporal punishment could, for example, undermine the parents' effort to socialize children after a spanking (Newsom, et al. 1983). Redd, Morris and Martin (1975), in an experimental demonstration study, found that parents who were negative and punishing toward children effectively achieved immediate child compliance but were avoided and rated as least preferred parents in later play situations.

ANGER

Corporal punishment can also evoke the feeling of anger from the child who may feel his goal was being frustrated by the action taken against him or that he was being unfairly punished. The immediate aggression children show for being punished is not an attack behavior, but a counterattack behavior. That is why upon being spanked, children can in anger, lash back at their parents either as a reflex or as an attempt to stop the spanking. If the anger persists, it can cause the child to begin to resent the punishing parent, which can be manifested in a decreased quality of parent-child interaction or in a decline in the child's mental health. The persistent use of corporal punishment would, over time, make the child associate the parent with painful corporal punishment, which can result in retaliatory aggression from the child (Berkowitz, 1983; Gershoff, 2002). Children whose memory of their parents only tells of frequent affliction with painful punishment may begin to fear and resent them until such disposition gradually erodes the bond of trust and closeness established between parent and child in early childhood (Gershoof, 2002).

FEAR AND DISTRESS

Corporal punishment also elicits fear and distress resulting from the inflicted pain it was meant to achieve. For corporal punishment to be effective as a disciplinary measure, it must evoke some level of emotional stress to ensure that the child attends to the disciplinary message (Lepper, 1983). In another study, it was found that children who watched a fear-inducing film were more compliant with a harsh adult than children who saw a pleasant film (Carlsmith, Lepper, & Landauer, 1974). The capacity of corporal punishment to evoke fear or distress is the reason for its effectiveness in making the child comply with the parent's demand (Macoby & Martin, 1983). When corporal punishment is used in a warm parent-child relationship, the child may misunderstand the punishment as a sign of his or her parent's withdrawal of love for him or her. In this case, the fear of losing the parent's love could compel the child to comply, in the short run, with the parent's wishes in order to restore the relationship (Macoby & Martin, 1983). The motivating effects of fear and distress resulting from corporal punishment were evident in a study by Larzelere and Merenda (1994) who found that children delayed repeating misbehavior longer if the corporal punishment for the misbehavior elicited very high distress. Fear and distress have unintended effects. That is why, fearing that they will be punished again, children may not be able to cognitively process and internalize the message which the parent meant the punishment to convey and so prefer the handy strategy of avoiding the punisher (Burgental & Goodnow, 1998). The purpose of parental corporal punishment will be defeated if children avoid their parents consistently due to the punishment as the parent-child relationship of trust will be eroded, undermining the parent's ability to influence the child's future behavior (Van Houten, 1983). In summary, corporal punishment leads to several negative emotions. The side effects are discussed in the following chapter to help parents make an informed decision as to what and how, if at all, corporal punishment should be used as a form of disciplinary measure in parenting.

CHAPTER 15

Side Effects Of Punishment

OVER AND ABOVE previous observations, studies have shown that punishment can decrease undesired behavior even for a short while. When this happens, the punisher is rewarded for using punishment. However, parents are advised to avoid spanking. How corporal punishment promotes long term compliance or moral internalization of acceptable behavior is unclear from psychological theory and research. This is because the goal of socialization should be to foster children's internalization of the reasons for behaving properly rather than being compliant due to coercion or fear of punishment (Hoffman, 1983), although research on learning has shown that corporal punishment can be effective in securing short-term compliance (Newson, Flavell, & Rincover, 1983). In contrast to immediate compliance, physical punishment does not promote long-term and internalized compliance to parental direction. Gershoff (2002), in his study, found that corporal punishment predicts less moral internalization and long-term compliance. As often as children receive such punishment, the less likely they would be to express empathy for others (Lopez, Bonenberger, & Schheider, 2001). However, a vicious circle can be in the making if the punisher and the one punished are reinforced for inappropriate behavior. This would be the case if the punisher takes delight in punishing and the recipient becomes fearful and submissive. Javo and colleagues (2004) observed that the negative effects of corporal punishment explain the reason for the increase in domestic violence today, while Larzelere and Johnson (1999) attributed such effects to bullying among teenagers. Again, the recipient of corporal punishment might become depressed or respond through one form of aggression or the other.

Another side effect of punishment is passive aggressiveness. This is because any kind of punishment often results in frustration, anger, or outright aggression. However, experience has shown that retaliatory aggression toward a punisher often leads to more punishment especially where the punisher is superior and more powerful (Huffman, 2010). As a result, children tend to control the tendency to resort to open aggression and would rather show their anger in subtle ways such as lateness to school or refusal to do their homework. Gilbert (2003) described this attitude as passive aggression.

Avoidance behavior can also be attributed to the effect of punishment. Recipients of punishment express hatred for the punisher by avoiding them. For example, if parents keep yelling at the child each time he or she comes home, the child may decide to go with a friend and delay coming home after school, just as the spouse will likely stay back in the office after the day's work if he or she knows that a nagging spouse awaits. Thus, punishment can create a distance between a parent and the child or between spouses (Huffman, 2010). Modeling for the child can also be jeopardized as a result of punishment. For example, if a parent spanks or hits a child for hitting another child, the punishing parent may unintentionally be teaching the child to practice the behavior which the parent was trying to stop.

Temporary suppression of the undesirable behavior may also be accounted for as an effect of punishment. It has been observed that children, for example, behave in a undesirable manner only when parents are away. Children unleash their worst behaviors because the punisher is not in sight. This is because punishment suppresses bad behaviors only temporarily when the punishing person or circumstance is present (Huffman, 2010).

Learned helplessness is another side effect of punishment. Shors (2004), Zhukov and Vinogrdova (2002) observed that people stay in an abusive relationship due to learned helplessness. When one repeatedly fails in an attempt to control the abusive relationship, the individual acquires a general sense of helplessness and stops short of trying and failing. This again is the case when the punisher possesses more power than the recipient.

The best principle in parenting remains reinforcing appropriate behaviors and discouraging inappropriate behaviors. Punishment, if used, must be only for the most extreme cases that may involve the child endangering himself or herself, or others. In the case of a combination of reinforcement and punishment, parents should provide immediate and clear feedback to the child as to why the behavior is undesirable, while punishment should be a response to inappropriate behavior that should be changed. Whether reinforcement or punishment is used, it is necessary that reward or discouraging action is taken within appropriate time. It is necessary, too, that for effective discipline, both reinforcement and punishment are consistent in application. For example, parents must be consistent with "no" when they refuse the child's request and not bend to say "yes" to the child's demand because she was throwing a temper tantrum. Finally, both reinforcement and punishment must come after the behavior and not before. The order matters because punishment that comes before the behavior can create frustration and resentment. Reward or reinforcement must come after the behavior. Most often parents do not assume their responsibility as parents early enough in the life of their children. As earlier noted, good parenting begins from the moment of conception, as the way and manner in which the mother nurtures and protects the infant while in the womb translates to how the child is cherished and loved when he or she is born. Thus, the early parent-child attachment relationship should begin immediately after birth and is critical in setting the right parenting foundation upon which the child models all other relationships throughout his or her lifespan.

AGGRESSION AND CORPORAL PUNISHMENT

The relationship between corporal punishment and a child's aggression has been one of the most debated side effects of parental corporal punishment. Most studies on this subject posited that corporal punishment was associated with increased child aggressive behaviors (Becker, 1964; Patterson, 1982; Radke-Yarrow, Campbell, & Burton, 1968; Steinmetz, 1979). The association of corporal punishment with aggressive behavior is borne out by the fact that corporal punishment, when excessive, models aggression (Bandura & Walters, 1959; Walters & Grusec, 1977). It also promotes hostility, which predicts violent behavior (Dodge, Petit, McClaskey, & Brown, 1986). According to Dishion and Patterson (1999), corporal punishment initiates the use of force and hateful behaviors between parent and child. White and Straus (1981) also observed that the early use of corporal punishment on children can result in modeling corporal punishment and legitimizing many acts of violence throughout the child's life. Simons, Lin, and Gordon (1998) found that children who suffered physical abuse in adolescence were found to be more violent in romantic relationships in adulthood. Compared to permissive parenting, parents' use of corporal punishment in childhood has been found to be a stronger predictor of adolescents' aggression eight years later. It should be noted that excessive use of corporal punishment in childhood would result in aggression in childhood as well as in adulthood (Cohen, Brook, Cohen, Velez, & Garcia, 1990). In addition, childhood corporal punishment has been linked to anti-social behavior and externalized behavior problems, including stealing, which may not be violent.

DELINQUENT, CRIMINAL, AND ANTISOCIAL BEHAVIOR

Over the years, many studies have implied that corporal punishment is at the root cause of criminal and anti-social behaviors in children and adults (Glueck & Glueck, 1964; Hetherington, Stouwie, & Ridberg, 1971; Wilson & Hernstein, 1985). Attribution theory explains the causes of human behavior and the association between corporal punishment and child delinquency. This theory explains that anti-social behavior results from an inability of corporal punishment to facilitate children's internalization of moral values. This is opposed to parents who believe positive reinforcement through corporal punishment could dissuade the child from unaccepted behaviors and promote moral behavior.

The social control theory posits that parental corporal punishment severs the parent-child relationship especially when corporal punishment is excessive or abusive. Such action diminishes the child's motivation to accept parental values and those of the society, which in turn, can result in low self-control (Hirschi, 1969). This same process can also explain the association between corporal punishment and adult criminality. For example, the fact that there is little to no use of corporal punishment in the criminal justice system is making the society rethink the use of capital punishment as a good measure for controlling violent crimes. Longitudinal studies by Glueck and Glueck (1950) and McCord (1979) found that the extent to which parents were aggressively punitive predicted their children's criminal behavior as adults.

QUALITY OF PARENT-CHILD RELATIONSHIP

One of the major disadvantages of the use of parental corporal punishment is the disruption of the parent-child relationship (Azrin & Holz, 1966). Corporal punishment, by its nature, evokes feelings of fear, anxiety, and anger in children. Some children can transfer the fearful feelings to the punishing parent and can disrupt a positive parenting relationship by inciting the child to be fearful and to avoid the parent (Mumme & Campos, 1998). In a situation where the child fears and avoids the punishing parent, such avoidance would erode the bonds of trust and closeness between parents and children (Van Houten, 1983; Parke, 1977).

MENTAL HEALTH

Not much study has been conducted to explore corporal punishment's role in causing mental health problems. It is known that harsh or excessive punishments contribute significantly to adolescents' distress and depression after ruling out the impact of age, gender, family socioeconomic status (SES), and history of physical abuse (Turner & Finkelhor, 1996). When children are forcefully subjected to painful discipline, it diminishes their feeling of self-confidence and increases feelings of humiliation and helplessness. Given the fact that corporal punishment affects the child's mental health, it is also expected to affect their mental health in adulthood (Gershoff, 2002). Corporal punishment and physical abuses are considered as a continuum. Children who suffered severe corporal punishment from their parents are likely to manifest an aggressive relationship in adulthood with family members like a spouse or child. This circle of abuse is corroborated, in part, because parents who had abused their children reported that most of their abusive experiences began as an effort to effect a change in children's behavior or to "teach them a lesson" (Coonntz & Martin, 1988). It can also lead to an intergenerational transmission of aggression in close and romantic relationships. The kind of message or interpretation the child derives from punishment determines the kind of effect corporal punishment will have on the child. This is important and the next chapter will dwell on exploring the various messages and interpretations children may take from corporal punishment and how it affects them positively or negatively.

PERCEPTION AND ACCEPTANCE OF PARENT'S DISCIPLINARY MESSAGE

It might appear from the above discussion that parental corporal punishment is totally bad and counterproductive or that corporal punishment sends a mixed message of good and evil. It is very easy to come away with a mixed message or the wrong message of the destructive side of corporal punishment. The aim here is to create an awareness of the danger of child abuse under the disguise of parental corporal punishment. As adults, parents should be knowledgeable of the right and wrong use of their parental authority while raising a child. While a clear message by parents and a clear perception of the message on the part of the child is central to the kind of effects parental punishment would have on the child's behavior through adulthood.

According to Grusec and Goodnow (1994) children who understand and accept a parent's disciplinary action are more likely to comply with the parent's wish to behave in a socially acceptable manner. Although corporal punishment is supposed to draw the child's attention to the message it is meant to convey, if parents do not clearly verbalize why the child is being punished, the child may misinterpret it (Hoffman, 1983). For instance, a parent may spank a child for running into the street, intending for the child to learn that such behavior is dangerous; however, the child may perceive the parent's response to mean that the child should not run into the street even when the parent is present. The emotional arousal described here could prevent the child from attending to or understanding the parent's message (Gershoff, 2002). Children would accept the parent's message which the punishment is intended to send if they perceive it accurately. Again, when children believe that their parents are acting in their best interests, or that the corporal punishment is appropriate and deserving for misbehavior, they will be open to accept the correction and its message (Grusec & Goodnow, 1994; Baumrind, 1997).

Similarly, hostile or harsh parent-child relationships could coerce the child to accept corporal punishment because she or he has known the parents as punishers who knew no other acceptable means of cautioning the child when they misbehave apart from corporal punishment. If the use of corporal punishment is the norm in a family, the children will be left with no other option but to accept it as a legitimate means of discipline (Gunnoe & Mariner, 1997).

In addition, Dobson (1996) argued that corporal punishment should be followed immediately by displays of affection for the child accompanied by explanations of why the behavior was unacceptable or wrong, whereas Rosemond (1994) argued that parents should be angry when they spank so that children will not mistake their parent's disapproval of the behavior. It is in the view of this author that both emotions should be used by parents in dealing with the erring child. The child must not be given such mixed reactions without explanation to help them realize that as parents we love them dearly but will disapprove of and dislike any kind of misbehavior. It is only in this fashion that authoritative and positive parenting that demands responsive care giving and firmness in discouraging wrong behavior is achieved.

Does the child's acceptance of corporal punishment make it an appropriate means of discipline? In a study to ascertain if children's acceptance of corporal punishment modifies its effects, it was found that children's acceptance of harsh corporal punishment did not alleviate the relationship between corporal punishment and poor psychological adjustment (Rohner, et al. 1991). Although all the variables were not examined in the study, it is unwise to draw conclusions until further research is conducted and all the variables considered. The various studies examined in this book to ascertain whether parental corporal punishment could be associated with particular child behavioral problems or whether it could cause the child's social competency outcome demonstrated a strong correlation between corporal punishment and a number of child behaviors and experiences (Gershoff, 2002). The studies provide a guide for parents to understand the direct, mediated, and moderated pathways by which their use of corporal punishment might be expected to affect their children either in adolescence or adulthood. Variation in the behavior of children of the same parents will, therefore, be dependent upon the attachment and total parenting style used in raising the child. Inappropriate application of any parental disciplinary technique can lead to negative child outcomes and must, therefore, be avoided by parents.

RELIGIOUS AFFILIATION AND PARENTAL USE OF CORPORAL PUNISHMENT

It has been speculated that parents with a religious background, especially a conservative religious background, find justification for the use of corporal punishment from ***The Holy Bible***. Some of these parents make reference to the common saying, "Spare the rod and spoil the child" or the passage of the Bible that says, "Discipline your son, make heavy his yoke, lest his folly humiliate you" (Sir. 30:13). Although this passage did not make any reference to use of corporal punishment as a technique to achieve compliance or discipline, conservative Christian parents believe it is appropriate to use corporal punishment as a disciplinary measure to keep in check children's moral, social, and prudential, misbehaviors. It is also expected to prevent future transgressions. Parents who viewed their religion as very important in their lives are prone, more than other parents, to emphasize the need to command the child's submission and obedience even if it means using traditionally strict childrearing skills. This group of parents asserts that "children should be seen and not heard," whereas some other parents, who also consider their religion important in their lives, would disapprove of corporal punishment as against their belief and an unnecessary or ineffective means of parenting (Jackson, Thompson, Christiansen, & Colman, *et al.* 1999).

However, Gershoff (1999) found that conservative Protestants, for example, believe that corporal punishment has a strong and consistent effect on child rearing. Conservative Protestant parents were found to use corporal punishment more than parents from other religious affiliations (Gershoff, 1999). The choice to use corporal punishment in child rearing by conservative Christian parents may not be unconnected with a religious belief that child misbehaviors deserve corporal punishment and that individual religious beliefs provide a guide for interactions in general and for parent-child relationships. These religious beliefs, then, counsel that nothing should be spared in the task of disciplining the child so as to rid the child of any negative interpersonal behaviors including disobedience to parental biddings (Greven, 1991). This class of parents uses the Bible as a parenting manual to guide their disciplinary actions. They refer to the wrath of God as a tool for disciplinary control, warning the child that "God will punish" the child for his or her bad behaviors. In this way, parents from a conservative Christian background teach their children morals and social norms founded on their religious parenting beliefs and behaviors. This group finds corporal punishment acceptable due to their belief in human nature as evil, sinful, and requiring punishment before it can be tamed or purified (Ellison & Sherkat, 1993). Although religious groups differ in the frequency with which they use corporal punishment in parenting, they do not differ in how much they use other disciplinary techniques such as reason, diversion, negotiation, threats, time-out, ignoring, withdrawal of privileges, or yelling.

In any case, conservative Protestant parents find their doctrine on corporal punishment as an effective instrument in parenting (Gershoff, Miller, & Holden, 1999). Parents from a conservative religious background are, therefore, less likely to subscribe to the findings that corporal punishment would result in child aggression, anger, resentment of parents, fear of authority, or rebelliousness. Even with this possible outcome, parents affiliated with certain religions believe in the effectiveness of corporal punishment in securing its paramount goal, which is the child's obedience to parental authority. Thus, they attend to the positive effects and discount any negative effects that disciplinary actions, which they have used with good Intentions, can have on the children. Conservative religious parents would prefer to use corporal punishment to address the child's moral and prudential misbehaviors rather than their social transgressions, with the belief that corporal punishment would be effective in preventing future misbehaviors. It is necessary, therefore, for parents to reevaluate how their religious beliefs affect their parenting skills (Gershoff, 2002). If such beliefs do not promote positive and warm parenting which has proven to prevent negative child outcomes, then there may be need for a reexamination of the skills of parenting delivered from the pulpits. While it may be true that religion can positively affect or promote positive parenting, it can also be misused when it is employed to justify negative child rearing practices such as physical abuse or beating children to inflict injury in the name of moral training. Rather, a parent's religious belief and church attendance should help to mediate or moderate the risk of child maltreatment (Brown, Cohen, Johnson, & Salzinger, 1998). Child abuse or maltreatment does not pass for discipline in parenting. Only moderate disciplinary action that has a clear message which characterizes authoritative parenting is permissible and effective in parenting. This position is further expatiated in the chapter which follows.

CHAPTER 16

Discipline And Adolescent Behavior Management

ALTHOUGH MODEST DISCIPLINE is key to authoritative parenting style, adolescent behavior raises more questions on disciplinary action for parents. While parents may be tempted to use disciplinary action as a way to control undesirable adolescent behavior, it is strongly encouraged that parents begin in childhood to impart discipline and develop good behavior management of their children. If authoritative parenting style is adopted by parents from these early years and parents learn to practice compassion and firmness with their children from childhood, early adolescent stress and storm will be less of a challenge for both parents and the adolescent. But if the parents have been permissive or lax in handling the behavior management of the child from childhood, the adolescent's rebellion and defiance will be much more challenging. Because the child has become accustomed to getting away with bad behaviors unchallenged, it will be more difficult for the parent to control the child's bad behavior in early adolescence.

Although it may be difficult to begin to implement good behavior management skills, parents can begin by setting their expected standards for the child. For example, parents can set a time when the child must be back home at night or on days when he or she must be home for dinner with the rest of the family. Such rules and standards must be consistently enforced. Training your adolescent to control his or her behavior is not just good for the family but for his or her general interrelationships at school and in the world. Otherwise, the child will have problems fitting into a social group where he or she will not have the freedom to behave as he or she would like. Children who had no home training or who grew up behaving as they like often get into trouble with others and the law. The child will now have greater difficulty learning to control himself or herself. Schools are not reformatories where children's bad behavior is corrected; however, public agencies may have to play this role when parents fail in their responsibility and the child has learned to have his or her way for many years. If the child is not helped while in school, he or she may have problems dealing with school authorities as well as with other public authorities in adulthood. Children who grow up with this kind of background may find it difficult to accept responsibilities in work places or obey laws in society. It is, therefore, better to discipline than not to discipline. Parents must consider discipline only when it is in the best interest of the child in the long run.

If parents shy away from saying no to the child's request when necessary because they feel refusing the child's request will make him or her feel bad and the child may not love them, they may be wrong. Good parenting involves both sensitivity to the child's needs and good behavior management. Being a single parent or a working parent who has to work outside the home and who has little time to spend with the child cannot be a justification for being permissive and not using the time spent with their child to demonstrate loving care and to teach good behavior. The greatest mistake parents will make in child upbringing will be to shy away from disciplining the child for fear that they will not love them when punished by the parents for their bad behavior. This is not true. In fact, the opposite is true! The child will not forgive a parent's permissiveness that allowed the child to do whatever she or he wanted, for this would have just allowed the child to grow up without self-control or any form of discipline. When the child grows up as an adult to face the realities of life, he or she is likely to hate the parents for not preparing the child for real life situations. For example, a story was told of a young man who had become a notorious armed robber. Eventually he was caught and tried in the court of law where he was convicted and sentenced to the death penalty. On the day he was to be given the electric chair, he requested his mother to come for his last wish before his death. He asked his mother to stoop close so that he could whisper into her ear. He said to the mother that he was going to die because she failed to discipline him and stop him from stealing at home. Then he immediately chopped off his mother's ears with his teeth before everyone. Although one might say such was an extreme case, it buttresses the point being made here as to why parents cannot choose to avoid disciplining their children under the guise of possibly being disliked or called mean by the child.

Children who may have developed moral consciousness may expect punishment for wrong doing because it relieves them of guilt feeling, builds character and self-discipline, and helps the child understand how to relate with those in authority in society outside of their homes (Caissy, 1994). Parents should, therefore, know that children require some kind of structure, rules, and limits to be able to learn self-control and discipline. By creating such standards and consistently enforcing them, they both restrict the child's behavior and protect the child from getting into trouble either at home or outside the home. Creating such rules provides physical safety and emotional freedom, without which the child will be no different than an animal. With such rules in place, the child knows his or her limits and knows that the child's parents will not allow anything that is bad for him or her. The child's expectations are clear, and he or she develops a set of values and standards, a sense of right and wrong. The rules and regulations that parents set for the child help him or her to prepare for adult life in the society where the child will not always be able to do what he or she wants because the laws of the society have set limits as to what is permissible, just like in the family.

To discipline a child does not, therefore, mean that he or she is not loved. When parents discipline a child, it is advisable to hug him or her, show affection, and praise the child when he or she behaves well. Such loving gestures reinforces the parents' love for the child while reiterating the goal of seeking what is for his or her best interests in life. Children learn very fast and will eventually come to understand and reciprocate with respect and love for the parents' care and concern for their wellbeing.

It is not right, either, for a parent to avoid disciplining the child when he or she is behaving badly by thinking that ignoring his or her wrongdoing will make the bad behavior go away. For parents to think it is too difficult to deal with the early adolescent by not disciplining him or her and so to choose the easy way out, i.e. to ignore the behavior, would amount to irresponsible parenting. If the child's bad behavior is not controlled at some point and the child is allowed to do things as she or he pleases, sooner or later the child will take control of the parents and, in some cases, of the entire family, where the child now dictates what happens in the family. Inappropriate behavior must, therefore, be dealt with in childhood and not allowed to escalate to the point of controlling such a child in adolescence when disciplinary problems are at their peak and will be almost impossible to correct. Parents must shun lax discipline because such practices will not ensure the proper home training of children. Without discipline, the child cannot learn right and wrong or feel a sense of physical security or emotional freedom.

BEHAVIOR MANAGEMENT STYLE

To set rules and regulations for effective early adolescent behavior management, parents should consider all the options and alternatives that are open to them. Whatever rules and regulations they put in place must meet the behavioral needs of the child and the parents' own values and standards. Ensure that the rules are carefully thought out and are enforceable. For example, one could have a rule concerning when the child must return home at night if he or she goes out with friends or goes to play. There is no harm if you anticipate some rules concerning dating even when the child is still young. Parents could set a rule that the child cannot date until he or she is seventeen or eighteen. With this rule at the back of his or her mind the child will not go dating before the set age. Parents could also involve their children in making the minor rules, for example, rules about when dishes are to be done, when to do laundry, use the telephone and television, and clean their rooms. The adolescent can be involved in deciding the penalty that might follow if these rules are not observed. After a rule is established parents must consistently enforce it; otherwise, the child will not take it seriously. The child will likely break the rules because he knows he will not be punished. To ensure consistent good behavior requires that parents consistently enforce the house rules as established. If the rules and penalties are not consistently enforced and applied, there is no way the child can understand the purpose or usefulness of the rule, because he or she will constantly take a chance that the parents will not act if the rule is violated. Parents should anticipate adolescents to test their seriousness about such rules by being defiant, as this is expected because of the early adolescent's rebellious nature. But the way and manner the first confrontation with your adolescent plays out will determine whether he or she will defy the rule in the future. Parents' resolve to consistently enforce the rule is the only way they can win the child over to control his or her behavior.

Whatever rules parents establish should be reasonable and reduced to a few important aspects of living and relationships in the family. Small matters should not be regulated; the child should not feel that he or she is living in a concentration camp. Early adolescents want to feel that they are getting away with something as they develop to adulthood. Whatever punishment parents decide to mete out upon violation of any of the serious rules should equally be thought out thoroughly. Such punishment must be fair, realistic and enforceable. Every punishment must be fair and commensurate with the seriousness of the behavior. Any violation of the rules deserving of punishment must be dealt with immediately or else the lesson the child is supposed to learn from the punishment will be missed. Parents should not mete out punishment when they are in a rage because of the tendency to pronounce unenforceable punishment. For example, a parent in a fit of rage says to the adolescent that he or she will not receive monetary allowance for five months. This is an unrealistic and unreasonably long time to deny the child a financial allowance. In addition, the parents are most likely to change their minds; consequently, such punishments in future will not deter the child from bad behavior in the future knowing parents will change their mind. It is, therefore, necessary to avoid making threats which are unrealistic and which cannot be enforced. If parents threaten a punishment for bad behavior, let it be reasonable and let the parents be ready to follow through; otherwise, future threats will not be taken seriously by the child.

Praise and reward the child when he or she shows good behavior and think through things before granting the child privileges and new freedom. For example, if a parent allows a child to go out on a date twice before he or she is of age, it will be difficult to stop this practice. Do not fall to the pressure of the child's report of privileges peers enjoy which the child does not have. Stick to the established rules and enforce them. The fact that other children are allowed to do what is forbidden in the family's home is not a justification for parents to allow it for their children if they feel it is not right (Caissy, 1994). As observed earlier, good behavior should be recognized and praised to encourage the adolescent in good behavior in the future. Acknowledge when they are paying attention and listening to instructions and not only when they do not listen. Being able to understand the early adolescent world is critical for parents, teachers, and all those who work with early adolescents and children in general.

Parents ought to have a high degree of patience and grace to be able to remain calm even when it is difficult to understand why the adolescent is acting out. And corporal punishment meted out with the intention to subdue and suppress the adolescent stress and storm cannot work to the benefit of either the child or the parent. Rather, such corporal punishment would amount to child abuse with very far reaching consequences for both the child and the parents. It is for such reason that the next chapter will be devoted to exploring the various ways the child can become a victim of abuse even in the home and how to determine child abuse and the trauma abuse which can impact both the child and his or her parents.

CHAPTER 17

Child Abuse And Trauma

ONE OF THE critical roles of good parenting is providing the protection of what Waters (1978) described as "safe haven," that is, to ensure protection of the child from doing any harm to himself or from others who may want to abuse the child physically or sexually. All forms of abuse, whether domestic or outside the home, whether physical, psychological or sexual, cause the child some degree of trauma which entails emotional injury, wound, or shock (Webster). Victims and survivors of abuse share equally in the traumatic experience associated with abuse. Victims of physical and sexual abuse may be immobilized by the incident and can be seen to have become survivors only when they can pick up the pieces by overcoming the traumatic memories and becoming active or mobile to function normally again. According to Figley (1985), survivors of debilitating abuse draw the strength of coping from the event while victims remain debilitated. This is because premeditated physical or sexual abuse is intended to destroy the will (Miller & Bersoff,1988) or murder the soul. Research conducted over the past decades indicated that a wide range of psychological and interpersonal problems are more prevalent among those who have either been physically or sexually abused than among individuals with no such experiences. Although a definitive causal relationship between such negative emotional difficulties and physical and sexual abuse has not been established, the probability of a positive correlation is reasonable.

The aim of this book is to help parents realize the enormous psychological problems the child survivors of physical or sexual abuse could face in adulthood. If left unacknowledged and unattended to by parents, it may seriously affect the child's wellbeing. Psychoanalysis is appropriate in exploring trauma issues from childhood abuses because most survivors dissociate from its emotional stress as a coping defense. Thus psychoanalytic psychotherapy not only analyzes the patient's childhood and how it is playing out in relationships outside the therapy, but also pays attention to the multivalent unconscious operations that are present in the inter-subjective relationship between patient and therapist. This is what happens when trauma is explored psychoanalytically through the four processes of discovery, namely: preparation, incubation, illumination, and reflection or interpretation.

As Judith Hermann (1992) observed, traumatized people suffer damage to the basic structures of self. They lose their trust in themselves, in other people, and in God (p.56). Considerable research supports this observation and suggests that many adults who have been physically or sexually abused as children experience distress and behavioral and interpersonal problems attributed to this trauma (Chu & Dill, 1991).

What is even most disturbing is that, despite the overwhelming emotional distress that victims undergo, any attempt by victims to express the atrocities against them or to seek help is to invite upon themselves the stigma which seems to constitute a major cultural problem. This stigma exacerbates the ordeals of the survivors of childhood sexual abuse. And like the traumatized survivors of childhood sex abuse, we need to understand the past in order to reclaim the present and the future. Physically and sexually abused individuals share in common the pain of trauma, stigmatization, and the need for help to be able to address the emotional disturbances resulting from the abuse. Receiving such help will enable the victim to function appropriately in human endeavors.

Fundamental to all forms of child abuse is the inability of the various governments to harness their natural and human resources to the advantage and economic benefit of the people. Thus socio-economic problems are among the factors that contribute to the unnecessary exposure of children to abuse and exploitation. Moreover, the disintegration of cultural values and the philosophy "I am my brother's keeper" is no longer obtainable in most cultures. As a result of urbanization, Western influence, consumerism, and an attitude of "get rich-quick," there has been mass rural-urban migration and the emergence of the urban poor. These migrants take on menial jobs and form the bulk of the traders in the streets and markets. Children in urban areas are quickly caught up in the daily struggle for survival and material gain. Although child abuse is not defined by a family's economic status, poverty remains a major social-economic problem that cannot be ignored if the problem of child sexual exploitation is to be checked.

FORMS OF CHILD ABUSE

The old saying of "spare the rod and spoil the child" is no longer acceptable in modern society. This philosophy is an outdated and unacceptable practice in modern parenting style. The reason is based on the assumption that any form of early child abuse has the tendency of causing the child a debilitating trauma that can affect his or her social and psychological development over time. Many studies in psychology have shown that early maltreatments and severe corporal punishment affect the child's ability to form lasting and satisfactory quality romantic relationships. Child abuse including all manners of child maltreatment, whether they be sexual, physical, psychological, or neglect, predict long lasting difficult intimate relationship effects in adulthood (Dilillo, Peugh, Walsh, Panuzio, Trask & Evans, 2009, in Bashan & Miehls).

Studies suggest that abuse occurs when corporal punishment goes beyond discipline. According to Miller (1988), any form of corporal punishment is capable of damaging important dimensions of a child's evolving sense of self. Physical abuse includes being strapped, slapped, hit with an object, kicked, bitten, smothered, and dunked or immersed in boiling water. Other forms of physical abuse include torture by extinguishing cigarettes on another's skin, locking a child in a closet, or confining the individual to a small space as in a prison. Emotional abuse can also be in a form of pointing a loaded gun at a child. All forms of abuse, whether physical, emotional or sexual result in catastrophic trauma.

Sexual abuse with children occurs when an older child or an adult uses a child or adolescent for his or her own sexual gratification. This includes incest. Incest with children occurs when the child is sexually violated by a parent, parent figure, older sibling, or other relative or significant person in the child's family life (Trocme & Wolfe, 2001, pp.20-21). Examples of other modes of sexual abuse against children include touching or fondling breasts and genitals, kissing, exposing one's genitals, masturbating, making sexual comments and any attempt to arouse a child or receive sexual gratification from a child such as showing a child pornographic pictures or films. Sexual abuse of children can, therefore, happen through contact which Trocme & Wolfe (2001) say involves an adult touching or fondling a child's sexual areas or kissing. This kind of abuse is most common, accounting for 69% of substantiated child sexual abuse cases (p.13). On the other hand, non-contact child sexual abuse will imply those situations where an adult forces a child to watch sexual acts, listen to sexual talk, or an adult exposing genitals to a child. This is said to account for 12% of substantiated child sexual abuse cases (p.13).

Again, the definition of sexual abuse as determined by Gold (1986) and Gulla (1996) may add to a more comprehensive understanding of what child sexual abuse implies. Gold defines sexual abuse as sexual contact, including touching a child under twelve years old by a post pubertal person at least five years older than the child. It is also a sexual contact between an adolescent thirteen to sixteen years old and an adult at least ten years older, or any sexual contact between any child or any adolescent under sixteen years of age and a person or persons who uses physical force (pp.94-95).

SIGNS AND SYMPTOMS OF CHILD ABUSE

Good parenting involves being involved in the life of the child. It also implies that parents should be watchful for the signs and symptoms that show that the child is hurting due to some abuse which he or she may have suffered from family, friends, or outright strangers. A healthy relationship between parent and child facilitates communication between them. The traditional methods of parenting that permitted corporal punishment are deemed wrong today because they inhibit this cordial relationship and lead children to deny suffering and humiliation. This denial, although it can be helpful if the child is to survive, will later cause emotional blindness for the child. Parental emotional blindness often results in parents no longer being able to read their children's happy and sad moods. Emotional blindness creates barriers in the mind erected to guard against dangers. Thus, early denied traumas become encoded in the brain. Even though no longer a threat, they continue to constitute an obstacle (Miller & Bersoff, 1998). The vicious nature of abuse can continue due to barriers in the mind that now lacks the ability to learn from new information, to put it to good use, or to shed old and outdated experiences.

Human mind retain memories of humiliations suffered in the past which drives us to unconsciously inflict on the new generation what we endured in childhood. Barriers in the mind make it difficult, if not impossible, to avoid this repetition, unless we firmly resolve to identify the cause of our behavior as deeply embedded in the history of our own childhoods. However, this rarely happens. Many of us often repeat what our parents, our parent's parents, and their parents before them had done. In a sense, we stubbornly and blindly keep repeating "Spare the rod, spoil the child."

According to Davies & Fraley (1994), children's symptoms of sexual abuse can be picked up early enough by responsive and caring parents who take note, for example, as to whether the child is failing or has poor grades at school, is showing decreased interest in school, is having difficulty concentrating, or is suffering from school phobia. Other indicators may include physical complaints for which no medical cause is found; headaches; gastrointestinal problems; oral, anal, or vaginal infections; urinary tract infections or nonspecific aches and pains. Children may further manifest signs of sexual abuse by engaging in sexualized or seductive behavior such as compulsive masturbation, inappropriate sexual behavior towards others, or exhibitionism portrayed often by an attention-seeking mode of dressing. Signs of sexual abuse in children may also be manifested through regressive behaviors such as drinking from a bottle, thumb sucking, and bedwetting or soiling. Finally, it could also be manifested through sleep disturbances such as insomnia, sleep walking, nightmares and night terrors.

Among adolescents the signs of sexual abuse can manifest themselves differently. According to Davies & Frawley (1994), sexually abused adolescents will continue to show signs of school problems through noninvolvement in extracurricular activities, truancy, and fear of speaking in class. Certain physical complaints are also observable in female adolescent victims of sexual abuse. These signs can be noticed during menstrual periods whereby the teen shows menstrual problems such as shame or fear about menses, severe cramps, depression during menses, pain or fear while inserting a tampon, inability to insert a tampon because of vaginal muscle contractions.

Furthermore, sexually abused adolescents may have problems with weight or body image. They often begin to gain excessive weight at puberty by engaging in binge eating. They can also begin to feel disgust and discomfort with their body. They may feel embarrassed and have a distorted view of their body, especially if they have a bulging or huge stomach. Other signs and symptoms are anorexia or bulimia, continued sleep disturbances, problems with sex or intimacy, promiscuity, prostitution, adolescent pregnancy, adolescent marriage, and complete avoidance of boys and dating. Sexual abuse can also manifest itself through other compulsive behaviors as running away from home, drug and alcohol abuse, self-mutilation, stealing, suicidal ideation or suicide attempts.

For Hagan & Case (1988), behaviors and conditions that may point to sexual abuse can appear in the form of complaints of pain while urinating or having bowel movements, indicating infection. There can also be symptoms of genital infections such as offensive genital odors indicating sexually transmitted disease. Signs that indicate evidence of physical trauma such as abrasions or lesions to the genital area may be signs of sexual abuse. Sexually abused teens can also have an unusual fear of being in a particular area of the house or some other place. For example, if a child suddenly became afraid of the bathtub or his or her bed, it could be indicative that something disturbing happened there. Other indicators include waking up during the night sweating, screaming, or shaking, or experiencing nightmares.

Sudden change in behavior like unusually aggressive behavior toward family members, friends, pets or toys can be a sign of sexual abuse. A child who engages in persistent sexual play with friends, toys or pets, who talks loudly, or who initiates sexual behavior not developmentally appropriate for the child's age towards other children or adults may also be exhibiting symptoms of Child Sexual Abuse, (CSA). Such children can also indicate sudden reluctance to be alone with a familiar person. Behavioral issues like periods of panic might be a sign of flashbacks of abuse episodes. Sexually abused children can also withdraw abruptly from activity with a club or group that was formerly enjoyed. Or they may ask an unusual number of questions about human sexuality, show an unexplained change in personality traits. For example, an outgoing child might become quiet and withdrawn. He or she may also develop an unexplained fear of males or females, fear of men with mustaches, or fear of men or women wearing a certain color or style of clothes. The child could make sudden requests for locks on the door and other safety precautions and ask questions about protection or safety. It could also be manifested as an extreme fear of undressing for a medical examination. Such children could become unusually dependent on parents when they were previously more independent. Sexually abused children can develop unexplained health problems because the trauma of the abuse can stress the child into being unhealthy physically and emotionally.

STIGMATIZATION

Stigmatization refers to internalized feelings of shame, guilt, and self-blame that arise from experiencing maltreatment, especially sexual abuse. In psychological abuse, stigmatization may arise from direct reprimand by the perpetrator. In other forms of maltreatment, stigmatization may develop in response to secrecy that often shrouds abuse, manifested in the way the family and community react upon discovery of the abuse from the victims. When stigmatization that results from maltreatment is not resolved in childhood, it may result in lack of openness, feelings of detachment, and general dissatisfaction in intimate relations (Walsh, et al. 2009)

Stigmatization is not just the use of the wrong word or action. Stigma is about disrespect; it is the use of negative labels to identify a person and, as such, it poses a barrier and discourages victims of sexual abuse and their families from acquiring the help they need due to the fear of being discriminated against. Labels lead to stigma, which means branding and shame (http://mentalhealth.samhsa.gov/pubs). It is mind boggling that most African cultures and traditions prohibit child sexual abuse, considering it to be an abomination. It does not allow room for excuses and a fair hearing for victims who, for fear of victimization, may decide to suffer in silence. Most often victims cannot seek redress or have disclosure support, especially when they do not have witnesses. However, this is a crime that is often committed in secret, making it hopeless and hard to prove. It gets worse when law enforcement agents, who should be handy in providing victims with reassurance, turn their backs on these individuals by apportioning blame not on the culprits but on the victims. They blame the victims' abuse on so-called immodest dress or the flirtatiousness of victims before their male aggressors.

Some of the reasons given by girls for not reporting sexual abuse were fear of stigma and ridicule, and a fear of reducing their chances of getting married if the abuse was made public. Abusers are sometimes relatives and family friends or familiar people and may be powerful people with widespread connections. About 80% of girls have seen the abuser before the day of the abuse. Also rejecting enticements and inaccurate reporting of enticements may be termed disobedience and disrespect (p.4). In most cases where secret gifts were taken by their would-be victim, the abuse is usually not made known to the parents. Sexual abuse of children is shrouded in secrecy, guilt, and fear. Therefore, offenders use intimidation and threats to keep the child from telling, but the number one reason children do not tell is that they are afraid they won't be believed. This often leads to their being stigmatized and victimized even when their stories are dismissed as false.

Many survivors, therefore, cannot share the ordeals of their abuse because they might, among other factors, be afraid of being shamed with the consequence of their horror being minimized, which could lead to being re-traumatized. They are denied the support they need to lead a healthy, normal life. But the cultural situation where such victims are not even listened to or believed by their family members can make matters worse since early and appropriate services are not sought because the victim does not want to be seen or labeled as promiscuous, "mentally ill" or "crazy." Stigma arising from this situation keeps victims from getting admission into schools, finding good husbands or jobs, or advancing in their work places. Stigma also leads to fear, mistrust, prejudice, and discrimination. All of these do not in any way help survivors of childhood sexual abuse; rather, they exacerbate their situation. Given this, there is a great need for a change of culture and attitude towards victims of sexual abuse.

TRAUMAGENIC PROCESSES

Traumagenic dynamics are found to be common in all manners of child abuse. The Traumagenic model states that the influence of childhood trauma can be accounted for by the dynamics of betrayal, traumatic sexualization, stigmatization, and powerlessness which the child experienced which negatively impacts children's cognitive and emotional development and view by the society. This situation creates trauma and distress by distorting the child's self-consent, world view, and affective abilities (Finkelhor & Browne, 1985). The dynamics of betrayal can manifest themselves in the aftermath of the abuse, which occurs upon the realization that a trusted family member whom the child looked up to for protection was their violator and the perpetrator of their abuse.

NEGLECT

Another form of child abuse is neglect, which refers to the breach of trust when adults who were expected to provide care and protection for the child deprive the same child whom they were supposed to protect, by neglecting their basic needs such of food, shelter, medical care, and supervision (Walsh, et al. 2009).

TRAUMATIC SEXUALIZATION

Traumatic sexualization refers to development of abnormal and inappropriate sexual behavior which resulted from sexual abuse. This condition can manifest itself in such difficulties as vulnerability to sexual assault, over-sexualization of adult relationships, or aversion to sexual relationships (Finkelhor & Browne, 1985).

POWERLESSNESS

There is a sense of powerlessness experienced by victims in every form of maltreatment. This dynamic refers to the lack of self-efficacy that results from uncontrollable and repeated boundary violations by highly valued individuals in the life of the victims. (Walsh, et al. 2009). Such imbalance of power paralyzes minors, impeding their ability to resist their aggressors' advances. This sense of powerlessness experienced in early child sexual or physical abuse undermines the survivor's sense of control in relationships over time. In this way, it renders victims ineffective in asserting their desires and views during conflict and decision-making with their future life-partners. In extreme cases, such an imbalance of power or control may become a risk factor for continued or additional victimizations within marriage or intimate relationships. On the other hand, anxiety over the issue of control and power may be paramount for victims who would want to exercise full control over relationship issues with their partners.

Many empirical studies with unmarried persons have shown that an experience of maltreatment is correlated with later psychological, physical, and sexual victimization of such individuals in a romantic relationship (DiLillo, Giuffre, Tremblay,

& Peterson, 2001; Whitfield, Anda, Dube, & Felitti, 2003). Again, it has been found that men and women who were abused or exposed to the adversity of maltreatment as children were more likely to engage in partner aggression as adults than children who were not exposed to any form of maltreatment and abuse (Anda, Felitti, Bremner, Walker, Whitfield, Perry, et al. (2006). This difficult relationship condition contributes to a low quality of relationship satisfaction and to shorter relationships. In a cross section study, for instance, couples with a history of maltreatment were found to be less satisfied in the romantic relationships than couples who had no history of abuse and maltreatment (Dilio & Long, 1999; Nelson & Wampler, 2000; Whisman, 2006). Other studies with couples who were either physically or sexually abused or neglected, were found to have higher rates of separation and divorce than spouses without such histories (Colman & Wisdom, 2004; Finkelhor, Hotaling, Lewis, & Smith; Whisman, 2006). The results of these studies lend credence to the theories that maltreatment or abuse increases the risk of numerous difficulties among individuals in committed relationships.

Child sexual abuse is one of the most damaging experience any child can have. This kind of abuse is discussed here because parents have the primary obligation to protect their children from all manners of abuse. Besides corporal punishment, child sexual abuse is one of the most common forms of abuse against children today. Its effects are even far more reaching than those of corporal punishment. The next chapter discusses the ramifications of child sexual abuse and the various ways victims manage the consequences.

CHAPTER 18

The Impact Of Child Abuse

EMOTIONAL HARM CAUSED by childhood sexual abuse appears to undermine normal healthy psychological development that would enhance children's ability to protect their sexual health. Victims of childhood sexual abuse display a broad array of behaviors which include social isolation, guilt, chronic depression, low self-esteem, vague somatic complaints, substance abuse, self- injurious behaviors and underlying resentments (Furnis, 1984; Shearers and Herbert, 1997; Beithchman et al., 1992). However, as abnormal as these behaviors may seem, care must be taken not to misinterpret them as typical adolescent behavior (Furnis, 1984). Other psychosocial and emotional disturbances that are associated with child sexual abuse include anxiety, feelings of worthlessness and powerlessness, inability to distinguish sexual from affectionate behavior, difficulty in maintaining appropriate personal boundaries and inability to turn down unwanted sexual advances, suicide attempts, problems with trust and intimacy, reproductive problems such as unwanted pregnancy and its complications, HIV/AIDS and sexual transmitted infections (STIs) that can cause cervical cancer, infertility and refusal to practice safe sex. All these behaviors may increase the risk of unintended pregnancy as well as sexually transmitted infections.

Sexually abused women are at increased risk for sexual difficulties ranging from avoidance of sex to compulsive sexual behavior (Browne & Finkelhor, 1986; Green, 1993; Polsuny & Follette, 1995). Finkelhor and Browne (1985) proposed that child sexual abuse might produce seemingly opposing outcomes, for example, aversion to sex versus sexual promiscuity which they attributed to traumatic sexualization. This refers to the shaping of a child's sexuality in an interpersonally dysfunctional manner, leading to lasting inappropriate associations with sexual activity and arousal. Studies suggest that children who experienced high levels of revulsion, fear, anger or powerlessness during CSA may be conditioned to associate sex with negative emotions and memories. These negative emotional reactions may subsequently lead to non-abusive sexual experiences in adulthood resulting in sexual dysfunction, including phobic reactions to sexual intimacy and avoidance of sex. In other cases, CSA experiences may teach the child to associate rewards, attention and affection with engaging in sexual behavior (Finkelhor & Brown, 1985; Merill, Guimond, De Kalb, & Milner, 2003).

Adults who are so sexually abused as children may use sex to meet nonsexual needs, for example, seeking love through sex, sexualizing non-sexual relationships, or using sex to manipulate others. Sexual promiscuity may result. Conceptualization of traumatic sexualization suggests that some adults sexually abused as children will engage in sexual activity with many partners, whereas others will engage in little sexual activity and have few partners (Finkelhor and Browne, 1985).

Adults who were sexually abused as children are generally found to have more sex partners than non-abused respondents. This has been documented in clinical populations and populations at high risk of contracting HIV (Cunningham, Stiffman, Dore, & Earls, 1994, Zierler et al., 1991) as well as in undergraduate (Johnsen & Harlow, 1996) and community (Wyatt, 1988) samples. However, a number of other studies have found no relationship between CSA and the number of sex partners (Bartoi & Kinder, 1998; Noll, Trickett, & Putnam, 2000; Widom & Kuhns, 1996). The failure of some previous studies to find a significant relationship between CSA and the number of sex partners may be due to the fact some women react to CSA with sexual avoidance rather than with increased sexual activity. In fact, Briere (2000) estimated that approximately ten percent of sexually abused women avoid sex in reaction to CSA experiences. On the other hand, women who react to CSA in different ways within a given sample might yield evidence of either increased or decreased numbers of sex partners among women who experienced CSA relative to those who did not or a null effect.

Again, there is evidence that adults sexually abused as children are more likely than non-abused adults to engage in dysfunctional sexual behavior (Briere et al. 1995). Dysfunctional sexual behavior referred to here is any sexual behavior that is self-defeating or maladaptive, such as having sex with strangers, having secret sex, and using sex to gain affection, to cope with distress, or to feel powerful. It always involves engaging in sexual activity to satisfy other types of needs. Dysfunctional sexual behavior implies also higher levels of sexual activity and larger numbers of sexual partners as observed by Briere (1995) and Runtz, et al. (1999). Further, it was hypothesized that the strategies sexually abused women use to cope with CSA in its immediate aftermath may exert a long-term influence on their sexual attitudes and functioning, thereby influencing their number of sex partners in young adulthood. Previous research has linked it to the use of avoidant coping, denial distancing, disengagement (Coffey et al. 1999) and self-destructive coping mechanisms like substance abuse (Johnson & Kenkel, 1991). Women who use self-destructive strategies to cope with CSA may also continue to use such strategies in adulthood.

For such women sex may be used as a way to escape or reduce stress, resulting in large numbers of sex partners.

Finally, it is proposed that the severity of CSA affects a number of sex partners, both directly and through its effect on coping and sexual functioning. This is due to the expectation that more severe forms of CSA would produce stronger effects on a range of outcomes, including coping, sexual functioning, and behavior. Previous studies have shown that CSA severity, assessed using global severity ratings, is positively associated with the number of sexual partners (Walser & Kern 1996).

Child sexual abuse experiences were assessed using a modified version of the Sexual Events Questionnaire (Finkelhor, 1979). Respondents were asked to report any sexual contact experienced before the age of eighteen with a family member or with a nonfamily member who was five or more years older. For each such experience, respondents reported they were asked to provide further information including their relationship to the perpetrator, whether physical force or threats had been involved, or whether it involved penetration and the number of times it happened (on a scale ranging from 0 to 99). Participants were classified as having experienced CSA only if they reported one or more contact sexual experiences before the age of 14 with someone at least five years older. Additional information concerned the severity of the experience. Combining several CSA characteristics into a single index of CSA severity likely provided a more reliable measure than specific characteristics considered individually (Fergusson & Mullen, 1999). Respondents received one point on the severity index for each of the following: penetration, force or threats, father or stepfather as perpetrator, more than one perpetrator and more than five incidents. The CSA severity index thus ranged from zero to five. In the present sample, 64% of participants had experienced intercourse, sixty-two percent reported force or threats, twenty-one percent identified a father or stepfather as the perpetrator, twenty-six percent identified more than one perpetrator, and fifty-three percent reported more than five incidents. Correlations for the five indicators comprising the severity index ranged from 0.24 to 42, yielding an overall scale reliability of 0.60. Thus it is concluded that the relatively low reliability of the severity index was not unexpected, as its constituent items assess related but distinct characteristics of CSA experiences in a cumulative fashion rather than as one unified factor.

COPING MECHANISMS AMONG VICTIMS OF ABUSE

Victims of CSA have been found to engage in several coping strategies to deal with the trauma of childhood sexual experiences in the weeks, months, and years after it first occurred. Known common coping systems include running away from home, using alcohol and drugs, contemplating suicide, avoidant coping, suppressing thoughts and feelings, avoiding reminders of the abuse, and staying home as much as possible. The sexual functioning of victims of CSA is also beset with various difficulties. They are prone to employ some measures of dysfunctional sexual behaviors that are self-defeating or maladaptive because of an indiscriminant potential for self-harm or use for a nonsexual purpose. Other related sexual concerns include sexual distress, sexual dissatisfaction, sexual functioning problems and unwanted sexual thoughts or feelings (Briere, 1995). Studies have found that sexually abused women and men who report experiencing sexual avoidance may have difficulty in relationships. Sexual problems can lead to feelings of inadequacy and a decrease in life satisfaction (Westerlund, 1992). A large number of sex partners and indiscriminate sexual contacts can also have severe consequences. It can increase a man or woman's risk for contracting a sexually transmitted disease, such as HIV/AIDS (Cunningham et al., 1994; Zierler et al., 1991) and for sexual assaults as an adult (S. R. Gold et al., 1999). Although decreasing self-destructive coping may be one way to reduce high-risk sexual behavior, learning adaptive coping strategies may teach women to satisfy their emotional needs in ways other than through sex and thus decrease their risk of being re-traumatized. In the next chapter, signs and symptoms of adult survivors of childhood sexual abuse are discussed. It becomes important that parents should take note of these signs so as not to mistake them as signs of early adolescent stress and storm.

TRAUMA OF CHILDHOOD ABUSE

Trauma can be defined as any life threatening event outside the range of normal human experience which as a result of its overwhelming impact supersedes the human capacity to control. Besides natural disasters like fire outbreak, accidents, flood, volcanic eruption, landslide, cyclones it could also be caused by human atrocities like war, armed robbery and sexual abuse *etc*. It is indisputable that the adult survivors of childhood sexual abuse suffer from some serious emotional pains as a result of their early life traumatic experience and consequent stigmatization that follows sharing of such experiences with family and friends. The seriousness of victims' pain depends on the severity of the sexual abuse, the level of emotional support, and family functioning. I will highlight some common signs and symptoms that can be found among adult survivors of childhood sexual abuse, followed by an analysis of the trauma which may result. The signs and symptoms of childhood sexual abuse represent the primary and secondary psychological impacts of sexual abuse. Despite the complexity surrounding the signs of childhood sexual abuse, children who have suffered sexual abuse often show no physical signs, and the abuse may go undetected unless a physician spots evidence of forced sexual activity. However, it leaves more permanent psychological and behavioral problems from mild to severe in the later life of victims if not detected and treated in time.

Polin and Roy (1994) gave one of the most comprehensive symptoms of childhood sexual abuse which is, for the most part, self-explanatory. It is important that anyone who cares for children for example, parents, guardians, clinicians, pastoral counselors know these symptoms. They include low self-esteem or feelings of worthlessness, fear of abandonment and other abandonment issues, acting out behavior, not knowing how to identify and process intense feelings in more productive ways, unexplained fears of being alone at night, nightmares, and feeling overly grateful or appreciative from small favors by others. Additional symptoms are boundary issues, lack of needing to be in control, power issues or fear of losing control. Eating disorders will include anorexia, bulimia and compulsive over-eating. Headaches, arthritis, joint pain, gynecological disorders, stomach aches and other somatic symptomology may also occur. Some victims may experience unexplained anxiety/panic when with individuals from childhood, extreme guilt/shame, and obsessive/compulsive behaviors not necessarily obsessive compulsive disorder. Other victims experience a history of being involved in emotionally and psychologically violent relationships, memories of domestic violence in childhood, sexual acting out, a history of prostitution, or performing in porn films. Distorted body image or poor body image, hypervigilance, a history of multi-victimizations in other forms, and extremely high or low risk taking can also result. Obsession with suicide at various times of the year or after triggering events has been known to occur. Wearing layers of clothing, even in summer, is also caused by body image issues. Lastly, sexually abused children suffer intense anxiety, seek to avoid gynecological exams and have unexplained fears of suffocation.

The above enumerated symptoms show that victims of childhood sexual abuse may present a very wide range of symptoms that cover four axes of diagnosis, namely psychiatric, personality disorders, medical conditions, and psychosocial stressors. While some of these symptoms are negative reactions to the emotional pains of sexual abuse, others are some kind of coping mechanism for the victims. However, this does not mean that a victim can manifest all the signs and symptoms enumerated. Only about five or seven of the above symptoms may be required according to ***Diagnostic and Statistical Manual of Mental Disorders*** DSM-V to diagnose a victim as suffering from the trauma of childhood sexual abuse. Symptoms can result in short or long-term negative effects, depending on the prevailing severity predictors in the victim. These include family structure, severity of abuse, and the duration and level of force or violence unleashed on the victim by his or her perpetrator. These factors will determine whether the victim would be able to resolve his or her issue of abuse or whether the issue will persist over time or lasting even to adulthood so as to stall the psychosocial development of the individual. Finally, victims of childhood sexual abuse who were not able to overcome the negative emotional disturbances associated with their sexual assault share one thing in common, and that is trauma, which this study will examine next.

ADULT SURVIVOR OF SEXUAL ABUSE

An adult who was physically or sexually abused as a child is an adult survivor of child abuse. This abuse may have had long-term effects on the survivor's life. In most cases, the victim of the abuse never discussed the abuse with others while it was occurring, especially if it was sexual abuse. This individual is learning now, as an adult, to deal with the effects of the abuse. Adults, like children and adolescents, manifest certain signs and symptoms of sexual abuse. According to Davies & Frawley (1994), adults who have been sexually abused often experience sleep disturbances like nightmares, insomnia, fear of the dark, or fear of someone breaking into the house at night. They may experience sexual dysfunction such as arousal disorder, sexual anesthesia, aversion to men, promiscuity, prostitution, and intense shame of self as a sexual being.

Other symptoms can be in the form of anorexia or bulimia, compulsive overeating, distorted body image, shame during pregnancy, feeling that it is wrong to be pregnant, parenting problems (especially with daughters), self-mutilation with pins and sharp objects, suicidal ideation, suicide attempts, low self-esteem, a chronic free-floating sense of guilt, chronic shame, depression, subjective feelings of being wholly and inherently bad, feelings of not belonging, difficulty trusting others (particularly men), social isolation, compulsive socializing and the need to please others, posttraumatic stress disorder (PTSD) symptoms, history of adult rape, sexual or physical victimizations and chronic dissociation (Davies & Frawley, 1994). Adult victims of sexual abuse may continue to experience these signs and symptoms until they receive the needed help in order to heal from the catastrophic effects of their abuse. Then they will no longer be victims but survivors of sexual abuse.

The term "survivor" is used, instead of the term "victim" because the individual has survived the childhood sexual abuse or adult sexual abuse. Thus, the term is used in recognition of the strengths of the individual who has survived. Most often, survivors do not remember the abuse until years after it has occurred. Usually something in adulthood will trigger the memory. According to Maltz and Holman (1987), some are never able to clearly recall the abuse. Jehu (1989) also observed that survivors often hold the distorted belief that they are responsible for the abuse perpetrated against them. This results in the feelings of extreme guilt and self-blame which make disclosure more difficult. Most abusers tell children that it is their own fault they are being abused, shifting the blame away from the abusers, where it belongs, and placing it on the child. Childhood sexual abuse is often characterized by severe physical, psychological, and spiritual problems which the author discusses here.

SYMPTOMS OF ABUSE TRAUMA

This part of the study will analyze what seems to be the last part of the negative impact of childhood sexual abuse. It can be said to fall under the third stage, which is more or less the long term consequence of CSA. Briere and Elliot (1994) described trauma as "the impacts of initial reactions and abuse-related accommodations on the individual's ongoing psychological development and personality formation." In other words, some individuals can overcome the experience, but others may be overwhelmed by it. Herman (1992) holds that "ordinary human response to danger like sexual assault is complex and involves integrated systems of reactions, encompassing both mind and body" (p.34). Threats, therefore, alter ordinary perceptions of victims. That is why sexual abuse can leave victims overwhelmed and hurt, because at that instance, victims of childhood sexual abuse are most often unable to fight off their assailants or flee from them, leaving them vulnerable to fatigue and pain. The implication is that the system of one's self defense becomes overwhelmed and disorganized. This situation leaves a profound and lasting change in physiological arousal, emotion, cognition, and memory (p.34). The entire human faculty is affected by the trauma, such that the physical, psychological, and spiritual components of the human person are not spared of such devastating incidents, leaving behind a certain enduring disruptive psychological syndrome called trauma.

In continuation of what is fundamental to understanding the cause and effect of child sexual abuse, this section of research will put into perspective the nature of the trauma of sexual abuse, with particular reference to the adult women survivors of childhood sexual abuse. In this study there is nothing to be gained in saying that some adults with substantial psychological problems do often have a history of child sexual abuse. Other studies of various troubled populations such as drug abusers, juvenile offenders, adolescent runaways, and adults with sexual dysfunction show that high proportions of these troubled individuals were sexually abused and victimized as children.

Finkelhor (1984) asserts that the case seems easily made, given the above studies, that a great fraction of those who were sexually abused and victimized in childhood are affected quite badly by their experiences (p.189). Inasmuch as one accepts the fact of the great harm child sexual abuse can cause the growing child, it should also be noted that other factors like stigmatization, toxic environments, and other pathological elements can contribute to or exacerbate the trauma. Central to the emotional disturbances experienced by victims of child sexual abuse are trauma and post-traumatic stress disorder (PTSD). Some observers have concluded that the true trauma of sexual abuse and victimization results not so much from the experience, per se, but from the alarmed reaction that such victimization elicits from a child's family, friends, and the community (p.197). This is why some researchers assert that all traumas destroy one's complex systems of self-protection and basic trust, the after effect of which can be far reaching as it varies widely across individuals and communities. What makes traumatic events extraordinary; therefore, is not necessarily because they occur rarely, but because they overwhelm the ordinary human adaptation to life and generally involve threats to life or bodily integrity, or a close personal encounter with violence and death.

Herman (1997) says that traumatic events "confront human beings with the extremities of hopelessness and terror, and evoke the responses of catastrophe" (p.33). Andreasen (1985) offered the common features of psychological trauma as "feeling of intense fear, helplessness, loss of control, and a threat to annihilation" (pp.918-924). The severity of trauma cannot be measured on any single dimension and, needless to say, are comparisons of horror as there are certain experiences that increase the likelihood of trauma harm. Herman (1997) observed that there are factors that could exacerbate the effects of CSA which include "being taken by surprise, trapped, or exposed to the point of exhaustion" (p.34). Herman (1997) maintained that the likelihood of harm is also increased when traumatic events involve physical violation or injury as in sexual abuse. Trauma can be experienced through exposure to extreme violence or witnessing grotesque deaths, for example, soldiers who experience deaths on the battle fronts.

In any case, the salient characteristic of trauma is its power to cause helplessness and terror. The immediate human responses to danger incorporate a complex integrated system of reactions which encompasses both mind and body. Threat arouses the sympathetic nervous system, causing the person in danger to feel an adrenalin rush and go into the state of alert for the immediate situation. It also alters the victim's ordinary perceptions, for example, the victim is often able to disregard hunger, fatigue or pain.

Many in this state of mind scale very high fences, run great distances for dear life or live without food or drink for days, which, under normal circumstances, they would be unable to do. Finally, threat evokes intense feelings of fear and anger. These changes in arousal, attention, perception, and emotion are normal adaptive reactions to trauma. In this state of mind, the threatened person is mobilized for strenuous action, either for battle or flight (p.34). Traumatic reactions occur when action is of no avail.

Children who were sexually molested are usually helpless and defenseless, increasing the enormity of their trauma. They can neither resist nor escape from their attackers, making their defense mechanism overwhelmed and disorganized. Such experience severs the normally integrated functions from one another. As a result, victims may experience intense emotions without clear memory of the event or may remember every detail of the event without emotion. Sometimes such persons find themselves in a constant state of vigilance and irritability without knowing why. At this stage "traumatic symptoms may become disconnected from their source and take on a life of their own" (p.34). Such fragmentation, whereby trauma tears apart a complex system of self-protection that normally functions in an integrated fashion, culminates in a disorder known as posttraumatic stress disorder, (PTSD).

POSTTRAUMATIC STRESS DISORDER (PTSD) IN ABUSE

The persistent manifestation of some of the earlier mentioned negative symptoms of CSA that disrupt the normal daily functioning of victims of child sexual abuse beyond a three month period will indicate that the natural psychological adjustment process of trauma of a sexually abused victim has derailed. At this point, the psychological reactions natural in the first few weeks become symptoms of PTSD. Foy, et al. (1993), defines PTSD as "the persistence of a natural process beyond its natural time frame for resolution." (p.622). The major features of PTSD are trauma-specific symptoms of intrusion, avoidance, and hyperarousal. A life threatening event such as childhood sexual abuse would satisfy this criterion. Hence, Saunders, et al. (1992), inferred that, "both clinical and nonclinical groups of adult sexual abuse survivors have been found to display more intrusive, avoidant, and arousal symptoms of PTSD than those not abused as children" (pp.189-204). Abuse trauma the major feature of PTSD among adult survivors of childhood sexual abuse will be expatiated.

INTRUSION

Intrusion refers to the presence, in some form, of persistent intrusive thoughts, including visual, auditory experiences and flashbacks, reminiscent of the original assault. Foy, et al. (1993), include "recurrent distressing dreams or flashbacks while awake about the traumatic experience" (p.622). These symptoms are usually relived long after the life threatening danger is past. Victims of trauma, therefore, cannot resume normal lives as the trauma repeatedly interrupts. Herman (1997) observes that "intrusion happens because such traumatic a moment is encoded in an abnormal form of memory, which breaks spontaneously into consciousness, both as flashbacks during waking states and as traumatic nightmares during sleep" (p.37).

Memories of such trauma may be triggered by any small event, thereby traumatizing the victim again. For survivors of childhood sexual abuse, their PTSD may stall their normal development mostly by the repetitive intrusion of the traumatic event or events into their life. It is worthy to note that traumatic memories are not encoded like the ordinary memories of adults in a verbal, linear narrative that becomes a part of an ongoing life story; rather they are encoded in the form of vivid sensations and images (p.38). For example Herman (1997) illustrated this with a child who had been sexually molested by a babysitter in the first two years of her life and could not, at age five, remember or name the babysitter.

Furthermore, she denied any knowledge or memory of being abused. But in his play, Herman (1997), enacted scenes that exactly replicated a pornographic movie made by the babysitter (p.38). It is this same visual and enactive form of memory, appropriate to young children that may eventually be carried over into the adulthood of childhood sexual abuse survivors. Traumatized people relive the moment of their trauma not only in their thoughts and dreams but also in some of their conscious actions. In this way, they put themselves at risk of further harm.

AVOIDANCE / CONSTRICTION

Avoidance refers to the presence of avoidance or constriction symptoms associated with trauma, such as fear of sexual relations following sexual assault. Foy, et al. (1993), gave an example of avoidance as "general numbing of responsiveness or the absence of strong feelings about the trauma" (p.622). In the face of a traumatic event, the self-defense mechanism shuts down entirely. It is at such a point that the molested child surrenders, escaping from her situation and getting out of the body not by action in the real world but rather by altering his or her state of consciousness. This is the response of captured prey to a predator or of a defeated contestant in battle. Herman (1997) maintains that "these alterations of consciousness are at the heart of constriction or numbing, one of the cardinal symptom of post-traumatic stress disorder" (p.42).

Some occasions of inescapable danger may evoke not only terror and rage but also, paradoxically, a state of detached calm in which terror, rage, and pain dissolve. Even though these events happen to the individual, it is as though they have been disconnected from their ordinary meanings. Perceptions may be numbed or distorted, with partial anesthesia or loss of particular sensations (pp. 42-43). The child may feel as though the event is not happening to him or her, as though the child is observing from outside his or her body as it is being violated by the offender. For the victim, it seems to be like a bad dream from which he or she will shortly awaken. Herman (1997) further says that these perceptual changes combine with a feeling of indifference, emotional detachment, and profound passivity in which the victim relinquishes all initiative and struggle. "This altered state of consciousness might be regarded as one of nature's small mercies, a protection against unbearable pain" (p.43). The example that is given below puts the issue of constriction and disassociation into practical experience, when Warshaw (1998) wrote:

> a rape survivor describes this detached state: "I left my body at that point. I was over next to the bed, watching this happen… I dissociated from the helplessness. I was standing next to me and there was just this shell on the bed…. There was just a feeling of flatness. I was just there. When I picture the room, I don't picture it from the bed. I picture it from the side of the bed. That's where I was watching from" (p.56).

Thus Cheston (1993), noted that "dissociation can take a number of forms from numbing, to out of the body experience, to creating another personality that flees the pain" (p.456), as could be seen from the above example. People generally use this natural capacity to reduce the horror and pain of acute trauma. A defense mechanism that is close to this is hypnosis, but hypnosis is always controlled by circumstances and by choice, whereas traumatic trances occur in an uncontrolled manner and usually without conscious choice. This notion confirms the view of Courtois (1999), that "avoidance may present at its extreme form a sort of dissociative amnesia" while Briere (2002), holds that avoidance, at lower levels, is a chronic suppression of negative thoughts or distressing and disruptive memories.

People who cannot spontaneously dissociate may want to self-medicate to achieve the same numbing effects by using alcohol or narcotics, engaging in self-mutilation, suicidality, and other coping or tension reducing activities. The adverse effect of an avoidance coping mechanism is that this tendency to avoid the distress of CSA may decrease the survivor's response to psychological assessment leading to significance under presentation of abuse history or effects. Owing to the danger of dissociation, any therapy assessment that requires the abuse survivor to recall or re-experience abuse-related events can activate upsetting thoughts or feelings that the victim was avoiding or motivate denial on the part of the victim.

HYPERAROUSAL

One of the consequences of traumatic experience is that the human system of self-preservation seems to go into permanent alert, as if the danger might return at any time. Herman (1997) posits that "traumatized people have an extreme startle response to unexpected stimuli associated with the traumatic event" (p.36). It also appears that survivors of sexual abuse cannot "tune out" repetitive stimuli that other people would find merely annoying. Victims respond to each repetition as though it were a new and dangerous surprise (p.36). These are persistent symptoms of arousal that were not present before the trauma. These symptoms reflect psychological changes in allostasis, hyperarousal of the adrenergic response system, resulting in behavioral expressions which manifest as PTSD symptoms.

Again, persons with PTSD are sometimes quick to react with irritability, hostility, anger, cynicism, confrontation, and anxious agitation at annoying circumstances. They are often restless, impatient, and quick tempered. Recent studies conducted by Bremner (2002), have shown that the basal ganglia area of the limbic system associated with anger and aggression are affected as part of the prolonged stress-response pattern (p.27). For some persons, especially those with a history of aggression or, like the sexually abused children and adolescents, those for whom self-defense is necessary for survival, the sub cortical brain structures associated with aggression appear to be in a state of kindling, a neurological ready-alert mode of functioning (p.27).

Hyperarousal in PTSD also influences thinking, concentration, academic performance, and other cognitive functions. The cognitive impairments of the executive function also include attention deficits. It is for such reasons that children who are sexually abused are most likely to drop out of school if they are not helped quickly enough; they may further manifest some form of irritability (p.27). PTSD disrupts the normal operation of the brain. It can be compared to stormy weather that disrupts radio and television reception, resulting in "lost" information and poor quality reception.

One of the major after effects of hyperarousal is hypervigilance. This is a behavioral disposition and a readiness to respond to stimuli, especially cues that have trauma-specific relevance to the victims' traumatic experience. Such persons are always on their guard; they scan their environment for cues, signs, or situations that signify a threat or potential problem. Hypervigilance consists of cognitive, affective, somatic, and behavioral perspectives. In their perception and cognition, persons with PTSD automatically and often unconsciously scan their environment for signs of threat based on their own trauma experience. They thereby activate the fight and flight stress response. Affective responses intensify fear, anxiety, anger, or terror. Somatically, there is an increase in hyperarousal experienced in the physical reactions of muscle tension, increased heart rate, blood pressure, respiration, and sweating. The person is then behaviorally ready to deal with fear and anxiety (p.28). Another problem often presented to people suffering from PTSD is decrease capacity to accurately self-monitor that is, to read their internal states of arousal, emotions, and thought patterns. This defect can also lead to their misinterpretation of other's intentions, actions and verbal expressions. Therefore, it is necessary for victims to seek help. The next chapter will, among other issues, expose some mental health perspectives in healing and counseling survivors of childhood sexual abuse.

As earlier observed, most child sexual abuse is unreported due to the stigma associated with it. The child may be too intimidated to report the abuse to parents especially when it is perpetrated by older persons. The situation becomes even more complicated when the abuse was committed by a parent. As a result, it becomes almost impossible to diagnose issues arising from such abuse or to seek help for the victim. However, the next chapter discusses some steps that could be taken in mental health counseling sessions to help victims.

CHAPTER 19

Some Perspectives In Mental Health Care For Abuse Victims

HELPING SURVIVORS OF child sexual abuse is imperative so that they can go back through the developmental stages and rebuild the sense of self which is critical to their overall emotional well-being. This is crucial as Cheston (1993), noted:

> When sexual abuse occurs the normal developmental tasks are interrupted or distorted for the victim. Some children respond by becoming fixated at a certain developmental stage, while others skip stages and become overly adult for their years. As adults, these clients react to situations in an immature, sometimes frightened manner that seems inconsistent with their age and status (pp.458-459).

Despite the defenses that survivors of child sexual abuse put up and the temporary relief such defenses provide them, the victims still feel hurt, angry, and empty. This means that coping mechanisms do not make victims healthy, but only make them live day by day, creatively clinging to a semblance of normalcy. It is noteworthy that when coping mechanisms fail or do not develop at all, victims are more likely to develop severe mental illnesses such as psychoses, suicide ideations, and addiction to drugs, alcohol, or gambling. They may engage in crime as a lifestyle, develop life-threatening eating disorders, use compulsive sex to meet intimacy needs, lie compulsively, and engage in self-mutilation, as well as many other abnormal behaviors as analyzed earlier on. Because most of these coping styles are counterproductive, as earlier observed, there is need for professional mental health therapy as the most significant means of setting victims free from their past trauma and becoming healthier in their present and future relationships, including their relationships with themselves and God.

SOME PERSPECTIVES ON THERAPEUTIC STAGES OF HEALING

With the diverse and complex effects of child sexual abuse, no single type of intervention is likely to be applicable or effective for all victims. This section will briefly examine the treatment strategies of Saywitz, *et al.* (2000), Hyde, et al. (1995), Davies and Frawley (1994), Herman (1992) and finally, Cheston, (1993), whose helping strategy for victims of sexual abuse will be analyzed in detail. The commonality in all of the above treatment practices is the standard fundamental principles of screening, assessment, and treatment planning. Due to the complexity of the effects of CSA on individuals and families, there is no practice of "one size fits all." Therefore, treatment plans should be individualized on the basis of the clinical assessment of the patient and the context in which treatment will take place.

Saywitz, *et al.* (2000), proposed what they described as multimodal treatment, which includes: individual, family, group, and pharmacological approaches. It also involves different levels of care; for example, the client could be an outpatient (partial), or as a victim of CSA an inpatient at different times during the period of recovery (p.13). They emphasized the importance of involving family or parents in one form or another in the treatment, especially if the client is an adolescent, in order to monitor the symptoms, develop strategies for preventing re-victimization, control their own distress, and normalize family functioning (p.13).

Another perspective on treatment of victims of CSA is that of Hyde, *et al.* (1995). This treatment process emphasizes the necessity that clinicians who treat victims of child sexual abuse think strategically. In other words, specific symptoms should be targeted with specific strategies. They described their treatment strategy as "abuse-specific treatment." They contend that abuse-specific CBTs are potentially helpful because "they incorporate well-established treatment strategies to target specific symptoms" (pp.1387-1399). This kind of treatment or intervention targets the chief symptoms of post-traumatic distress, for example re-experiencing the event with intrusive thoughts or flashbacks, avoidance of reminders, and hyperarousal. These are targeted with gradual exposure and desensitization, stress inoculation and relaxation training, and interruption and replacement of upsetting thoughts to regain control over thoughts and feelings. Depressive symptoms are targeted with coping-skills training and correction of cognitive distortions. Behavior problems that interfere with functioning are targeted with conventional behavior-management strategies (pp.1387-1399).

The abuse-specific treatment is another method available in the repertoire of therapeutic options for therapists who work with victims of childhood sexual abuse.

Again, Davies and Frawley (1994), taking the psychoanalytic perspective of treating survivors of CSA, evaluated the level of regression encountered by therapists in clinical work with victims of CSA. They insist on speaking directly to the victim's persona and understanding therapeutic stalemates from the victim's perspective. This means "taking into account the victims' unique ego organization and system of internalized object relations which changes profoundly, the nature of the analytic work" (p.77). For reasons like this, it is imperative that every treatment plan should be tailored to suit the individual victim's need.

Davies and Frawley (1994), therefore make the following therapy recommendations for the therapist treating victims of CSA. First, speak directly to the child persona in the adult survivor; this helps to recover the traumatogenic memories. It is a way of getting in touch with the split self that exists outside of the victim's conscious awareness. Secondly, speaking to the child persona is the most effective way to work in the patient's transference-counter transference. This, they infer, hinders the patient's current interpersonal relationships that make them ongoing victims of real or perceived abuse and intensify dissociative barriers. Finally, the analyst must establish an alliance with the child persona as this will change the original traumatic experience of isolation and despair and result in bringing about internalization of a new therapeutic object relationship that will produce a permanent change in the internal structure of the victim (pp.77-78). Although Davies and Frawley (1994), affirm the need to work with the dissociative states of the survivor, they caution that the process could be a complex and problematic one.

Herman (1992), basically identified three stages to working with survivors of childhood sexual abuse. Primary to therapy is establishing the victim's safety, both in his or her home situation and with the therapist. The second is remembering and mourning, which implies processing the traumatic material. Finally, the third stage will be fostering social reconnection, which will include having to start normal life once again after the victim has reconnected with any dissociative part of the self or relationship (p.155). Herman is quick to add that because of the complex nature of CSA, no single course of recovery follows these stages through a straight-forward linear sequence as traumatic syndromes defy any attempt to impose such simpleminded order (p.155). Herman (1992), confirms that traumatic syndromes like that of CSA are a complex disorder that requires a complex treatment as well. Once a safe environment has been ensured, the counselor can begin to develop a therapeutic relationship.

The last therapist whose therapeutic theory will be analyzed in some detail is Cheston (1993), whose process is psychodynamic in nature. He proposed a six stage process of healing survivors of CSA. Paramount to the therapeutic proceedings is the establishment of a working alliance. Gelso and Carter (1985), defined this working alliance as "the emotional alignment that occurs between the reasonable or working sides of the client and therapist" (p.208). They suggest that this alignment is fostered and fed by a strong emotional bond, agreement on goals, and agreement on tasks. Developing a therapeutic relationship may be particularly important for adult survivors because these individuals often have significant difficulties in trusting other people. Regardless of clinicians' differing technical approaches to therapy, the quality of the therapeutic relationship is of singular importance in treatment with victims of sexual abuse. This is critical because the relationship with the therapist must be the foundation of the therapeutic process with survivors, as it provides the context in which the traumatic memories and accompanying affect can be addressed. Through such a reliable relationship, the therapist can begin to help a survivor of CSA to understand why it is important to process what happened to him or her as a child. For example, a survivor of childhood sexual abuse whom Gelso (1985), refers to here as Dana at 35, described her experience after being in therapy for some time.

> I entered therapy at 27 and have been working off and on most of those years with five different therapists. I had some concrete memories of "what happened" for years, but never dealt with them in

therapy because I was 'too ashamed' and because 'I feared that I might have wanted it to happen'. None of the therapists ever asked me about sexual abuse as a possibility, and I never revealed the memories I did have access to (p.208).

Though this may not be a result of her inability to establish a therapeutic relationship, it is possible that this client did not establish adequate rapport with her therapist in order to decrease resistance and freely discuss her issues in therapy sessions. It is equally important for the therapist to discuss confidentiality with the client as a part of forming a therapeutic relationship. It is therefore, possible that a client like Dana may prefer to repress her CSA due to fear of betrayal and the trauma associated with CSA. Some survivors, at times cope with abuse by "putting it behind them" and thus are unaware that their current life difficulties are connected to the childhood trauma.

Olio (1993), citing Butler (1978) and Herman (1981), agrees that therapists may miss or underestimate the relevance of the abuse experiences as victims may report these incidents without apparent distress. Basically, this lack of affect, they maintain, reflects the victim's life-long pattern of using denial and dissociation rather than the absence of damage or a successful resolution of the childhood trauma. By the time a survivor of CSA receives the help he or she deserves, the individual may have been sexually or otherwise abused over a period of time. The person will have built up an array of defenses to protect himself or herself, and contact with the individual may be difficult (p.7).

Having established a working relationship with at least one person, that is the therapist, prior to treatment, the next step will be the first stage to recovery, which is the decision to heal or what Cheston (1993), referred to in Bass and Davis (1988), as "taking the risk" to explore the chaotic, harmful, childhood environment. To heal requires psychological fortitude and the ability to risk looking at the very painful experience that the client has been trying to avoid for years (p.463). Survivors of childhood sexual abuse grow up mistrusting virtually everybody, having been betrayed by a trusted person who violated their personal and physical boundaries. They greet every situation with mistrust. The victim needs to be affirmed and confirmed in the fact that he or she is not alone, will not be abused, and can begin to have a trusting relationship with a least one person. To ask the victim to trust anyone again requires a great deal of time, effort, testing and risking. Thus, treating a survivor of childhood sexual abuse cannot be completed in a brief therapy approach. This is why the therapist must take time and slowly navigate and explore the layers of trauma involved, while at the same time expecting setbacks and many acts of testing the relationship.

The second stage in Cheston's (1993), stages of recovery is helping the client to acknowledge the reality of the abuse instead of denying it. The therapist at this point will aim to help the client have a total recall of the horrific events of abuse. Attention will be paid to the facts of time frames, incidence, persons involved and the effects of the abuse (p.467). The objective of this stage for Cheston (1993), is to gently confront the denial, if any, confirm the sexual abuse, affirm the victim as not being responsible for his or her misfortune, and ask the victim to join in the process of healing. Again, he says the therapist's concern at this stage will be to help the survivor face the reality of the abuse and not the pain. For Cheston (1993), therefore, it seems that having to reexamine the trauma memory is a very important component of his treatment of survivors of CSA.

Ford, et al. (2007), working with the philosophy "if it don't itch, don't scratch," would not subscribe to Cheston's (1993) method. They noted that since traumatic events like CSA happened in the past, there should be no need to reopen old wounds and cause the individual to experience further distress or to be preoccupied with memories that are better treated as "water under the bridge" (p.477). They proposed that the recovery trauma of CSA neither requires nor necessarily includes dredging up or repetitively recalling trauma memories but, instead, can be accomplished by helping the survivor to manage and even gain control over the unwanted trauma memories that are core symptoms of PTSD (p. 477).

Ford, et al. (2007), further hold that the skill for managing the trauma of child sexual abuse will be to provide the atmosphere for such survivors to make thoughtful choices about whether or not to reexamine trauma memories and if the victim agrees, to decide how, when, and with whom. Following this process, they affirm that it will be an informed choice rather than a re-traumatizing or further destabilizing experience (p.478). Having to process the trauma memory is not a necessary condition for the recovery of victims of CSA according to Ford, et al. (2007),

It must be noted here that the Cheston's (1993), view of recalling client's memories of abuse is, therefore, not shared by all therapists. This may not be a major treatment issue, since some victims have only a patchy or vague memory of their abuse, but where the memory is intact, facing its denial will be the informed choice of the patient as Ford, et al. (2007), proposed. However, Davies and Frawley (1994) affirm Cheston's view but in the extreme situation of CSA effect resulting in dissociation. They recommend that the therapist engage in "speaking directly to the child persona as the most effective way of recovering all of the traumatogenic memories" (p.78). Nevertheless, they acknowledge this as the more severe end of the split self that exists outside of conscious awareness. Having to make the unconscious conscious at this stage, or in treatment generally, may have more healing benefits than dangerous outcomes, depending on the patient's choice and the therapist's strategy.

The third stage for Cheston (1993), will be to help the survivor face the pain of abuse.

This means breaking the silence of the secret so that it can be effectively brought out into the counseling session (p.467). It is this author's opinion that Cheston supposes here that the memory of the abuse is still fresh in the mind of the victim. For him, while stage two deals more with the intellectual understanding of the abuse, the third stage moves into deeper realm of "knowing" emotionally the pain of grieving. Cheston (1993), maintains that there is no more talking around the subject; if the time is ripe, "the silence of doubt, denial, intellectualization, and repression is lifted" (p.468). The therapist's role at this point will be to let the victim of CSA know that he is present, allowing the catharsis to wax and wane naturally. Cheston (1993) maintains that the client should be left alone: "silence will serve you well, the pain is the only sound" (p.468). Once the client does not fear or recoil from the pain, but faces it, experiences it, and embraces it, he or she will begin to move into stage four. Again, Cheston (1993), did not recommend what should be done if the client begins to fear or recoil from his or her pain.

Let us note here that even though Cheston (1993), uses this method, some other therapists may not ascribe to it because, for them this might result in retraumatizing patients of CSA. Herman (1992), for example, is of the view that patients of CSA may want to deny their pain out of a sense of pride. According to Herman (1992), some patients feel that acknowledging psychological harm grants a moral victory to the perpetrator in a way that acknowledging physical harm does not (p.159). Like Cheston (1993), however, Herman (1992), in her remembrance and mourning process, advocates that patients of CSA tell their trauma "story completely, in depth and in detail" (p.175). The essence of this practice, she holds, is to have the experience and pain integrated into the survivor's life and story. Traumatic memory in contrast to life story "is wordless and static," it does not develop or progress in time, nor does it reveal the storyteller's feelings. Most importantly, Herman (1992), like Ford, et al. (2007), notes that the onus to confront one's horrors from the past rests with the survivor of CSA, as the patient recollects his or her memories. Herman further maintains that the need to preserve safety must be balanced constantly against the need to face the past. Herman (1992), like Cheston (1993), holds that avoiding the traumatic memory leads to stagnation in the recovery process, while processing it hastily leads to a fruitless and damaging effects, reliving of the trauma (p.176).

There will be no need, therefore, for the therapist to help the victim of CSA to face his or her trauma memories, as Cheston (1993), suggests, if the patient does not want to go there. The patient dictates the pace and takes the lead in treatment.

According to Cheston (1993), the fourth stage cannot be rushed because if the client moves too quickly, "the defenses of suppression, intellectualization, and denial may be used and the healing will not be complete" (p.469). This stage for Cheston (1993), is important because it is one in which the client is helped toward wholeness. For Cheston, this is the stage of the integration of intellectual knowing, emotional pain, spiritual estrangement, the abused child, the adult and the social relationship. Saywitz, et al. (2000), would prefer CBT treatment for victims of CSA at this stage in order to resolve issues and feelings of about their sexual abuse as highlighted by Cheston above. Saywitz, et al. (2000), contend that when the abuse is the source of distorted cognitions that underlie depression, some direct discussion of the abusive event is often indicated for cognitive restructuring to be effective. However, if the discussion is not carefully conducted, it may contaminate the child's report and the disclosure process (p.2).

This process, Cheston (1993), affirms, will aim at bringing the child to the intellectual realization that his or her misconception of the abuse being the child's fault was invalid. Once this fact is established, then the client must speak to his or her child "persona" and say, "None of this was your fault, you were just a child." This is necessary because the victim is likely to think it was his or her fault that he or she was abused or may have loved the abuser and may feel that he or she has betrayed the abuser by talking about the abuse and feeling all the emotions of the past (p.471). It is an adult's absolute responsibility to refrain from abusing children. Once this is internalized by the victim, he or she will be helped to affirm that the individual does not deserve to be abused, and that he or she can and will avoid abusive situations (p.472). Using this process, each of the other misconceptions in the individual's life will be reconstructed into new reality statements. In other words, if the therapist is able to change the thought process of the victim, the victimized person will be able to eliminate the symptoms.

The fifth stage of recovery for Cheston (1993) is to deal with the anger and other negative emotional disturbances and feelings that survivors of childhood sexual abuse might have. This stage has to deal with the intense rage and bitterness that the victim feels toward the abusive father, uncle or whoever the perpetrator might be. There are many opinions among therapists as to how to deal with patients' anger. Cheston (1993) proposes that the patient, at this stage, should be encouraged to sit still and feel the emotion, to emote by crying, yelling, and pounding a pillow. For Herman (1992), in her process of mourning, victims of CSA must come to terms with the impossibility of getting even with the perpetrator. When the victim is allowed to vent rage in safety, this helpless fury will gradually change into a more powerful and satisfying form of anger which Herman called "righteous indignation" (p.189). This transformation of rage to righteous indignation serves to free the survivor from the prison of the "revenge fantasy" where the individual is with the perpetrator alone, which Herman described as "a wish for catharsis" (189). This whole process helps the victim to regain his or her sense of power without becoming a criminal by taking revenge. Herman holds that for the survivor to give up the fantasy of revenge does not mean giving up the quest for justice and the effort to bring the perpetrator to account for his crime (p.189). Most therapists agree that grieving the loss is one experience which victims cannot bypass, but if they adequately mourn their traumatic experience both the fantasy for revenge and rage for the perpetrator will begin to wane.

Finally, Cheston (1993) in his sixth stage proposes resolution and reconciliation. This involves acceptance and rapprochement. As noted earlier, survivors need to understand and forgive themselves of anything they perceive that they did, felt, or thought at the time they were actively victims and later after the abuse ended. It is an ongoing process, which continues even after therapy is completed. Herman (1992) subscribes to Cheston's view here because Herman's approach to healing depends on the discovery of restorative love in the survivor's own life. It does not require that this love be extended to the perpetrator (p.190), since survivors may never have knowledge of who their abusers were. Herman (1992) notes that once the victim has come to understand the reality of his or her sexual abuse, the individual will begin to reconnect to his or her former relationships, working to create a new future, and incorporating the traumatic experience into his or her life. A survivor of child sexual abuse who reached this final stage of recovery was quoted by Herman as saying,

> Okay, I've had enough of walking around like I'd like to brutalize everyone who looks at me wrong. I don't have to feel like that anymore. Then I thought, "How would I like to feel? I wanted to feel safe in the world. I wanted to feel powerful. And so I focused on what was working in my life, in the ways I was taking power in real-life situations (p.197).

This means that this survivor will begin to let go at this stage. For Cheston (1993), the conversation will now change, and the survivor's topics of conversation will now revolve around moving forward with his or her life. Subject matters this time might include current relationships, career development, or parenting issues (p.476). The survivor will make an effort to look at the positive side of life to move forward.

To move in this direction, the survivor will begin by accepting and loving himself or herself again, which includes physically taking care of oneself, emotionally caring for one's needs, intellectually using one's gifts to the fullest possible extent, establishing healthy relationships and feeling spiritually connected. If the survivor can now function normally and continue growing, her own termination can occur slowly over a period of time to avoid showing the signs of rejection and abandonment to which childhood sexual abuse survivors can be sensitive. Saywitz, *et al.* (2000), Hyde, *et al.* (1995), Davies and Frawley (1994), Herman (1992) and Cheston (1993) are only a few of the numerous other therapeutic models for treating survivors of CSA. The other side of the coin in healing survivors of childhood sexual abuse will be to address any spiritual damage the survivor may have suffered or the disassociated spiritual aspect.

Another side to clinical mental health care for victims of child abuse is the pastoral care perspective discussed in the following chapter. Parents may choose to seek help for an abused child from a Christian counselor or pastoral counselor who uses both secular sciences and religious insights in providing help and healing to patients who seek a religious based intervention. Such intervention becomes very necessary if the victim is suffering from faith-based problems such as God-image, guilt, or forgiveness.

CHAPTER 20

The Pastoral Care Of Abuse Survivors

THE DIFFERENCE BETWEEN mental health and pastoral counseling is that while secular mental health counseling uses only psychological tools to help patients of sexual abuse, pastoral counseling uses theological and spiritual means in addition to psychological tools. Cooper-White (2006) maintained that pastoral psychotherapy brings additional tools to psychotherapy because, apart from the psychological process, there is the component of theological reflection and the conviction that healing is a sacred process desired and supported by God so as to live a fulfilled life (p.136). In dealing with adult survivors of abuse, it is imperative to be aware of the tripartite nature of humankind as comprised of body, mind, and soul. When an individual is sexually abused it is not only the body and mind that is impacted, but also the soul. In the discussion of the theology of the human body in the Chapter One, it was emphasized that the spirituality of human sexuality originates from its divine essence.

Therefore, the violation of the human body implies the defilement of that body which is the temple of the soul.

The result of such violation is that the child will not only hold all loving adults in distrust but also, if the child has been taught the goodness and omnipotence of the Christian God, the victim may hold God in distrust. This might spell a grave consequence with the child's God image. For patients of CSA their major problem may be the split self, which is now compartmentalized. This is why a spiritual director, for instance, cannot complete the healing process required in such an individual. There is need for referral to a secular mental health counselor who will work with the patient on the issue of his or her trauma. Only a pastoral counselor who is fully trained to use both psychological and spiritual tools can work with the patient without making a referral. Chapter Four dealt with the issue of dissociation in survivors of CSA from the perspective of both secular and pastoral counselors. Chapter Twenty-One dealt with the various perspectives of pastoral counseling in the case of CSA. Chapter Twenty-Three will analyze the spiritual care component to pastoral counseling which naturally should be the last part of restoring the patient's dissociated spiritual component or restoring his or her distant relationship with God, if any, since the survivor's abuse.

The trauma effects in the life of a sexually abused survivor make him or her feel alienated. It will be the aim of the pastoral counselor during the therapeutic process to address each alienated piece of the individual as well as each person or group who is alienated. Cheston (1993) noted that each step of the pastoral counselor will be to help the patient to identify the lost part or person, affirming the importance of the lost piece, accepting the part or person back into the self. Secondly, she should set appropriate boundaries for how much importance the part of self or person will have in the victim's future (p.484).

This process is a long one fraught with many setbacks. Given the preponderance of child sexual abuse, pastoral counselors and spiritual care givers should understand as much as possible about the symptomatology of and treatment planning for those adult survivors of childhood sexual abuse. The contribution of pastoral counselors to the entire problem of sexual abuse is significant because childhood sexual abuse raises many issues of faith. Secular counselors may well address the issue of sexual abuse, but they often ignore the faith dimension so critical to the healing process of the client. It is by considering the spiritual dimension that therapy can achieve the integration of the various personal dimensions, namely: intellectual, physical, social, emotional, and spiritual.

Cheston (1993) observed that victims of CSA who have been taught in the church that God is a loving parental figure may doubt this position because of their disconnection with God. Some abused survivors may end up losing their faith, especially if the perpetrator is a priest, or because "when they were being abused they cried out for help from God, and when the abuse did not stop, they felt abandoned by a cruel and uncaring God" (p.481). The major treatment goal for the pastoral caregiver here will be to help the patient resolve feelings about his or her abuse and abandonment by God. Thus, if a client raises a theme with such religious content and the therapist is unable to address it, but ignores or dismisses it as personal, this may interfere with the exploration and resolution that counseling provides. The job of a pastoral counselor is to aid the client in seeing ways that God has been supportive over the years, which made him or her able to survive the abuse. This activity may not be embraced by the client at first because of bitterness and pain (p.481). As the client moves through the stages of therapy and is supported in feelings of anger and hurt, the individual will begin to see some areas in his or her life where God has been active. It is not the duty of a pastoral counselor to persuade the victim to forgive the perpetrator, even if he demands forgiveness, nor to further demand that the victim forget what happened. This practice could be counterproductive, especially when it presses on the abused to ignore his or her feelings, since this persuasion could mean reinforcing the fact that the perpetrator can do what he or she wishes and escape accountability. It is within this area that the many child abuse laws make sense.

The clergy member, most often, is the one on the spot and represents the front lines of mental health delivery for many individuals, especially in the developing countries where the priests and pastors are considered as masters of all trades. This is so because pastors are often the first person to be contacted by parishioners in crisis. Pastoral counseling may serve as the sole professional resource for many who may never seek treatment from other mental health professionals. Because of this key role, it is important that pastoral counselors be aware of the types of traumatic events which produce symptoms of post-traumatic stress disorder. By recognizing risk in parishioners who have experienced these traumas, the clergy can take active steps to help in the crisis and thus reduce the risk for PTSD. Each of these individuals needs a place to experience acceptance and nurturing. The pastor is expected to provide this containment and safe environment. Cheston (1993) gives a rule of thumb for pastoral care givers in their bid to help survivors of childhood sexual abuse. Pastors should show non-judgmental acceptance and validation of the survivor, set the psychological tone for helping. Support, alliance, and advocacy are appropriate role expectations for the helper. It is assumed that post-traumatic distress is primarily related to the traumatic experience and not personality or spiritual "weakness." It is recognized that trauma transformation is a lifelong process. Losses from traumatic experiences may not be compensable, but they can be grieved. The right to self-determination is retained by the survivor. Pastoral self-care is assured (p.631).

When pastoral caregivers do not meet the above expectation, the healing process may derail with the result that Lovinger (1994) observed, "Counselors must understand that the client's anger over un-empathic or abusive approaches is a response to disappointment and hurt" (p. 209). Thus if the pastoral counselor's reaction is loving acceptance and affirmation of the strong feeling, the patient is more likely to breathe a sigh of relief, feel a little less afraid and more hopeful, and express other taboo feelings. This outcome is one that the patient cannot accomplish alone. To be able to do this, the patient must make recourse to his or her higher power. Beginning to trust God and prayer will not be easy at the beginning, but victims should be encouraged to do so as this will enable them to begin to feel the freedom to talk about their anger at God for "abandoning them" so many years ago. In working with survivors of childhood sexual abuse, the pastoral caregiver must not lose sight of the treatment goal which is comprised of a client's particular interest in exploring such religious issues as shame and guilt, God's punishment and forgiveness or forgiveness, sin, and grace.

GUILT AND SHAME

According to Cooper-White (2006), all patients, except perhaps those who are sociopathic, will bring varying degrees of shame about their "inner objects" (p.209), which in the case of survivors of CSA, were formed as a result of their sexual abuse. For Cheston (1993), guilt is a feeling that is experienced when someone has done something that one judges to be wrong. Shame, on the other hand, is a feeling of unworthiness about oneself just because of a failure or weakness (p.485). The sexually abused person typically feels both inappropriate guilt and unjustified shame. Most survivors of childhood sexual abuse are often obsessed with self- blame, resulting from feelings that their guilt cannot be forgiven by God. This is because the victim fears that his or her relationship with God has been damaged. Lovinger (1994) adds that shame which develops earlier than guilt occurs also when the client's integrity or body has been violated as a result of the sexual abuse (p.210). Shame and guilt, therefore, are very important emotions to deal with in pastoral counseling of survivors of childhood sexual abuse.

Guilt, for Lovinger, is often displaced and in a detailed process clients feel guilty about some ideas or feelings associated with their sexual abuse. "Shame compared to guilt is harder to expunge in counseling and takes prolonged time. Shame can diminish only by desensitization if the therapist is non-judgmental and reliable" (p.210). Shame resulting from CSA can also be a part of the difficulty some victims encounter in keeping a relationship.

Furthermore, Lew (1990), from his working experience notes that what works at this point for some victims is prayer. He noted that, "some incest survivors report that prayer provides them with feelings of calm, comfort, and connection with a strength that goes beyond them" (p.485). It is necessary to note Koenig's (2002) caution that some experts advise that physicians including therapists never initiate spiritual activities with patients. Instead they rely on the patient to take the first step. This is because of the factor of power dynamics discussed earlier. In this case, because of power differentials between patient and physician, "whenever the therapist initiates a spiritual exercise such as prayer, an element of coercion which the victim does not want enters the picture" (Koenig, 2002. p.40).

Beginning to trust God and pray will not be easy at the beginning, but victims should be encouraged to pray if they so desire since God's grace can be found in the most unlikely places and situations. Then will they begin to feel the freedom to talk about their anger at God for "abandoning them" so many years ago. Patients may begin to feel that because they expressed their anger, resentment, and sense of betrayal at God they are going to be struck dead, or worse, that loved one will be harmed. They are almost sure that they are going to hell. Cheston (1993) maintains that some of this response will be in direct relation to how the pastoral counselor reacts to the sexually abused individuals' feelings and emotions (p.486). Thus if the pastoral counselor's reaction is loving acceptance and affirmation of the strong feeling, the patient is more likely to breathe a sigh of relief.

SIN, RECONCILIATION, AND FORGIVENESS

Lovinger (1994) defined sin as "deliberate violation of God's law" (p.213). This sense of sin is partly the guilt feeling which some victims of CSA experience. The victim's intense sense of sinfulness may arise from anger at someone else, often the perpetrator, but turned inward to avoid self-awareness. Without sounding judgmental, many therapists agree that pathology and sin are not the same. If through psychotherapy and pastoral counseling therapists are able to heal every psychological wound, Cooper-White (2006) asks, would we be able to bring about a utopian world free of sin? (p.118). Even though sin and pathology overlap, they remain distinct issues to be dealt with according to their nature and to the expertise of the therapist. Victims of CSA who accuse themselves of sin are often scrupulous about their behavior, which is a desire to be perfect and a sign of defective conscience. Lovinger (1994) notes that conscience does three things: warns one against wrongdoing, makes one feel bad if one does so, and rewards the individual for doing well. While the conscience can do well in the first and second goals, it does not in the third (p.214). Conscience by itself cannot mete out punishment to the victim but can accuse the victim of moral failure, especially if the victim has a scrupulous conscience even when the victim of CSA is not culpable.

Groeschel (1983) will posit that a tool in such struggle for recovery and deliverance is confession, in a sacramental or non-sacramental way. The Sacrament of Reconciliation, he contends, is a powerful means for personal perfection when used wisely and well. Survivors of CSA who are not Catholics can access this help in a non-sacramental manner by confessing to another informed and prayerful person whom they trust, probably their pastoral counselor. This is similar to the confession required in the fifth step of Alcoholics Anonymous (p.107). Confession in this situation may serve as a great relief for such victims of scrupulous conscience who feel that they will be punished by God for being victims of sexual abuse. Confession to one's higher power most probably will open the soul to the forgiveness of God.

As earlier noted, the life of a victim of CSA may become alienated from the once trusted abuser, the victim himself or herself, others whom the victim sees as non-protective, God, and authority. These disconnected parts of the victim are usually taken care of during the therapeutic process, where each alienated piece is addressed. Cheston (1994) recommends that the purpose of each step of therapy should be to identify and accept the lost part or person back into the person (p.484). In this stage of therapy, it is assumed that the pastoral counselor has dealt with all the dissociated parts, but that the fallout of the abuse experience which borders on self-acceptance and reconciliation with one's higher power stands in the way of total recovery. Here the victim is helped to realize that his or her sexual abuse was not a deliberate violation of God's law, but of the abuser, that the victim does not deserve any punishment of God, but that the abuser does if the abuser does not make amends. The example of Freda, as related by Cheston (1994), tells the whole story of reconciliation.

Freda had alienated all males from her life. She believed that the world was better off without them. She knew, however, that a world without men would end. And she also had to affirm that her experience was not every person's experience. She next looked at her male side and recognized its strength in her life and accepted that it is not maleness that is bad but abusive maleness that is bad. Finally, she embraced that males were OK, but that as a victim she needed to proceed carefully building any male friendship lest she fall back into the role of victim with another male (pp.484-485).

Authorities differ over the need for forgiveness as a part of healing in the life of victims of childhood sexual abuse. Lew, (1990), and Bass and Davis (1988), assert that forgiveness can impede healing. They assert that if one has strong religious ties, particularly Christian ones, one may feel it is one's sacred duty to forgive. This just is not true. If there is such a thing as Divine forgiveness, it is God's job, not that of the victim (p.482).

It takes the responsibility from the child and puts it on the shoulders of society and its representatives. The perpetrator can demand forgiveness from the child and threaten the child if he or she does not forgive, but a court of law will not be so easily manipulated and will hold the abuser accountable for his or her actions.

Sanford (1988) disagrees with many writers by citing that forgiveness is freedom, letting go. Remitting the behavior of another and remitting pain, guilt, and rage to God allows the victim to move toward health. This kind of letting go can take a long time. Again, Lew (1990) and Bass and Davis (1988) believe that forgiveness is not necessary for health. They maintain that forgiveness in the early stage in treatment is not necessary and does not make the victim to become better. In fact, forgiveness too early can block health. However, Cheston (1993) noted that forgiveness at the last stage of therapy is almost always necessary to obtain health (p.483). It is at this point that Sanford is correct. Forgiveness becomes freedom. In all, using the word forgiveness underscores the point that there is something within the victim that needs forgiving. The indelible mark such abuse leaves on the victim's life and the ruptured relationship with others and with the victim's higher power is one that the victim may not be able to forgive or cope without grace.

GRACE

Grace is a gratuitous favor or gift of God which most survivors of childhood sexual abuse find difficult to see in their broken lives. However, it does make a great difference in the process of recovery for those who take recourse of it. According to May (1988), Grace for Christians is the dynamic outpouring of God's loving nature that flows into and through creation in an endless self-offering of healing, love, illumination, and reconciliation. It is a gift that we are free to ignore, reject, ask for, or simply accept. And it is a gift that is often given in spite of our intentions and errors. At such times, when grace is so clearly given unrequested, uninvited, even undeserved, there can be no authentic response but gratitude and awe (p.17).

It is in the realization of CSA victims' helplessness that the pastoral counselor can most honestly and completely counsel the patient to turn to the power of grace. Grace is the hope and the power that can truly vanquish the destructiveness of CSA. It is the duty of the pastoral counselor and spiritual caregiver to help the survivor of CSA to take recourse of grace which is possible by reconnecting to his or her higher power for final freedom from the pains of abuse. May (1988) posits that grace is the invincible advocate of freedom from the pains of sexual abuse and expression of perfect love for oneself, God and neighbor (p.16). With a victim's heart, mind and attention clogged with the trauma and hopelessness resulting from the abuse, the pastoral counselor at this stage of recovery brings into the counseling room the last tool of spiritual power by encouraging the patient to turn to a higher power if the patient finds it helpful. Cheston (1993) gave a very good example of how victims could be helped to recognize God's presence in their life when he narrated the experience of a woman with whom he was working and who saw nothing that God had done for her:

> One woman with whom I was working saw nothing that God had done for her. She still believed in God but had the image of a cruel, punitive God. Over the course of therapy she refused to discuss her faith which she called "nil." But then one day she was describing her youngest child as a "gift from God." I asked her to pause and reflect on the statement. She said, "God didn't rape me, my uncle did. God didn't make it happen, my uncle did. I just do not know if God was there when I was crying out for help." On further pondering she said, "God

did answer my prayer for it to stop because it did stop one month later. I guess I forgot to ask God to make it stop now." As counseling continued, she saw many ways in which God's love was present in her life. One way was the wonderful escape she had in her out-of-body experience during the rape. She claimed that it was the only thing that kept her sane. Seeing her out-of-body experience as a blessing from God gave her the impetus she needed to say "thank you" in prayer. While she did not return to church immediately she did begin praying and reading inspirational books. She claims to feel more peaceful and reconciled to her supreme being (p.481).

At this point, the pastoral counselor helps the victim to learn how to look at and count her graces which are abundant in his or her life. Some of these graces may include one's spouse, child, job, best friend, successes in life and loving gifts. These experiences help survivors to see where God is in their lives. Grace, according to Cheston (1993), is not recognized until the pain of abuse has been felt and acknowledged (p.484). This is why the spiritual component of pastoral counseling may come after the normal stages and process of mental health counseling. As the pain wanes, a victim will begin to experience other positive emotions that will lead to thankfulness and recognition of where grace has become life-giving and life restoring to the survivor of childhood sexual abuse.

As noted earlier in this study, the pastoral counselor and care giver is often the first and at times the last place of call for members of the community who have trauma issues such as child sexual abuse, fatal accidents, fire disasters, floods, landslides, tornadoes or hurricanes. In Nigeria, for example, where the number of trained secular mental health counselors is inadequate, a fully trained pastoral counselor no doubt will have more than his fair share of opportunities to provide services to patients who have mental health issues. As observed in Chapter Two, one the greatest challenges for pastoral counselors remains the tremendous patronage ill-trained pastoral caregivers receive from Nigerians suffering from various kinds of mental health and spiritual problems. Oftentimes, due to the insufficient training some pastoral counselors received, they lack the knowledge for diagnosing mental health issues; instead, they have often classified every mental problem as a spiritual issue. Thus, the neo-Pentecostalism that seems to classify every mental health problem as demonic possession is dangerous to mental health of such individuals and should be addressed through seminars.

CONCLUSIONS AND RECOMMENDATIONS

Like some researchers in the field, I have observed that child sexual abuse is one of the most discouraging discoveries of our age. Most cultures abhor any sexual violation of children, who are regarded as innocent and pure. Their attitude is built around their religious, ethical and moral life which is inseparable from their communion with God the creator and ancestral spirits. This bond that unites them is so fragile that any act of immorality, especially incest will amount to a violation of this bond and will attract the wrath of the gods on the whole community. It is noteworthy that some people do not often reckon with the psychological and emotional impact of child abuse. However, the psychological impact as seen from this study is serious and should be a concern of parents, pastors, health care providers, governments, humanitarian organizations and the entire countries.

One of the major discoveries of this study is the systemic close family ties that exist in some traditional societies. Most importantly, these close family ties seem to have been the factor that has long been mitigating the negative emotional disturbances of victims of childhood sexual abuse, especially among victims who share their abuse incidents with their families. On a personal note, for example, when a relation of mine was violated by armed robbers who attacked her and her classmates in their school residence hall, every member of the family rallied around her, showed concern, and helped her to get through the trauma of the abuse and sought medical care. However, victims who keep their sexual assault secret due to the resulting stigma, or who have preexisting mental health issues, most probably will not go unscathed from such a traumatic experience. For according to Saywitz, *et al.* (2000),

> Sometimes sexual abuse exacerbates already existing developmental delays or potentiates ongoing psychological, behavioral, or interpersonal difficulties. With placement in foster care, some sexually abused children suffer consequences, including the loss of family and friends that cause additional symptoms distinct from the abusive incident itself (pp. 1040-1049).

Again, family ties and an extended family system are fast giving way to the nuclear family system due to Western influences and the economic situations of today. In such cases, it can no longer be taken for granted that children are going to be safe, as they were before now, in many traditional communities. In addition to this is the issue of dysfunctional family as noted in Ada's case in Chapter Two. Many societies today are experiencing more cases of divorce than at any other time in history. For this reason, many children are being displaced from their homes and being put in orphanages or sent to extended family members. These family members often put the children in harm's way, because the children are often those who are sent to hawk wares for their madams in the homes where they are placed thereby exposing them to child sexual predators. From reasons like these, one can infer without fear of contradiction that child sexual abuse is an immense problem in general because of the gradual break down in family life and law and order as fueled by unemployment and poverty.

The prevalence of childhood sexual abuse today is due not only to the dysfunctional character of some families, but also to the culture of keeping sexual abuse secret in the family, a practice that has done more harm than good. It has in no small measure encouraged child sexual abuse. Moreover, the paucity of statistics and information on the prevalence of childhood sexual abuse is largely due to the fact that society in general still regards discussions on sexual matters as taboo. Other contributing factors are the Western influences on traditional society through radio, television, internet, movies and magazines. The effects of globalization facilitated by the internet, communication, modern transportation, print media and electronic media on the moral values of the peoples cannot be overemphasized. The sex explosion experienced in Europe and America more than two decades ago as expressed in nudity and pornography did not bypass the traditional societies and their people's way of life. It has in many ways affected the moral values of the people. Nudity and child pornography are no longer issues in both developed and developing countries.

The idea of a compassionate God in world religions seems to have allayed the fear associated with certain child sexual abuse like incest. Consequently, people no longer dread the consequences of breaking the laws of the ancestors, for example, child sexual abuse. But the irony is that Christian religions have equally strict moral principles and child sexual abuse is a serious sin against God, but the idea of a merciful and forgiving God in the Christian religion seems to make such acts less serious.

One of the commendable steps government has taken to address the issue of CSA is the introduction of sex education in high schools. This is a shift from the secrecy under which sex abuse thrives. This step will not only help break the secrecy surrounding CSA and its effects but also educate teens on the dangers of sexual promiscuity and its health implications such as the spread of HIV/AIDS and other STDs. Another important contribution sex education can make in keeping CSA under check is teaching teenagers to be aware of child molesters and strangers who lurk in the shadows seeking ways to kidnap and rape children. Sex education will enlighten them to report such incidents and actual sexual abuse to their teachers and parents. In this way the culture of secrecy under which childhood sexual abuse thrives will be broken and victims will be able to talk about or report cases of sexual abuse to those in authority. Sex education for teenagers will be a proactive means of preventing the spread of HIV/AIDS and STDs among teens but also one of the ways of preparing children to fight off adults who may want to violate them by reporting them to their parents and authorities.

Again, poverty and urbanization have also made children prone to sexual abuse as children are dangerously exposed to sex predators. It is necessary for government to also deal with poverty and unemployment, which constitute the root dispositions of child sexual abuse, by providing jobs for parents so that they can take care of their children responsibly.

Moreover, due to the perceived widespread instances of child sexual abuse, parents and guardians must take the safety and security of their children seriously. This implies that parents should be close to their children and ask questions when they observe some abnormal behaviors from their children. The government should remove the burden of reporting child sexual abuse from the victims and parents by enacting laws mandating human service providers to report cases of child sexual abuse to law enforcement agents and the appropriate authorities for investigation and prosecution as being practiced in many States in the United States of America.

This author's general evaluation of this study gives rise to a basic hypothesis for this field that childhood physical or sexual abuse victims are less adjusted in day to day functioning. Any attempt to address CSA should be comprehensive and include building the capacity of law enforcement and judiciary, as well as social services, to be able to deal effectively and promptly with suspected or confirmed cases of child sexual abuses. Prevention of CSA should also include efforts on the part of agencies to understand some of the motivations behind the behavior of perpetrators as briefly exposed in this study in order to put in place appropriate prevention programs. Prevention and response initiatives are required to be able to deal adequately with the social, moral, mental, and health issues associated with CSA. Considerable effort should be made to raise awareness of the issue of CSA among children, families, and communities. There should be public education about the underlying causes of CSA, parental-monitoring education, life-skills workshops for adolescents, and support groups for high-risk children. Another strategy may be enhancing sex education in schools to teach children the concepts and skills that promote protection from sexual abuse.

The ability of health professionals can do much to limit the potential negative health impacts of the abuse. Heath care providers should also be trained in the act of treating victims with the required compassion and sensibility, for by so doing, a healthcare provider can also reduce the victim's immediate distress and act as a role model to family members whose support is so critical to a child's recovery. Since we live in a modern society, some traditional practices that promote child sexual abuse should be repealed.

Having known the problems that sexual abuse can cause its victims, it will be necessary to train more mental health and pastoral counselors to help in both community enlightenment on the negative consequences of CSA and treatment of victims of child and childhood sexual abuse. In addition, victims of CSA should be made to understand that it is their right to report any unsolicited and unwarranted sexual abuse to the appropriate quarters without fear of stigmatization.

When all these recommendations are carried out, the mental health and pastoral counselors will be able to face the challenging effects of childhood sexual abuse and the right and dignity of children will be restored. Good parenting that protects children from all forms of abuse will forestall the potential outbreak of mental health problem cases that might militate against the goal of raising a happy and successful child.

REFERENCES

Ainsworth, M. D. S. Blehar, M.C., Waters, E., & Wall, S. (1978). *Patterns of Attachment: A psychological study of the Strange Situation.* New York: Basic Books.

American Academy of Pediatrics. (1997). Breastfeeding and the use of human milk. Pediatrics, 100, 1035-1039.

American Academy of Pediatrics (2002). "Sexual Abuse." Retrieved on 12/19/2007. From http://www.medem.com

American Academy of Child & Adolescent Psychiatry (2004). Responding To Child Sexual Abuse. Retrieved on 12/19/2007, From http://www.aacap.org

Arnett, J. J. (2000). Emerging adulthood: A theory of development from the late teens through the twenties. *American Psychologist*, 55, 469-480.

Alfie, K. (2005). Unconditional Parenting. New York, NY: Atria Books.

Azrin, N.H., & Holz, W.C. (1966). Punishment. In Gershoff, E.T. (2002). Corporal Punishment by Parents and Associated Child Behaviors and Experience: A Meta-Analytic and Theoretical Review. *Psychological Bulletin*, 128, 4, 539-579.

Bartholomew, K. (1990). Avoidance of intimacy: An attachment perspective. *Journal of Social and Personal Relationships*, 7, 147-178.

Bartholomew, K. and Horowitz, L.M. (1991). Attachment Styles Among Young Adults: A test of a four-category model. *Journal of Personality and Social Psychology*, 61 (2), 226 244.

Bass, E. and David, L. (1988). The Courage to Heal. New York: Harper & Row.

Baumrind, D. (1980). New directions in socialization research. American Psychologist, 35, 639- 652.

Baumrind, D. (1995). Child maltreatment and optimal caregiving in social contexts. New York: Garland.

Bandura, A., & Walters, R. H. (1959). *Adolescent aggression.* New York: Ronald Press.

Baumrind, D. (1967). Child care practices anteceding three patterns of preschool behavior. *Genetic Psychology Monographs*, 75, 43–88.

Bartholomew, K. (1990). Avoidance of intimacy: An attachment perspective. *Journal of Social and Personal Relationships*, 7, 147-178

Baumrind, D. (1973). The development of instrumental competence through socialization. In A.

D. Pick (Ed.), *Minnesota Symposia on Child Psychology* (Vol. 7, pp. 3–46). Minneapolis: University of Minnesota Press.

Becker, W. C. (1964). Consequences of different models of parental discipline. In M. L. Hoffman & L. W. Hoffman (Eds.), *Review of child development research* (Vol. 1, pp. 169–208). New York: Sage.

Belkin, L. (92012). The Huffington Post. Humiliating Children In Public: A New Parenting Trend? From www.huffingtonpost.com/lisa. Retrieved on July 10, 2014.

Berger, K.S. (2013). The Developing Person Through the Life Span (8th ed.). NY, NY: Worth Publishers.

Berlin, L., & Cassidy, J. (1999). Relations among relationships: Contributions from attachment theory and research. In J. Cassidy & P. R. Shave (Eds.), *Handbook of attachment: Theory, research and clinical applications* (pp. 688–712). New York: Guilford Press.

Berman, W. H. & Sperling, M. B. (1994). The structure and function of adult attachment. In M. B. Sperling & W. H. Berman (Eds.) Attachment in adults: Clinical and developmental perspectives (pp.3-28). New York: Guilford.

Bowlby, J. (1969). *Attachment and Loss:* Vol. 1. Attachment (2nd). In Feist, J. & Feist, G.J. (2009). Theories of Personality (7th ed.). New York, NY: McGraw Hill.

Bowlby, J. (1973). *Attachment and loss: Vol. 2. Separation.* New York: Basic Books.

Bowlby, J. (1982b). *Attachment and loss:* Vol. J. Attachment (2nd ed.). New York: Basic Books. (Original work published 1969).

Bowlby, J. (1988). *A secure base.* New York: Basic Books.

Bowlby, J. (1998). *A secure base: Parent-child attachment and the healthy human development.* New York: Basic Books.

Broderick, P.C. and Blewitt, P. (3rd). (2010). *The Life Span: Human Development for Helping Professionals.* Upper Saddle River, NJ: Pearson.

Bretherton, I. (1992). The Origins of Attachment Theory: John Bowlby and Mary Ainsworth. *Developmental Psychology.* Vol. 28, No. 5, 759-775.

Brown, J., Cohen, P., Johnson, J. G., & Salzinger, S. (1998). A longitudinal analysis of risk factors for child maltreatment: Findings of a 17-year prospective study of officially recorded and self-reported child abuse and neglect. *Child Abuse & Neglect, 22,* 1065-1078.

Buchanan, C. M. (1998). *Parents' category-based beliefs about adolescence: Links to expectations for one's own child.* Manuscript submitted for publication.

Bugental, D. B., & Goodnow, J. J. (1998). Socialization processes. In W. Damon (Series Ed.) & N. Eisenberg (Vol. Ed.), *Handbook of child psychology: Vol. 3. Social, emotional, and personality development* (5th ed., pp. 389–462). New York: Wiley.

Caissy, G.A. (1994). Early Adolescence: Understanding the 10 to 15 Years Old. Cambridge, MA: Perseus Books Group

Carlsmith, J. J., Lepper, M. R., & Landauer, T. K. (1974). Children's obedience to adult requests: Interactive effects of anxiety arousal and apparent punitiveness of adults. *Journal of Personality and Social Psychology, 30,* 822–828.

Carr, A. & Pike, A. (2012). Maternal Scaffolding Behavior: Links With Parenting Style and Maternal Education. *Developmental Psychology*, 48, 2, 543-551. Doi: 10.1037/a0025888

Caspi, A. (2000). The child is father of the man: Personality continuities from childhood to adulthood. Journal of Personality and Social Psychology, 78(1), 158-172.

Cassidy, J., & Shaver, P. R. (1999). *Handbook of attachment: Theory, research, and clinical applications*. New York: Guilford Press.

Cassidy, J., & Kobak, R. (1988). Avoidance and its relation to other defensive processes. In J. Belsky & T. Nezworski (Eds.), *Clinical implications of attachment* (pp. 300–323).

Cheston, S.E (1993). Counseling Adult Survivors of Childhood Sexual Abuse. In R.J.Wicks &R.D.Parsons (Eds.). Clinical Handbook of Pastoral Counseling Vol.2 (pp.447-488). Mahwah, NJ: Paulist Press.

Cohen, P., Brook, J. S., Cohen, J., Velez, N., & Garcia, M. (1990). Common and uncommon pathways to adolescent psychopathology and problem behavior. In L. N. Robins & M. Rutter (Eds.), *Straight and devious pathways from childhood to adulthood* (pp. 242–258). New York: Cambridge University Press.

Cooper, M. L., Pioli, M., Levit, A., Talley, A., Micheas, L. & Collins, N.L. (2006). Attachment styles, sex motives and sexual behavior: Evidence for gender-specific expressions of attachment dynamics. In G. S. Goodman, & M. Mikulincer (Eds.), *Dynamics of romantic love: Attachment, caregiving and sex* (pp. 234-274). New York: Guilford Press.

Coontz, P. D., & Martin, J. A. (1988). Understanding violent mothers and fathers: Assessing explanations offered by mothers and fathers of their use of control punishment. In G. T. Hotaling, D. Finkelhor, J. T. Kirkpatrick, & M. A. Straus (Eds.), *Family abuse and it consequences: New directions in research* (pp. 77–90). Newbury Park, CA: Sage.

Collins, N. L., Ford, M. B., Guichard, A. C., & Allard, L. M. (2006). Working models ofattachment and attribution processes in intimate relationships. Personality and SocialPsychology Bulletin, 32, 201-219.

Collins, N. L., & Read, S. J. (1990). Adult attachment, working models, and relationship quality in dating couples. *Journal of Personality and Social Psychology, 58,* 644-663.

Crittenden, P.M. (1985). Maltreated infants: Vulnerability and resilience. Journal of Child Psychology and Psychiatry and Allied Disciplines, 26, 85-96.

Darling, N., Cumsille, P. & Martinez, M.L. (2007). *Adolescents as active agents in the socialization process: Legitimacy of parental authority and obligation to obey as predictors of obedience.* Journal of Adolescence, 30, 297-311.

Davies, J. & Frawley, M.G. (1994). The Adult Survivor of Childhood Sexual Abuse. New York: Harper Collins.

Dishion, T. J., & Patterson, G. R. (1999). Model building in developmental psychopathology: A pragmatic approach to understanding and intervention. *Journal of Clinical Child Psychology, 28,* 502–512.

Dobson, J. C. (1996). *The new dare to discipline.* Wheaton, IL: Tyndale House.

Dodge, K. A., Pettit, G. S., McClaskey, C. L., & Brown, M. M. (1986). Social competence in children. *Monographs of the Society for Research in Child Development, 51*(2, Serial No. 213).

Eisenberg, N., Fabes, R. A., Bustamante, D., Mathy, R. M., Miller, P. A., & Lindholm, E. (1988). Differentiation of vicariously induced emotional reactions in children. *Developmental*

Ellison, C. G., & Sherkat, D. E. (1993). Conservative Protestantism and support for corporal punishment. *American Sociological Review, 58,* 131-144.

Feeney, J. A. (1998). Adult attachment and relationship-centered anxiety: Responses to physical and emotional distancing. In J. A. Simpson & W. S. Rholes (Eds.) Attachment theory and close relationships (pp.189-218). New York: Guilford.

Fortuna, K., Roisman, G.I., Haydon, K.C., Groh, A.M., & Holland, A.S. (2011). Attachment States of Mind and the Quality of Young Adults' Sibling Relationships. Developmental Psychology, Vol. 47, No. 5, 1366-1373.

Fraley, R.C. and Shaver, P.R. (2000). Adult Romantic Attachment: Theoritical Developments, Emerging Controversies, and Unanswered Questions. *Review of General Psychology,* Vol. 4, No. 2, 132-154. Retrieved October 28, 2010, from www.hptt://web.ebscohost.com.library.capella.edu.

Fraley, R. C. (2005). *Information on the Experiences in Close Relationships–Revised (ECR-R) Adult Attachment Questionnaire.* Retrieved August, 25 2010 from http://www.psych.uiuc.edu/~rcfraley/measures/ecrr.htm

Finkelhor, D. and Browne, A. (1985). The traumatic impact of child sexual abuse: American Journal of Orthopsychiatry. 55:530-41.

Gershoff, E.T. (2002). Corporal Punishment by Parents and Associated Child Behaviors an Experience: A Meta-Analytic and Theoretical Review. *Psychological Bulletin*, 128, 4, 539-579.

Gelles, R. J., & Straus, M. A. (1988). *Intimate violence*. New York: Simon & Schuster.

Gershoff, E. T. (1999). Short-and long-term effects of corporal punishment on children: A process model and meta-analytic review. Manuscript submitted for publication. Gordon, T. (1975). Parent effectiveness training. New York: Plume.

Gershoff, E.T., Miller, P.C., & Holden, G.W. (1999). Parenting Influences From the Pulpit: Religious Affiliation as a Determinant of Parental Corporal Punishment. Journal of Family Psychology. 13. 3, 307-320.

Gershoff, E.T., (2002). Corporal Punishment by Parents and Associated Child Behaviors and Experiences: A Meta-Analytic and Theoretical Review. *Psychological Bulletin*. 128, 4, 539-579.

Gick, M.L., & Sirois, F. (2010). Insecure Attachment Moderates Women's Adjustment to Inflammatory Bowel Disease Severity. *Rehabilitation Psychology*, Vol.55, No. 2, 170-179.

Roisman, G.I. personal communication, April 13, 2006.

Glueck, S., & Glueck, E. (1964). *Ventures in criminology*. Cambridge, MA: Harvard University Press.

Gulla, R.M.(1996). Ethics in Pastoral Ministry. Mawah, NJ: Paulist Press.

Gordon, T. (1975). Parent effectiveness training. New York: Plume.

Greven, P. (1991). Spare the child: The religious roots of punishment and the psychological impact of physical abuse. New York: Knopf.

Grolnick, W. S., Deci, E. L., & Ryan, R. M. (1997). Internalization within the family: The self- determination theory perspective. In J. E. Grusec & L. Kuczynski (Eds.), *Parenting and children's internalization of values: A handbook of contemporary theory* (pp. 135–161). New York: Wiley.

Grusec, J. E., & Goodnow, J. J. (1994). Impact of parental discipline methods on the child's internalization of values: A reconceptualization of current points of view. *Developmental Psychology, 30,* 4–19.

Gunnoe, M. L., & Mariner, C. L. (1997). Toward a developmental–contextual model of the effects of parental spanking on children's aggression. *Archives of Pediatric and Adolescent Medicine, 151,* 768–775.

Hall, G.S. (1904). *Adolescence: Its psychology and its relation to physiology, anthropology; sociology, sex, crime, religion, and education* (Vols. 1 & 2). Upper Saddle River, NJ: Prentice Hall.

Hazan, C., & Shaver, P. R. (1987). Romantic love conceptualized as an attachment process. *Journal of Personality and Social Psychology, 52,* 511–524.

Hazan, C. & Zeifman, D. (1999). Pair bonds as attachments: Evaluating the evidence. In J. Cassidy & P. R. Shaver (Eds.) Handbook of Attachment (pp. 336-354). New York:

Herman, J.L. (1992). *Trauma and recovery*. New York: Basic Books.

Hetherington, E. M., Stouwie, R. J., & Ridberg, E. H. (1971). Patterns of family interaction and child-rearing attitudes related to three dimensions of juvenile delinquency. *Journal of Abnormal Psychology, 78*, 160–176.

Hollist C.S. & Miller, R.B. (2005). Perceptions of Attachment Style and Marital Quality in Midlife Marriage. Family Relations, 54, 46-57.

Holmbeck, G., & Hill, J. (1988). Storm and stress beliefs about adolescence: Prevalence, self- reported antecedents, and effects of an undergraduate course. *Journal of Youth & Adolescence, 17,* 285–306.

Huffman, K. (2010). Psychology in Action (8th ed.). Hoboken, NJ: Wiley.

Jackson, S., Thompson, R. A., Christiansen, E. H., Colman, R. A., Wyatt, J., Buckendahl, C. W., Wilcox, B. L., & Peterson, R. (1999). Predicting abuse-prone parental attitudes and discipline practices in a nationally representative sample. *Child Abuse and Neglect, 23,* 15–29.

John, P. II, (1997). The Theology of the Body: Human Love in the Divine Plan. Boston, MA: Pauline Books & Media.

Larzelere, R. E. (2000). *Child outcomes of non-abusive and customary physical punishment by parents: An updated literature review.* Unpublished manuscript, University of Nebraska Medical Center, Omaha, and Father Flanagan's Boys' Home, Boys Town, NE.

Larzelere, R. E. (1996). A review of the outcomes of parental use of nonabusive or customary physical punishment. *Pediatrics, 98*(4, Pt. 2), 824–828.

Lawson, D.M. & Brossart, D.F. (2009). "Attachment, Interpersonal Problems, and Treatment Outcome in Group Therapy for Intimate Partner Violence". *Psychology of Men & Masculinity,* Vol. 10, No. 4, 288-301. Retrieved on November 10, 2010 from http://web.ebscohost.com.library.capella.edu

Lay, K., Waters, E., & Park, K. A. (1989). Maternal responsiveness and child compliance: The role of mood as a mediator. *Child Development, 60,* 1405–1411.

Lepper, M. R. (1983). Social control processes and the internalization of social values: An attributional perspective. In E. T. Higgins, D. N. Ruble, & W. W. Hartup (Eds.), *Social cognition and social development* (pp. 294–330). New York: Cambridge University Press.

Lew, M. (1990). Victims No Longer. New York: Harper & Row.

Lindabl, K., & Obstbaum, K. (2004). Entering the canon: A tribute to Chess and Thomas. *PsyCRITIQUES.* (np).

Ling, H. & Qian, M. (2010). Relationship Between Attachment and Personality Disorder Symptoms of Chinese College Students. Social Behavior and Personality, 38 (4), 571- 576.

Lopez, N. L., Bonenberger, J. L., & Schneider, H. G. (2001). Parental disciplinary history, current levels of empathy, and moral reasoning in young adults. North American Journal of Psychology, 3, 193–204.

Lovinger, R.J. (1994). Religious Issues. In Ronch, J.L., Ornum, W. V., Stilwell, N.C., (Eds.). The Counseling Sourcebook. New York: Crossroad.

Karabinus, David S. (2009). Flow cystometric sorting of human sperm: MicroSort clinical trial update. Theriogenology, 71, 74-79.

Kobak, R. R., & Sceery, A. (1988). Attachment in late adolescence: Working models, affect regulation, and representations of self and others. *Child Development, 59,* 135–146.

Koenig, H.G. (2006). Spirituality in Patient Care. Randnor, PA: Templeton Foundation Press.

Kirkpatrick, L. & Davis, K. (1994). Attachment style, gender, and relationship stability: A longitudinal analysis. *Journal of Personality and Social Psychology, 66,* 502-512.

Kohlberg, L. (1976). Moral stages and moralization: The cognitive development approach. In Broderick, P.C. and Blewitt, P. (3rd). (2010). *The Life Span: Human Development for Helping Professionals.* Upper Saddle River, NJ: Pearson.

Klohnen, E.C., & Bera, S. (1998). Behavioral and experiential patterns of avoidantly and securely attached women across adulthood: A 31-year longitudinal perspective. Journal of Personality and Social Psychology 74: 211-223.

Kochanska, G. (1993). Toward a synthesis of parental socialization and child temperament in early development of conscience. *Child Development, 64,* 325–347.

Kochanska, G., & Thompson, R. A. (1997). The emergence and development of conscience in toddlerhood and early childhood. In J. E. Grusec & L. Kuczynski (Eds.),

Parenting and children's internalization of values: A handbook of contemporary theory (pp. 53-77). New York: Wiley.

Kuczynski, L., & Hildebrandt, N. (1997). Models of conformity and resistance in socialization theory. In J. E. Grusec & L. Kuczynski (Eds.), *Parenting and children's internalization of values: A handbook of contemporary theory* (pp. 227-256). New York: Wiley.

Kurtz, J.E. (2006). Human Dignity and the Plague of Pornography. Two Pastoral Letters. Diocese of Knoxville.

Patterson, G. R. (1982). *Coercive family process.* Eugene, OR: Castalia.

Parke, R. D. (1977). Some effects of punishment on children's behavior Revisited. In E. M. Hetherington & R. D. Parke (Eds.), *Contemporary readings in child psychology* (pp. 208-220). New York: McGraw-Hill.

Percy, A. (2006). Theology of the Body Made Simple: Australia: Connorcourt Publishing Pty Ltd.

Powers, S. I., Pietromonaco, P. R., Gunlicks, M. & Sayer, A. (2006). Dating couples' attachment styles and patterns of Cortisol reactivity and recovery in response to a relationship conflict. *Journal of Personality and Social Psychology, 90,* 613-628.

Maccoby, E.E. & Martin, J.A. (1983). Socialization in the context of the family: Parent-child interaction. In Broderick, P.C. and Blewitt, P. (3rd). (2010). *The Life Span: Human Development for Helping Professionals.* Upper Saddle River, NJ: Pearson.

Main, M. & Solomon, J. (1990). Procedures for indetifying infants as disorganized/disoriented during the Ainsworth Strange Situation. In M.T. Greeberg, Cicchetti, D. & E. Cummings

(Eds.), Attachment in the preschool years. Chicago: University of Chicago Press.

Main, M., Kaplan, N. & Cassidy, J. (1985). Security in infancy, childhood, and adulthood: A move to the level of representation. In I.Mahoney, I., Pargament, A., Tarakeshwar, K.N., & Swank, A. (2001). Religion in the home in the 1980s and 1990s: A meta-analytic review and conceptual analysis of links between religion, marriage, and parenting. *Journal of Family Psychology, 15,* 559–596.

Main, M. & Weston, D. (1981) Quality of attachment to mother and father: Related to conflict behavior and the readiness for establishing new relationships. Child Development, 52, 932-940.

May, G.G. (1988). Addiction & Grace. San Francisco: Harper Collins Publishers.

McCord, J. (1997). On discipline. *Psychological Inquiry, 8,* 215–217.

McCord, J. (1979). Some child-rearing antecedents of criminal behavior in adult men. *Journal of Personality and Social Psychology, 37,* 1477–1486.

Mikulincer, M. & Shaver, P.R. (2007). Attachment in Adulthood: Structure, Dynamics, and Change. New York: Guilford Press.

Miller, J.B. & Hoicowitz, T. (2004). Attachment contexts of adolescent friendship and romance. *Journal of Adolescence,* 22(6), 191-207.

Miller, J.G., & Bersoff, D.M. (1998). The role of liking in perceptions of the moral responsibility to help: A cultural perspective. Journal of Experimental Social Psychology, 34, 443-469.

National Clearinghouse on Child Abuse and Neglect Information (2000).

Naude, H., Marx, J., Pretorius, E., & Hislop-Esterhuyzen, N. (2007). Evidence of Early Childhood defects due to prenatal over-exposure to vitamin A: A Case study: Early Child Development and Care, 177, 235-253.

Newsom, C., Flavell, J. E., & Rincover, A. (1983). The side effects of punishment. In S. Axelrod & J. Apsche (Eds.), *The effects of punishment on human behavior* (pp. 285–316). New York: Academic Press.

Patterson, G. R. (1982). *Coercive family process.* Eugene, OR: Castalia.

Piaget, J. (1965). *The moral judgment of the child* (M. Gabain, Trans.). New York: Free Press. (Original work published 1932)

Pinker, S. (1994). The Language instinct. New York: Morrow.

Realmuto, G.M., August, G.J., Egan, E.A. (2004). Testing the goodness-of-fit of a multifaceted preventive intervention for children at risk for conduct disorder. *Canadian Journal of Psychiatry*, 49(11), 743-752.

Reis, S. & Grenyer, B. F. S. (2004). Fear of intimacy in women: Relationship between attachment styles and depressive symptoms. *Psychopathology,37,* 299-303.

Redd, W. H., Morris, E. K., & Martin, J. A. (1975). Effects of positive and negative adult child interactions on children's social preference. *Journal of Experimental Child Psychology, 19,* 153–164.

Roisman, G.I. Personal communication, April 13, 2006.

Rohner, R. (1986). The warmth dimension. Newbury Park, CA: Sage.

Rohner, R. P., Kean, K. J., & Cournoyer, D. E. (1991). Effects of corporal punishment, perceived caretaker warmth, and cultural beliefs on the psychological adjustment of children in St. Kitts, West Indies. *Journal of Marriage and the Family, 53,* 681–693.

Rohner, R.P., & Britner, P.A. (2002). World-wide mental health correlates of parental acceptance-rejection: Review of cross-Cultural and intracultural evidence. Cross-Cultural Research: *The Journal of Comparative Social Sciences,* 36(1), 35-47.

Rosemond, J. K. (1994). *To spank or not to spank.* Kansas City, MO: Andrews & McMeel.

Saey, Tina Hesman, (2008). Epic genetics: Genes' chemical clothes may underlie the biology behind mental illness. Science News, 173, 14-19.

Saywitz, K.J. et al. (2000). Treatment for Sexually Abused Children and Adolescents. American Psychological Association, Inc. Vol. 55, No. 9.

Sibley, C. G. & Liu, J. H. (2006). Working models of romantic attachment and the subjective quality of social interactions across relational contexts. *Personal Relationships, 13,* 243- 259.

Sibley, C.G. & Overall, N.C. (2008). Modeling the hierarchical structure of attachment representations: A test of domain differentiation. *Personality and Individual Differences,44,* 238-249.

Skinner, B.F. (1953). Science and human behavior. New York: Macmillan.

Simpson, J. A., Rholes, W. S., & Phillips, D. (1996). Conflict in close relationships: An attachment perspective. J. of Personality and Social Psychology, 71, 899-914.

Simpson, J.A., Collins, W.A., Tran, S., & Haydon, K.C. (2007). Attachment and the Experience and Expression of Emotions in Romantic Relationships: A Developmental Perspective. Journal of Personality and Social Psychology. Vol. No. 2, 355-367.

Smetana, J.G., Crean, H.F., & Campione-Barr, N. (2005). *Adolescents and parents changing conceptions of parental authority: New Directions for Child and Adolescent Development.* 108, 31-46. In Broderick, P.C. and Blewitt, P. (3rd). (2010). *The Life Span: Human Development for Helping Professionals.* Upper Saddle River, NJ: Pearson.

Straus, M. A. (1994a). *Beating the devil out of them: Corporal punishment in American families.* New York: Lexington Books.

Stams, G-J. J., M.Juffer, F., van IJzendoorn, M.H. (2002). Maternal sensitivity, infant attachment, and temperament in early childhood: The case of adopted children and their biologically unrelated parents. *Developmental Psychology,* 38(5)806-821.

Sroufe, L. A., & Fleeson, J. (1986). Attachment and the construction of relationships. In W Hartup & Z. Rubin (Eds}, *Relationships and development* (pp. 51-71). Hillsdale, NJ: Erlbaum.

Stroufe, L. A. & Water, E. (1977). Attachment an an organizational construct. Child Development, 48, 1185-1199.

Thomas, A., & Chess, S. (1977). Temperament and development. New York: Brunner/Mazel.

Thomas, A., & Chess, S. (1987). Roundtable: What is temperament: Four approaches. Child Development, 58, 505-529.

Thomas, A., & Chess, S. (1991). Temperament in adolescence and its functional significance. In R.M. Lerner, A.C. Peterson, & J.Brooks-Gunn (Eds.), Encyclopedia of adolescence (Vol.2), New York: Garland.

Tuttle, C. (2012). The Child Whisperer: The Ultimate Handbook for Raising Happy, Successful, Cooperative Children. Live Your Truth Press.

Turner, H. A., & Finkelhor, D. (1996). Corporal punishment as a stressor among youth. *Journal of Marriage and the Family*, 58, 155–166.

Ugoagwu, P.C. (2012). The Impact of Attachment Styles on the Quality of Romantic Relationships Among African American Adults as Measured by Support, Depth, and Conflict. A *Doctoral Dissertation*. Capella Minneapolis.

Van Houten, R. (1983). Punishment: From the animal laboratory to the applied setting. In S. Axelrod & J. Apsche (Eds.), *The effects of punishment on human behavior* (pp. 13–14). New York: Academic.

Vygotsky, L. S. (1978). *Mind in society: The development of higher psychological processes*. Cambridge, MA: Harvard University Press.

Thompson, R. A. (1999). Early attachment and later development. In J. Cassidy & P. R. Shaver (Eds.), *Handbook of Attachment:*

Theory, Research and Clinical Applications (pp. 265- 286). New York: Guilford Press.

Ward, L.M. (1992). Does television exposure affect emerging adults' attitudes and assumptions about sexual relationships? Correlational and experimental confirmation. Journal of Youth and Adolescence, 31, 1-15.

Waters, E. (1978). The reliability and stability of individual differences in infant-mother attachment.*Child Development, 49,* 483–494.

Waters, E., Cronwell, J., Elliott, M., Corcoran, D., & Treboux, D. (2002). Bowlby's secure base theory and the social/personality psychology of attachment styles: Work(s) in progress. *Attachment & Human Development, 4*(2).

Waters, E., & Cummings, E. (2000). A secure base from which to explore close relationships. *Child Development, 71,* 164–172.

West, C. (2003). Theology of the Body: Explained : A Commentary on John Paul II's "Gospel of the Body." Boston, MA: Pauline Books & Media.

Wilson, J. Q., & Herrnstein, R. J. (1985). *Crime and human nature.* New York: Simon & Schuster.

Zimmermann, P., Maier, M. A., Winter, M., & Grossmann, K. E. (2001). Attachment and adolescents' emotion regulation during a joint problem solving task with a friend. *International Journal of Behavioral Development, 25,* 331–343.